INVENTING ADOLESCENCE

INVENTING ADOLESCENCE

The Political Psychology of
Everyday Schooling

JOSEPH ADELSON

Transaction Books
New Brunswick (U.S.A.) and Oxford (U.K.)

Copyright © 1986 by Transaction, Inc.
New Brunswick, New Jersey 08903

Library of Congress Catalog Number: 85-16495
ISBN: 0-88738-026-3 (cloth)
Printed in the United States of America

Library of Congress Cataloging in Publication Data
Adelson, Joseph.
    Inventing adolescence.

    1. Adolescence.   2. Public schools—United States.
3. Students—United States—Psychology.   I. Title.
LB1135.A33   1986   305.2'35   85-16495
ISBN 0-88738-026-3

Contents

Preface

This book contains a fair sampling of most of the topics I have written on—primarily adolescence, education, and the growth of thinking. With one exception it does not include those papers which present and analyze quantitative findings. About fifteen years ago I began to give less time to such writing and more to essays discussing ideological problems in psychology and education, thereby complicating a flourishing if staid academic career.

It was a period of utopian giddiness in American society, marked by an increasing addiction, so I felt, to false or shallow ideas about human nature and much else. Those ideas had begun to hold psychology captive, and what was worse, *psychology* had become a key medium for their propagation. My own major area of interest—adolescence—was affected early and deeply, through the construction of such quarter-truths as the *generation gap*, and even more so by the invention of *the radical young*, that quantum leap upward in the continuing elevation of the species. In the fullness of time I was drawn—no, driven—to writing on these and related issues, the last straw being a conference during which I witnessed a university president pandering shamelessly to a group of college seniors, praising them on the basis of "scientific data" presuming to document their moral and intellectual superiority to the rest of us. That brought home how quickly and decisively a political doctrine, offering itself a science, can capture a vulnerable audience and become accepted truth.

Well, those were wild times, what with Vietnam and all that, and there were excesses everywhere, and we now live in an era of ruefulness and Republican landslides. One would think that would translate into a more sober, less politicized social science. Not at all, far from it, to the contrary. What was once occasional is now commonplace, what was once ingenuous is now deliberate. We take for granted that certain psychological topics are occupied by certain points of view; others need not apply. What is different now is the boldness with which politics, or one's "values," are given priority over disinterested inquiry. What is different too is that the central institutions of social science are so casually deployed for ideological ends—both the professional journals and the scientific meetings of the American Psychological Association are now given over, in no small degree, to unabashed *parti pris*. The newest paper included here, "Terrorizing Children," written with Chester Finn, discusses the worst case yet—the devising of a mental health crisis, and the capture of convention time, journal space, and congressional hearings, all to a blatantly political end, and all under the banner of research.

We begin to see the costs. Our must sophisticated audiences regard us skeptically. Legislators, judges, bureaucrats, educators, neighboring professionals and scholars, all of whom would not long ago have given our findings credence and our counsel respectful attention, now treat us warily, at moments cynically. Some will tell you that the expert opinions of social science are not worth much, that we affect the trappings of science without approaching its achievements, and above all that we tend to find only what we want or mean to find. These judgments are no doubt too severe and too sweeping, but they are part of the price we pay for our collective hubris, past and present, for the inflated claims and unredeemable promises so many of us have made in the name of social science. Many of these essays try to tell how and why it happened.

Acknowledgments

Chapter 1: "What Happened to the Schools?" *Commentary* (March 1981).

Chapter 2: "How the Schools Were Ruined," *Commentary* (July 1983).

Chapter 3: "Why the Schools May Not Improve Much," from *Challenge to American Schools: The Case for Standards and Values*, ed. John H. Bunzel (Oxford: Oxford University Press, 1985). Copyright © 1985 by Oxford University Press. Reprinted by permission.

Chapter 4: "The Social Sciences vs. the Humanities," from *Challenge to the Humanities*, ed. Finn, Fancher, and Ravitch (Holmes & Meier, 1985).

Chapter 5: "Living with Quotas," *Commentary* (May 1978).

Chapter 6: "Looking Back," *Daedalus*, vol. 103, no. 4 (Fall 1974). Reprinted by permission of *Daedalus*, Journal of the American Academy of Arts and Sciences, Boston, MA.

Chapter 7: "The Teacher as a Model," *American Scholar* (Summer 1961). Copyright © 1961 by the United Chapters of Phi Beta Kappa.

Chapter 8: "The Political Imagination of the Young Adolescent," *Daedalus*, vol. 100 (Fall 1971). Reprinted by permission of *Daedalus*, Journal of the American Academy of Arts and Sciences, Boston, MA.

Chapter 9: "Rites of Passage," *American Educator* (Summer 1982). Reprinted by permission of *American Educator*, quarterly journal of the American Federation of Teachers.

Chapter 10: "Inventing the Young," *Commentary* 51(5):43–48 (1971).

Chapter 11: "What Generation Gap?" *New York Times Magazine* (January 4, 1970). Copyright © 1970 by the New York Times Company. Reprinted by permission.

Chapter 12: "Adolescence for Clinicians," from *From Research to Clinical Practice*, ed. G. Stricker (Plenum, 1984).

Chapter 13: "The Psychodynamics of Adolescence," from *Handbook of Adolescent Psychology*, ed. Joseph Adelson. Copyright © 1979 by John Wiley & Sons, Inc.

Chapter 14: "Psychology, Ideology, and the Search for Faith," *The Public Interest*, no. 46 (Winter 1977): 119–125. Reprinted by permission of *The Public Interest*. Copyright © 1977 by National Affairs, Inc.

Chapter 15: "Orwell: The Self and Memory in *1984*," from *The Future of 1984*, ed. E. Jensen (University of Michigan Press, 1984). Copyright © 1984 by the University of Michigan.

Chapter 16: "Still Vital After All These Years," *Psychology Today* (April 1982).

Chapter 17: "The Dream as a Riddle," *Psychiatry* 29(3):306–309 (1966). Copyright © 1966 by The William Alanson White Psychiatric Foundation, Inc. Reprinted by special permission of The William Alanson White Foundation, Inc.

Chapter 18: "Letty in Pogrebinland," *Commentary* (May 1981).

Part I
Recent History of the Schools

1

What Happened to the Schools?

It is only recently, and only by hindsight, that we have been able to appreciate the enormous stresses imposed upon the schools in the immediate postwar era. The most visible of these was demographic in origin. There was an extraordinary increase in the number of youngsters to be educated, requiring a vast expansion of the public schools, and ultimately of the colleges and universities. That expansion was carried out remarkably well, or so it seems to me; there were strains, inevitably, but these were compensated for by a sort of euphoria about doing so much so energetically in so short a period of time—not merely the building of physical plant but the recruitment and training of a large body of teachers and administrators. It was a euphoria that extended to the idea of education itself. Education came to be seen as a sort of universal solvent for the problems of the polity. The utopian tendencies in the American mind were to some large degree invested in the schools, in the notion of perfectibility through learning. As we shall see, there was to be a great fall, indeed one we are still witnessing, but I think it is fair to say that through most of the 1950s the authority of the schools rested upon a sense of inner confidence—they believed in themselves because we believed in them, and we believed in them because they were the repository of so many of our fondest hopes, for ourselves, for our children, for the nation.

There were other outcomes of the demographic pressure, which we are just now beginning to understand and—ruefully—appreciate. One of these was the effect of generation size, that is, not merely the numbers involved in a generation but its size relative to the total population. A baby-boom generation is a crowded one; economic and other opportunities are fewer, and more fiercely competed for. In the fullness of time, we see in that generation an increase in social pathology, and more specifically increases in the rate of suicide, homicide, delinquency, illegitimacy, alcoholism, and the like. That at least is the breathtakingly bold theory proposed recently by a number of economists and demographers, most forcefully by Richard Easterlin.[1] Whether or not the hypothesis is true—and we shall soon know, for it is a hypothesis that tests itself, and that predicts that we should soon be seeing declines in these indices—the fact is that beginning in the 1960s the schools found themselves confronting, rather suddenly, new and unexpected problems in

3

discipline, in student motivation, and in collective morale. Perhaps one ought to stress how quickly it took place. As it happens, my three children, born within a five-year span, went to the same high school. The oldest tells me that he knew no one who used drugs; the second, two years younger, says that drugs were being used, but only by deviant youngsters, the emotionally troubled, and the socially outcast; the third, in school three years later, says that the occasional use of drugs was commonplace and that regular and heavy use was to be found among a substantial minority of his fellow students.

The size of the postwar generation had yet another effect that was not immediately evident. School systems enlarged, accelerating a long-standing tendency toward the consolidation of school districts. The figures are quite astonishing. In 1932 there were around 127,000 school districts in this country; now there are about 16,000.[2] There were many things at work in producing that attrition; the Conant Report on the high schools, published in 1959, placed a particular emphasis on the educational advantages of consolidation. The outcome was a substantial increase in system size, and with it, inevitably, a shift to bureaucratic modes of organization. That shift in turn brought with it a series of changes in the nature and practice of authority in the schools. The change was from traditional modes of authority, that is, direct and personal, to legal and contractual modes, in which the emphasis is placed upon conformity to rules and legal codes.[3]

The distinction between traditional and legalistic modes of authority is far from a new idea, in fact, it is a central concept in the writings of the pioneers of contemporary sociology, especially Max Weber. But the trend toward legalistic modes of authority, though discernible since at least the nineteenth century, was relatively slow in coming to the schools. When it did come, it could not have arrived at a less propitious time, at least so far as discipline was concerned. Just at the moment when social pathology was beginning its ominous rise, educators began to find themselves being buried in paper, and what was worse, constrained in the performance of disciplinary authority by increasingly complex regulations involving the rights of students, these in turn following upon court decisions that produced a widespread anxiety about litigation.

I remember quite vividly a sort of watershed event in my own experience of the schools, as a parent. This took place a little more than ten years ago. I attended what was advertised as an urgent meeting of the PTO at the junior high school my son attended. Arriving there, I learned that the meeting had been called to discuss some disturbing incidents taking place near the school: some of the older, roughneck children were bullying and extorting money from some of the younger children on the way to and from school. There had been many complaints from parents to the principal but the answers had not been satisfactory. So the PTO had decided to make the issue public. A youngish assistant principal had been sent to calm the multitudes, and I have rarely seen anyone quite so unhappy—he stammered, he mumbled, he hemmed and hawed, he shifted from foot to foot, and his message to us was that they would do their best but that probably not much could be done.

It was a long and rancorous meeting. The assistant principal, though defensive and embarrassed, provided us with a resumé of the legal education he himself had been receiving, at the hands of the police and of the school's attorney. That course of instruction told him not what he could do but all the many things he could not do. The audience listened, incredulous, then angry and disgusted. At one point one parent shouted something to the effect that this would not have happened in the old days, and brought forth the name of a revered principal of the recent past who had exercised a benign form of curbside justice. But those days were gone forever.

I do not want to sentimentalize the good old days, nor do I want to focus exclusively upon problems of discipline, important as they are—it is the leading complaint parents bring against the public schools. Yet we see in this example how forces and ideologies both extrinsic and alien to the schools and to education—in this case, the courts and the adversarial spirit—have begun to penetrate the practice of education in the United States in regard to not only discipline but other realms of educational policy as well.

Perhaps the most important source of the school's diminished authority is the growth—I am tempted to say the cancerous growth—of judicial and bureaucratic intervention, generally at the federal level. The initial occasion was desegregation and racial equity in education; somewhat later, questions of sexual equality were addressed. Yet one now senses that these issues were used merely as pretexts, that a sort of iron law of federal expansiveness had come into play, which at this moment shows few signs of recession. It is an extremely troubling development because neither the courts—given their adversarial style—nor the bureaucracies—given their tendency toward Byzantine inefficiency—are the appropriate forum for the discussion or the making of educational decision.

Let me illustrate by an example close to home—and I mean that literally, for the case I have in mind took place in my own hometown, Ann Arbor, and in fact in my own home neighborhood. I refer to the black English litigation. The case began when a group of radical activists, largely white, sued the school system on behalf of a group of black families. It was their claim that the poor academic progress of the children was due to the fact that their native language, so to speak, is black English, and instruction takes place in standard English, a language these children do not fully comprehend. As a solution, the teachers were to be trained to understand black English, and to respect its linguistic autonomy.

To anyone on the scene, the doctrine being proposed was not far from frivolous. Some of the children in question are from poor families. In at least some cases, family life is unstable and demoralized. School attendance is irregular, among other reasons because the families move so often (I am told, for example, that about half of the plaintiff families have already left the district). Given these circumstances, it is hard to imagine how language can be singled out as the prime reason for poor achievement. Nor is there any reason to believe that these youngsters do in fact speak black English exclusively, or cannot understand standard English. They watch television daily, they talk easily with white classmates; all those with direct and extensive experience with these youngsters report that black English is a variant dialect that can be turned on and off depending on circumstances, in much the same way that many middle-class southern children learn to speak both standard English and "country," and switch back and forth between the two depending on whom they are addressing.

Hence, there was no reason to believe that black English functioned as a foreign language, or that it acted as an impediment to learning. Nevertheless, a federal judge decided to hear the case, much to everyone's surprise; and much to everyone's astonishment he agreed with expert testimony that black English was linguistically a distinctive language, and hence a probable factor in the poor school performance of these youngsters. The remedy ordered was that the teachers be compelled to attend a series of lectures wherein they would be instructed on the linguistic merits and integrity of black English. That remedy has now been tested, and the results are precisely what our common sense would lead us to expect: it has not made the slightest difference in the achievement of the children. In short, the nullity of the outcome follows directly from the silliness of the suit, the foolishness of the judicial holding, and the fatuity of the remedy.[4]

What should trouble us most about this case is the ease with which the judge intruded himself into the heart of the educator's domain, into what is to be taught, how it is to be taught, and how teachers are to be trained to teach it. What qualifies a judge to do so? What qualifies a judge to pronounce on the linguistics of English dialects? What qualifies a judge to pronounce on the causes of scholastic achievement, and the means needed to enhance it? The answer is, nothing at all; yet the judiciary now takes it upon itself—here as elsewhere—to settle the most recondite technical and scientific questions. What began as judicial activism in the cause of equality has by some demonic inner logic become a kind of judicial narcissism, wherein the competence of the mediating institutions of U.S. life is systematically diminished by judicial vanity. Here is Martin Shapiro, a distinguished student of the law, now at Berkeley, on this matter:

Our newspapers tell us of judges who forbid the transfer of Air Force squadrons from one base to another, delay multi-million dollar construction projects, intervene in complex negotiations between public employers and their employees, oversee the operation of railroads, and decide the location of schools. In the course of these litigations we have seen judges blithely intervening in precisely the kinds of massive and complex technical matters about which they would have automatically disclaimed competence twenty years ago. Judges now joyously try their hands at everything from the engineering of atomic reactors to the validation of IQ tests. They run school districts, do regional land use, redesign welfare programs, and calculate energy needs. They make policy decisions with massive financial and political consequences for every level of government. They destroy and redirect the building of educational, electoral, tax, and public-utility systems that are the products of thousands of hours of legislative negotiation and hundreds of complex statutes. Today there seems to be no public policy issue, no matter now massive, complex, or technical, that some judge somewhere has not felt fully capable of deciding aided only by the standard processes of litigation.[5]

Shapiro goes on to write that one defense of this process is that the judge is in a position to decide among the rival technical experts of the two parties, and thus free of the domination that technicians exercise over laypersons, who generally see only one side of the issue. Shapiro says that although that may be true in theory, "in reality the judge often cannot understand the technical testimony on either side, has no mode of independently evaluating the accuracy of either, and is reduced to an act of faith in one side's technicians or the other's. The judicial weighing of technical testimony often comes down to a law clerk, fresh out of law school with no technical background, juggling footnotes to support whatever guess the judge is making."

Nor is the judiciary alone in its zeal to administer the schools. Congress has done more than its share, in a series of ill-advised acts of legislation, as has the executive through the bureaucracies. In short, all three branches of government and, furthermore, separate or overlapping or competing units within these branches take it as their privilege to intervene in education. They do so with almost no regard to the financial costs involved. And once they have done so, their decisions, however erroneous or short-sighted they turn out to be in practice, prove nearly impossible to modify or rescind. The fruits of judicial and bureaucratic intervention are painfully evident to those of us in the university: a professor in Georgia jailed for three months in a tenure dispute; or a federal functionary blithely sitting in on university classes to monitor potential bias; or the extraordinary and thus far unchecked growth of a bureaucracy both within and without the universities determined to compose racial and sexual quotas, to rectify an unproved and unlikely pattern of discrimination.

Thus the authority of education—at all levels—is weaker today, far weaker, than at any other moment in memory. The schools do not fully govern themselves; they do not freely choose their own goals; they are not guided by their own values. Above all, they cannot bring themselves to resist these false or meretricious or merely foolish ideas imposed on them by others. Here I come to the point I want to stress, that our inability to resist those ideas stems in part from our inability to develop or sustain a coherent idea of ourselves, and of our own essential values.

In their relation to the federal courts and to the bureaucracies, the schools have had to confront institutions that, like Isaiah Berlin's famous hedgehog, know but a single thing, that thing being a distended and distorted idea of equality, distended in that it puts equality above all other values, and distorted because it has transformed the original idea, of moral equality, the idea of Jefferson and Lincoln, to the idea of numerical equality, that all groups must be represented equally in all statuses.[6] A corollary idea is the notion that variations in achievement are due only to error or malevolence, which in practice amounts to a charge either of negligence or willed malice in the schools. In their defense of their single idea, the courts and bureaucracies behave not like the ordinary hedgehog but like a fierce and demented one, which knocks down anything that gets in its way—in short, a hedgehog with the ambitions of a fox. Whether the schools could in fact educate the courts on their narrow idea of equality is unclear; that idea has the fatal attraction of a vulgar belief understood to be advanced. Yet one can say with some confidence that they will be unable to do so until they are ready to plead publicly the traditionalist values they hold privately.

Far more than any other institution in U.S. society, the schools have become an arena for the struggle between the values of traditionalism and of modernity. Among the values of traditionalism are merit, accomplishment, competition, and success; self-restraint, self-discipline, and the postponement of gratification; the stability of the family; and a belief in certain moral universals. The modernist ethos scorns the pursuit of success; is egalitarian and redistributionist in emphasis; tolerates or encourages sensual gratification; values self-expression as against self-restraint; accepts alternative or deviant forms of the family; and emphasizes ethical relativism.

I think we do well here to distinguish between the universities and the schools, the former having been simultaneously the seedbed, staging area, and ultimate haven of the modernist temper. Not entirely, of course, because important segments of the university—I have in mind the sciences and some of the professional schools—have been largely immune to the modernist spirit, especially so with respect to the values of merit and success. On the whole, however, the intellectual debacle of the universities, which began in the 1960s and continues to this day—a debacle the symptoms of which were and are grade inflation and various curricular travesties—was the inevitable result of a tacit submission to modernist ideology. I want to quote a marvelous pair of sentences from Lionel Trilling, who wrote that "ideology is not acquired by thought but by breathing the haunted air. The life in ideology, from which none of us can wholly escape, is a strange submerged life of habit and semi-habit in which to ideas we attach strong passions but no very clear awareness of the concrete reality of their consequences." Breathing that haunted air, the haunted air of modernism, meant that we no longer remembered what we believed in, or why. I recall my first recognition of this, in the late 1960s, when our faculty faced a student demand for a new bachelor's degree, the major reason being the desire of some students to escape the requirements for a modest degree of proficiency in a foreign language. Heart-rending stories were told of students possessing the highest degree of sensitivity and moral conscience yet failing the French examination for the third time, and thereupon being cast out into the darkness. What struck me most was the apparent inability of our faculty, collectively, to frame a cogent response, to argue the case for language. And listening to that debate, or rather that nondebate, I felt I was gazing into the void. For if one could not answer the question, why language? one could not, if pressed, answer the questions, why mathematics? why science? why literature? why history? why anything else?

The situation in the schools—I mean here secondary education in particular—was, and is, far different, more complex, sadder. In their fall from public favor, the universities got their just deserts, in choosing to live that "strange submerged life of habit and semi-habit" in which passionate ideas are taken to be without consequence. But U.S. public schools rarely generate values; they more often merely absorb and reflect them. As John Dewey once told us, the educator is uniquely sensitive to what he takes to be the needs of his constitutents. He accommodates; he serves; he aims to please. He is the least arrogant, the least petulant, the least willful of all professionals; and sad to say, the most lacking in self-esteem. In a morally unified and harmonious era, the schools can serve the public intention readily. In an era marked by a multiplicity of aims, or by competing aims, the schools tend to become ambivalent, or confused, or inhibited—often all three at once.

In the postwar period, the schools were to do everything at once. They were to help us beat the Soviets into space; they were then to liberate poor and minority youngsters from the heritage of slavery and oppression; they were shortly thereafter to help middle-class children free themselves from their bourgeois constraints; and then someone noticed that the SAT scores had plummeted, and so they were to fix that too. It was never quite clear how these separate aims were to be achieved simultaneously, although it was commonly believed that it might be done through some revolution in method or technology. As I have written elsewhere: "The story of education in this period is a story of experiments—an abundance, a cornucopia of reforms and breakthroughs, each introduced breathlessly, each kept afloat by publicity, and each sinking out of sight, soon to be replaced by more publicity, and more disappointment—The New Math. Head Start. Computer instruction. Programmed learning. Closed-circuit TV. Community control. Contract teaching. Open classrooms. Sensitivity training.''[7]

It is now fairly clear that the schools took on too much, and by doing so without sufficient caution or demurral, they were implicitly promising more than they could fulfill. Furthermore, what the schools had accepted for their agenda was not necessarily responsive to the interests and values of the ordinary families they were serving. It has been an abiding strength of U.S. education—and a source of its weakness as well—that it remains close to the needs of that essential constituency. But as the postwar era wore on, the schools found themselves trying to serve not only local interests but also the larger goals of public policy. In addition, the schools were being persuaded by our governing elites—the universities, the foundations, and the mass media—to accept the claims of the modernist spirit. In pressing these claims upon the schools—as always, in the name of progress—these elites were in fact helping to separate school from family. It is quite clear what ordinary citizens want from public education—one can discover this in casual conversation, even in a relentlessly progressive community like my own, or by examining, as I have recently done, the evidence on parental opinion about the schools. They want there to be more discipline, both in personal conduct and in maintaining academic standards.[8] They want there to be a greater emphasis on moral education, in teaching children about right and wrong. In short, the demands of the American family upon the schools reflect the spirit of traditionalism—children are to be literate, ambitious, well-behaved, and morally virtuous.

I would not want to say that the schools took the side of modernity. As is their wont, they tried to do both things at once, that is to retain the loyalty of the bourgeois family and yet offer the impression—to themselves and to others—of being "with it," contemporary, alert, and alive to the new values of the putative future. It has not quite worked, not really. If you are going to hold children to high standards of achievement, you cannot at the same time, secretly, feel that ambition is a crass or ignoble motive. If you are going to teach children to be virtuous—that is, to be brave and loyal and honest—you must yourself possess a strong sense of what is right and wrong, and you cannot in one silent part of your mind feel that there are no moral absolutes, that virtue and vice are meaningless because they are understood differently among the Kwakiutl. The compromises attempted were never quite satisfactory. Thus, if you cannot bring yourself to teach values, thinking that to be old-fashioned, or absolutist, or authoritarian, you can instead teach values clarification, wherein the parental wish for instruction in ethics is met by engaging the child in a pseudo-Socratic dialogue, ethically neutral in appearance. Yet some parents have come to feel—and I think correctly— that the very mode in which the questions are framed is a way of introducing, surreptitiously, the agenda of modernist ethics. That same uneasiness is to be found in other areas. With respect to sex education, one often feels that there is considerable deception or self-deception at work, that the bland and ingenuous intentions of instruction—to reduce illegitimate pregnancies and venereal disease, etc.—are little more than a means of introducing the panoply of modernist views of sexuality, one that tolerates sexual experimentation, glamorizes homosexuality, and so on. In the long run, these efforts at compromise further diminish the authority of the schools, in that they diminish our sense of their probity: we come to feel either that they do not know what they are doing, or that they are trying to put something over on us.

In either case the parent is further alienated from the school. That the assault on traditional education was a struggle about values did not escape the attention of ordinary citizens, who quickly came to believe that their children's schools were becoming trendy in curriculum, gimmicky in methods, lax about standards, and confused about purposes. They came to feel that the schools were abandoning their interests, were devoted to ideals they found alien, and were doing a poor job of teaching besides. Accordingly, they began to withdraw both emotional and financial support from the schools. That cooling of interest, that readiness to look elsewhere, is one of the most striking changes in the attitude in the United States toward the public schools. Twenty years ago there were few families with children to educate who would have considered anything but the public schools, for to do otherwise, or even to ponder it seriously, seemed to suggest a rejection of the democratic spirit, a rejection of a tacit social contract. That is not the case today. Most parents, of course, do choose public education, but the choice is not reflexive; one sees little of that profound allegiance to the idea of public schooling that marked an earlier generation.

What role has the family itself played in the current crisis of the schools? One cannot deny that the family is not what it used to be, that it has come under severe pressure, that it has lost at least some of its self-confidence and thus its sense of authority, especially in relation to the adolescent young. The most palpable evidence we have are the statistics on social pathology among adolescents I alluded to earlier. Edward Wynne has taken the lead in assembling this evidence and making it more widely known; the homicide rate for white males ages fifteen to nineteen has more than doubled in a fifteen-year period, as has the rate of illegitimacy for young white females, as have reported cases of gonorrhea. It is likely that much of this is associated with the decline in family stability, with increases in the divorce rate and the number and percentage of single-parent households. Interestingly enough, U.S parents, when surveyed about the lack of discipline that so troubles them, are quite ready to point their finger not only at the schools but also at the failure of some families to raise their children properly.

Nevertheless, what is true of some families is not true of all, and indeed may not be true of most. To an extraordinary degree, Americans remain attached to the family, both as an idea and as an emotional reality. I have yet to see an opinion survey that does not report a secure and happy family life as the central value in most people's lives. Nor ought we to believe, despite the lugubrious statistics just cited, that adolescence as a whole has become a disaster area. We now have a series of studies on the adolescent self-image, collected over a period of years, by the eminent psychiatrist Daniel Offer and his colleagues.[9] These important findings tell us two things. First, that there has indeed been some loss of morale, that the American adolescents studied in the 1970s are less self-confident, less self-controlled, less trusting of others than an equivalent group studied in the 1960s. Yet, second, that that erosion is on the whole modest. After a painstaking examination of the evidence, the authors conclude that the degree of pathology, alienation, and rebelliousness in the adolescent population need not alarm us; overall, these studies confirm what each and every empirical research ever done has shown, that the vast majority of teenage youngsters are competent, purposeful, at ease with themselves, and closely bonded to their families and their values.

Given the prevailing mood of social commentary on the young, on the family, on the common culture of this country, this appraisal may strike the reader as complacent to the point of eccentricity. So be it. But we must bear in mind that there are economic and class interests at stake, that to portray the family as feeble and failing is to make a case for a further expansion of the bureaucracies, in the name of helping those who cannot help themselves. That was the hidden message of that recent fiasco, the White House Conference on the Family, of the Carnegie Commission Report on Children, and of almost all other official efforts to instruct us on the imminent collapse of the family. I have tried to suggest that the school's authority has been needlessly enfeebled by the ministering angels of the state. The family has so far resisted that benevolence, to its credit, and to the advantage of us all.

Notes

1. *Birth and Fortune* (New York: Basic Books, 1980).
2. These figures are taken from Paul Bohannan, writing in *Science* (December 1980): 17–18.
3. The same point was made by Gerald Grant in his address to the conference "Crisis of Authority in the High School," University of Southern California, 1981. Also see a penetrating discussion by N. P. Emler and R. Hogan, "Developing Attitudes

Toward Law and Justice: An Integrative Review,'' in *Developmental Social Psychology*, edited by Brehm and Gibbons (London: Oxford University Press, 1981).

4. This may seem harsh but, on the contrary, my brief account does not capture the full bizarreness of this case or the strange character of its judicial reasoning. For an excellent summary and analysis, see Nathan Glazer's ''Black English and Reluctant Judges, *Public Interest* (Winter 1981): 40–54.

5. ''Judicial Activism,'' in *The Third Century*, edited by S. M. Lipset (Stanford, Calif.: Hoover Institution Press, 1979), p. 125.

6. I have borrowed here from the important book by Terry Eastland and William J. Bennett, *Counting by Race* (New York: Basic Books, 1979).

7. ''Battered Pillars of the American System: Education,'' *Fortune* (April 1975): 143.

8. For a trenchant analysis of how modernist assumptions about the nature of achievement have damaged the competence of the schools, see T. Tomlinson, ''The Troubled Years: An Interpretive Analysis of Public Schooling Since 1950,'' *Phi Delta Kappan* (January 1981): 373–76.

9. D. Offer, E. Ostrow, and K. Howard, *Adolescence: A Psychological Self-Portrait* (New York: Basic Books, 1981).

2

How the Schools Were Ruined

Writing a full half-century ago, Walter Lippmann (1925) pointed out that every optimistic book written on democracy concludes with a chapter on education. In the years since, we have seen no change in the avidness with which Americans—those consummate, ultimate democrats—pursue their optimistic, at times millennial hopes for schooling. Even when we are gloomy, our sadness is that of the disappointed yet ever hopeful lover. A few months ago I participated in the taping of a series of programs, for the National Humanities Center, on the state of U.S. secondary education. Of the five discussants, three were morose, and two ambivalent. For nearly a full day the panel complained about the public schools: their mediocrity, their low standards, the loss of discipline, the flight to the private schools, legislative intrusion, the dearth of science and mathematics teachers, the prevalence of drug use, minimum competence testing (necessary but troubling), the low SAT scores of prospective teachers, and much, much more. Apparently overwhelmed by this catalogue of woes, the moderator concluded by asking the group to comment on what it foresaw for the next ten years. Every face brightened as the discussants reported their consensus: things would be far better; demographic trends were favorable; there would be fewer students and we already had in place a splendid educational plant; social pathology showed signs of ebbing; the legislators had at last learned their lessons and were beginning to butt out; SAT scores would soon begin to show a rise, school administrators were feeling more confident; and parents were making themselves heard. All in all we could look forward to a glorious decade.

That peculiar ambivalence has been noted by a number of thoughtful observers of U.S. education. Diane Ravitch (1981) has pointed out the swings between utopian zeal and a tendency to blame the schools for "failures" that are not genuinely their responsibility. Indeed, we can note that very ambivalence in Lippmann himself. One thinks of him as a writer concerned almost exclusively with the large political issues—foreign policy, the philosophy of democratic government, public opinion—yet to a truly surprising degree he was preoccupied with education, which he saw as vital to a democratic nation, and which he wrote about persistently through a long career. Much of the time his tone is elegiac, as he looks back nostalgically to the triumphs of public education in the past, and as he laments the increasing failure of the schools to teach the Western cultural tradition. And at other times he gives way to urgency, even passion, as in his stirring Phi Beta Kappa oration (1941), calling for the nation to resume its great tradition of excellence in education.

During the past quarter-century, sentiments on the success of education have fallen and risen and fallen, as they so often do, though on the whole they have been more elated than depressed. In the heart of that period, circa 1960 to 1975, we witnessed what can only be called a frenzy of exalted expectations on the prospects of schooling. The present mood is despondent, and I suspect more so than ever before in our history, certainly more so than in the memory of most of us. A great many feel that we are not merely coming down from a high but that the high is itself to be blamed for the depths in which we now find ourselves—that the reforms of the late 1960s, undertaken thoughtlessly, giddily, produced the shallowness of learning and ennui of spirit we find so commonly in the schools.

The degree of disaffection amounts almost to disgust. Here is a sampling of opinion compiled in just the last week. The chancellor of a southern university comments to the *New York Times* that "the quality of secondary education is just awful"; an eminent political philosopher begins a powerful essay on higher education by writing that "students in our best universities do not believe in anything, and those universities are doing nothing about it, nor can they" (Bloom 1982). A noted investment banker, being interviewed on our country's loss of economic competitiveness, mentions almost off-handedly that an important part of the problem is our educational system. One of our most distinguished academicians, in a new preface to a classic book on U.S. education, says: "The once proud and efficient public school system of the United States—especially its unique free high school for all—has turned into a wasteland where violence and vice share the time with ignorance and idleness" (Barzun 1980).

Part of us wants to believe that this is rhetorical excess, reflecting the disappointment of those inflated hopes mentioned earlier. Yet the data we now have on school achievement tell us precisely the same thing. We have a masterful analysis of these findings by Barbara Lerner (1982), which will put to rest any surviving complacency about our nation's educational system. Her article concentrates on two types of comparisons: historical and international. As to the former, she marshals evidence from a number of studies showing a substantial decline in the competence of students during the past quarter-century, especially at the high school level. The decline of SAT scores is by now so well known as to have become a journalistic cliché, but Lerner points out that this key finding is corroborated by almost every other reliable study of the performance of students then and now. The international comparisons are equally dispiriting. Examining the massive (twelve volumes) research by Torsten Husén's team, Lerner concludes that our country comes off quite poorly: "Out of nineteen tests, we were never ranked first or second; we came in last three times and, if comparisons are limited to other developed nations only, the U.S. ranked at the bottom seven times." To attempt to discount the poor U.S. performance, the argument is sometimes made that many more of our youngsters remain in school to the senior year; hence are comparing bodies that differ considerably in academic selectiveness. Lerner examines this argument skeptically, putting particular stress upon the fact that the two countries that have retention rates very close to our own—Japan and Sweden—both score extremely high on these comparisons.[1] The Japanese—to no one's surprise—outscore all others, and it may be worth noting that many observers credit its superb, and very demanding, primary and secondary education for that nation's economic prowess.

Nor is the impression of widespread crime and violence in the schools without equally impressive empirical confirmation. The most recent large study we have was carried out by the National Institute of Education (some of its details are reported in Toby 1980), and it tells us that crime in the schools is substantial. For example, about 7 percent of all junior high school students report having been assaulted within the past month of the survey; a slightly higher number report having been robbed during the preceding month. Well over 10 percent of teachers report being victimized by thefts during that period. This is a topic we will return to a bit later in this essay; I mention these figures now to make the point that the widespread disaffection about U.S. schools is neither hyperbolic nor hysterical nor based on fancy but, rather, is rooted in an accurate perception of what the schools—a great many of them—are like.

How shall we understand this apparent decline in both civility and competence? Is there some fault in the national temper? Paul Samuelson believes we may be seeing a diminution of the U.S. work ethic, as a response to more general economic changes in the country. There is a substantial body of opinion that holds that the country "has had it," especially with respect to economic innovation and productivity, the corollary hypothesis being that the slackness often seen in the schools reflects a more general failure of will. We have caught the "English disease," so it is said, and are now experiencing that loss of energy that laid low Great Britain's economy. The good times of the post-World War II years took some of the edge off. Economic enterprise, technical innovation, and intellectual drive must have behind them some stimulus to effort or to risk taking; for various reasons, these motives declined in force during the past quarter-century, as an unwarranted self-satisfaction took over the national consciousness.

Another version of this theme stresses cyclical variations, shifts from era to era in the emphasis given certain values. In a seminal essay, Daniel Bell

(1972) refers to the "issue-attention cycle," referring to the waxing and waning of values over time. Writing in 1972, he notes that a decade earlier "excellence" had been at the center of national concern, and that it had receded, to be replaced by "equality." A decade later the wheel continues to turn and we are seeing a renewed interest in excellence, and if not a dethronement of the rampant egalitarianism of a decade ago, at least some signs of a dialectic between the two values. (This is another topic this essay will address.)

Whether one believes that long-range secular trends are at work, or whether we ought to be looking at shorter-range variations, most of us are gradually coming to understand that the variables we want to be looking at are ideological or, if you will, philosophical. One dubious habit of ours is to see our problems as concrete or "practical" and hence to search for technical solutions. That has in fact been a prominent feature of our thinking about the schools during the period in question. It has begun to dawn on us that at least some solutions are to be found in the realm of ideas and ideals, that we will be slow to recover past levels of achievement and decorum without giving some thought to some of the transformations in the American sensibility. In what follows I will try to explore some ways in which "ideological" changes have influenced U.S. education during the past twenty-five years, looking at transformations in four areas: authority, educational theory, the idea of merit, and the movement to modernist values.

Authority

If you spend any time at all in the schools, you soon realize that a great many of those nominally in authority have a sense of having lost it. Some feel that loss so keenly that they feel unable to go on and, if they can do so, leave the schools or simply go through the motions until they can retire. About twenty years ago, in the course of doing some research in the secondary schools, I met a junior high school principal who was widely admired, by his staff, his students, and their parents. He ran his school by a sort of omnipresence: He knew all of the children by name, and knew their families, and often their family histories. He tended to make decisions—about discipline, for example—quickly, informally, often intuitively, sometimes taking the child aside to talk, sometimes (though less often) by talking to the parents.

A few years later I was surprised to learn that he had resigned as principal, and had decided to return to teaching. I learned that he had left the job because he felt he could not adjust to a new administration, which had determined to set things in order, and was particularly concerned about the freewheeling manner in which many principals ran their schools. They were being told not to settle so much on the spot, and on their own authority. They were to keep records, to set up fixed procedures, to report things more completely to the central administration, and the like. It did not take this man long to decide that the fun had gone out of the job, and so he returned to teaching, and shortly thereafter to retirement.

This story does not necessarily bring tears to the eyes of the school people I tell it to. They are likely to say that an unfettered principal may be a fine thing so long as he is the salt of the earth, but if he were a petty tyrant, I would then feel somewhat differently, would want some controls, or at least some monitoring and accountability. There is, of course, something to be said for that—indeed it is the traditional argument for bureaucratic and jur-idical controls, that these provide evenhandedness and equity to those under the sway of authority. This is not the place to argue the issue, though it is worth pointing out that in a public school system in a democratic society, there exist other means of recourse if there are wrongs to be redressed. In any case, the decision of the central school administration to tighten things up had little to do with any wish to assure evenhandedness. It had to do entirely with the need to protect the school system against litigation, to comply with an increasing number of federal regulations, and to meet the demands of activist groups. It is fair to say that the central administration, in wresting authority from the principals, was itself responding to the loss of its own authority, as it was forced to meet the actual and projected demands of other groups and institutions, groups that for the most part had only a special or temporary interest in schools and schooling, and rarely in the question of educational quality.

That sense of lost authority is felt most strongly at the secondary school level. A high school principal may tell you, as one told me, that he finds himself answerable to the students, their parents, his teachers, his superin-tendent, the school board, the local press, and the rules and regulations coming from the state legislature, the Congress, and various courts. As it happened, this man is unusually effective and rather enjoyed these challenges, which he took to be a test of his mettle, and a test he could pass easily. But a great many of his colleagues do not have his panache and, faced with a multitude of conflicting pressures, tend to retreat to bureaucratic authority, avoiding decisions and commitments until the proper rules can be found, cited, and applied. That paralysis of authority—genuine authority—is transmitted to teachers and students and others, and soon enough becomes the expected ethos to which everyone accommodates.

The effects are seen most clearly in the area of discipline. The extraordinary growth of litigiousness, and of litigation, meant that school administrations—and ultimately teachers and principals—became gun-shy, fearing that a wrong move would land them in the courts or on the front pages of the local press. Much of the time, of course, that fear is exaggerated, but there were enough instances of gratuitous litigation to reinforce anyone's caution—or paranoia. In my own school district, a judge took it upon himself to overturn a standard disciplinary penalty meted out in a case of serious vandalism by a high school student. That a case of this sort is taken to court, that a judge decides to accept it, and that he rules in favor of the defendant—all of that suggests a profound change in the atmosphere of education and in the authority of the schools. Gerald Grant (1982) has provided us with some illuminating—and depressing—reports stemming from his extensive survey of U.S. high schools. Some of his observations are worth quoting in full:

> Jurisdiction is so narrowly defined that a student who comes to a school principal after lunch complaining of being beaten up is asked which side of the street he was standing on when the beating occurred. If he was across the street, it would be out of the school's jurisdiction and hence of no concern to the principal. Often when students need help, teachers are afraid to intervene for fear of legal reprisals. One teacher, explaining why she hadn't interfered with a girl who clawed another in her classroom, said, "You'll only be after trouble if you physically handle them." Another teacher was still shaking as she told us about a group of students who had verbally assaulted her and made sexually degrading comments about her in the hall. When we asked why she didn't report the students, she responded, "Well, it wouldn't have done any good." "Why not?" we pressed. "I didn't have any witnesses," she replied.

These vignettes focus upon the helplessness of teachers, but we should also note the thuggishness of the students depicted. As I have written elsewhere (Adelson 1981), the loss of authority in the schools could not have come at a worse time for those deputed to run them. Many youngsters remain in the upper grades of high school who would have left in an earlier era; and among these a small but significant number are resentful and fractious. More important still, we have seen a rise in the number and proportion of antisocial adolescents—there was an astonishing increase in *all* indices of social pathology among the young during the past quarter century, in assaults, suicides, homicides, drug use, out-of-wedlock pregnancy. The economic demographers—notably Richard Easterlin (1980)—argue that in a crowded youth cohort, that is, when the proportion of the young to the total population is high, we are liable to find a rise in such phenomena, an indirect effect of the demoralization that many youngsters feel when they recognize that their economic prospects are marginal, that they are losing out to more talented competitors in a tight market.[2] There were also larger families, which meant a decrease in the number of intellectually able youngsters. Hence, in the postwar era, the schools confronted a horde of youngsters, a large percentage of whom were academically weak and/or antisocial. It was at that very moment that they found themselves stripped of their accustomed powers.

The weakened authority of teachers and principals also led to a weakening of academic demands. Teachers coping with unruly students could not give themselves fully to instruction; those coping unsuccessfully lost the esteem of all students. A demoralization often set in that diminished the will to set and abide by high expectations. Gilbert Sewall (1982) says that his study of a large number of high schools persuaded him that in most of them students rather than teachers decide how much work they will do. Students seem to agree; a large number of high school youngsters, when polled, say they are not given enough homework. It seems evident from these and other reports (see below) that during the late 1960s a sense of impotence overcame many of those managing and teaching in the schools, producing in turn that inanition of purpose necessary for sustained academic effort.

The crisis of authority in the university system did not involve discipline—except during moments of upheaval—so much as it involved the erosion or collapse of academic standards. One hardly needs to belabor the matter, for the crisis in the universities was the most publicized set of events in education during the quarter-century we are considering.[3] The academic faculties lost much of their control over curriculum, grading, intellectual standards, and above all the tacit definition of what the university ought to be. Those losses have not been made up.

One might argue, as Robert Nisbet (1971) and many others did, that the faculties lost their authority because they did not have a strong definition of the university to begin with, that in particular the specifically pedagogical functions of higher education had been treated by many of them with derision or had at most been given lip service. Hence there was an intellectual flaccidity, a confusion of inner purpose, that left the universities unable to defend themselves against the anti-intellectualism of the student movement. Be that as it may, the events of the late 1960s had as their primary effect—and perhaps as one of their latent purposes—a serious decline in intellecutal quality. The social sciences were the most grievously affected, in my view, especially those disciplines, such as psychology and sociology, that proved particularly attractive to the youngsters of the 1970s. One found that credit was given in courses where neither work nor attendance was required; there were a number of embarrassing moments when departments discovered that ''A'' grades had been given to students who had dropped out of the course at the beginning of the semester. In some cases instructors guaranteed an ''A'' grade for any student enrolling, either as a protest against the Vietnam war or merely against the competitiveness of academic life. Some courses in psychology became therapy groups or other exercises in self-expression. In other instances the subject matter was entirely politicized; one of my sons, attending an Ivy League university, found that the introductory psychology course (and the only one given that year) consisted exclusively of denunciations of capitalism. To be sure, these cases were in the minority and the faculty as a whole, even in affected departments, did not participate nor even approve. There was a great deal of muttering and handwringing, but little action taken. There proved to be little spirit in most departments to impose restraints on the faculty for fear of diminishing academic freedom. It was all seen as a kind of fever that could be left untreated because it would ultimately run its course. The uninfected faculty thereupon retreated even further into research or specialized graduate education, and withdrew even more decisively from the pedagogical missions of the university.

We now find that a blessed amnesia has begun to settle over us, and with it a tendency to minimize the impact of that period, on the grounds that the consequences were limited. In fact they were extensive, enduring, and have yet to be repaired. Consciously or otherwise, many teachers simply gave up requiring sustained effort from their students. In many instances this was done cynically, in others out of despair. Some teachers came to believe that the entire academic enterprise had been so compromised by the failure to resist student demands that the game was no longer worth the candle. In other instances a mood of manic zeal persuaded some teachers that they were living in a Golden Age so far as student achievement was concerned. There has never been a more self-celebratory moment in the history of U.S. higher education. College authorities told anyone who would listen that they were privileged to be teaching the most talented group of students the planet has ever seen; many students solemnly agreed.

That self-congratulation produced—or perhaps merely rationalized—the notorious grade inflation that dominated higher education, and that persists. Each year GPAs rose, ultimately to dizzying heights. In some universities the average GPA was at a level that had once been reserved for the highest academic honors, which forced a change in long-standing criteria for the awarding of such honors. One saw the same phenomenon, less concretely but far more vividly, in reading the letters of recommendation written by university teachers about students applying to graduate and professional schools. Where a few years before these letters had on the whole been positive but measured, they were now uniformly euphoric. During this period I served a term as chairman of admissions to our graduate program in clinical psychology and, wishing to test the hypothesis that these letters were no longer credible, decided to read every one of the more than one thousand recommendations submitted that year to see whether I could find anything other than words of extreme praise. As it happens I did find one, from a most unusual source— the abbot of a seminary who said in no uncertain terms that the applicant, one of his seminarians, was mistaken in his view of himself, and of his readiness for graduate school. Every other letter was enthusiastic, and a great many were ecstatic, claiming that the applicant was the most brilliant in the past five or ten or fifteen years of the writer's experience. There were of course a great many gifted candidates in our pool of applicants, but about one-third to one-half were mediocre at best, and these students received equally glowing commendation. One might read three such intoxicated letters regarding an applicant who could not compose a coherent complex sentence, and whose transcript showed that there had been no college-level instruction in mathematics or science or language or philosophy or history.

And that was, of course, the inevitable and inherent counterpart to the inflation of grades: a devalued curriculum and debased standards of achievement. There was a general retreat from required courses, or sequences of courses, and from the ideal of a general, liberal education. What was most troubling was that the liberalization of the curriculum seemed to have nothing behind it, aside from the pious notion that coercion deadens enthusiasm, which in turn inhibits learning. Those in favor of a core curriculum seemed too disheartened or confused to argue their case persuasively. Perhaps the most depressing experience I can remember from that period was listening to a general faculty discussion on whether we ought to institute a new bachelor's degree, the only purpose of which seemed to be to enable some students to escape requirements they found noxious, especially languages. Listening to that listless discussion made it clear that many of the faculty could no longer "remember the answers," that the vision of a liberal education had been eclipsed, and that the only arguments being brought forth were crassly utilitarian—that languages were useful acquisitions, and the like. Yet one also knew that most of those sitting there so mutely could achieve a Churchillian eloquence in defense of other and narrower propositions, for example that their department absolutely had to have two instead of one course in nonparametric statistics.

As we all know, the colleges not only offered junk courses of their own but, by lowering admissions standards, encouraged the high schools to use junk courses for admission to the university. Or was it the other way around? Do the high schools, through their failure to educate their students adequately, make them unfit for college work? There is no way we will ever answer those questions, except to agree that each pulled the other down, and despite some grumbling here and there, neither objected too vehemently to the pulling down. In all likelihood, both secondary and higher education were being responsive to the same obscure but compelling forces in American life, which involved a peculiar mixture of inflated self-esteem on the one hand, along with an exhaustion of will on the other.

Remedies

The zeal for education in the United States provides the energy for programs of innovation and reform. It is hard to think of another country where we find so many proposals for the improvement of schooling. The zest for reform was evident throughout the postwar period and, as always, reflected larger social and ideological preoccupations. The Conant Report was one of the most influential documents in this century's history of education, in helping to establish as normative the idea of a consolidated high school able to offer all students the abundance of opportunities so often not available in smaller and more provincial schools. A second landmark event was the Sputnik "crisis," which led to substantial improvements in the scientific curricula and an infusion of federal money into mathematics, science, and technological education. These were establishment ventures, in that their intention was to strengthen the existing system rather than to overturn it. In no sense were the aims utopian; they were within reach, given sufficient energy and effort, and in both cases the goals were readily achieved and became an enduring part of the pattern of education.

The movements for reform that succeeded these—let us place them in time from about 1960 to about 1975—are not so briskly characterized because they move in many different directions. But they can be placed into two general categories, which we will call "technological" and "liberationist." The technological direction encompasses a wide variety of proposals, some narrow, some quite far-reaching, wherein we find some effort to manipulate the materials or specific processes of learning. The simplest examples involve exploiting for the classroom technical devices originally developed for other purposes. The use of cassette tapes for language and other instruction is one obvious example, as is the use of closed-circuit television. In most instances these techniques are meant to hasten learning or extend it but do not aim at any radical transformation of the teaching process. Although their introduction is often announced by inventors and early enthusiasts as "revolutionary," they generally survive as ancillary methods woven into the quotidian activities of the classroom.

There are other modes of technology that are—potentially—more ambitious and even radical in intention. The microcomputer is one such device—again, potentially—in that it may have the capacity to transform the very processes of learning, though whether it will do so remains to be seen. Another approach that is "technological" is programmed learning, through the systematic use of reinforcers (à la Skinner), and its close cousin "contract teaching." Though neither of these necessarily involves mechanical or electronic devices, their aim is to rearrange and rationalize the learning process itself, basing themselves upon a technology of response acquisition. The Skinnerian and other behavioral approaches to education were at their inception utopian, in that they promised not merely the transformation of the classroom but a formula for the remaking of human behavior in society itself. These approaches have, however, proved themselves adaptable, in that they can be borrowed from piecemeal. It is my impression that the Skinnerian emphasis these days is seen in a more deliberate effort on the part of classroom teachers to reward students, both in general and as they acquire specific skills.

It is the second direction of reform—the liberationist—that had a more profound initial impact on education. These movements define themselves as radical. They see as a major aim of education to undo the constraints imposed by excessive socialization. They believe that conventional child-rearing chains the "true self," and with it creativity and the capacity to learn easily and joyously. Conventional education then reinforces that enchainment; it merely completes what traditional child-rearing has left undone. Liberationist writing posited—at times merely implied—a "true self" that is essentially virtuous, and it is that optimism about human nature, that tacit denial of original sin, that was part of its attraction in an era marked by political utopianism. The movement was often thought to stem from Dewey, in that it aimed to be "progressive"; my own view is that much of the time it donned Deweyan colors much as a wolf may dress in sheep's clothing. The immediate sires of most postwar progressive writing were A. S. Neill, Wilhelm Reich, and Paul Goodman. The ultimate progenitor is Rousseau (or some sides of him), and before him the Gnostics and Cathars.

Liberationist writing was a bold attempt to redefine the purpose and practice of education, in part by redefinitions of human psychology. The student was to be seen not as recalcitrant but as avid (under the correct circumstances), and the teacher was to be seen not as a drill master so much as a partner or inspirational leader. Subject matter was to take second place to the perfection of the self: the cultivation of sensitivity, creativity, and the like. The writing is by turns polemical, hortatory, and evangelical; it stands in sharp contrast to the modesty and cautiousness of formulation that we find in other presumably "experimental" writers on education, such as William James, John Dewey, and Jean Piaget.

Given these sweeping aims, aims that went far beyond "method" as we ordinarily understand that, there tended to be little concern with the actualities of the classroom and of instruction—John Holt is an exception. Revolutionary movements tend to be both totalistic and sectarian, that is, on the one hand they aim to produce conversion in the auditors and enlist them totally in the cause, and on the other, a sense of exclusivity develops within the movement itself. For these reasons, the new progressivism did not take over U.S. schooling—far from it. It proved to be self-limiting. In those few communities where it enjoyed a large constituency, there might be some effort to satisfy it by offering special programs, or in some cases by setting aside one or two special schools. But it rarely went beyond that because the more radical the program proposed, the more certain there was to be community resistance. My hometown of Ann Arbor is quite instructive in this regard. It hired an ultraprogressive school superintendent who was able to establish an open-classroom school at the elementary level, and two small liberationist high schools (one soft-shelled, the other hard-shelled), and do little else. The very fact of a liberationist regime meaning business served to mobilize the conservative elements of an extremely liberal university community, to the degree that they were able to elect a school board and in time depose the superintendent and appoint a centrist administrator.

Yet I would not for a moment want to imply that the liberationist movements were without effect; to the contrary, they were to be deeply influential. They were able to give credence and respectability to the idea that the cultivation of "the total personality" was as important a goal as the acquisition of subject matter and of cognitive skills. Hence it became easier to establish coursework on such topics as "family living" and "personal adjustment" in lieu of conventional offerings in history and the social sciences. By far the major impact of liberationism was the adversary stance it took to the existing system of public education, and to those who taught and managed in that system. The messages of the movement were these: the schools are extremely dull places for the young; the teachers were rigid and unimaginative, and could not engage the enthusiasm of their students; the secondary schools have as their essential but unspoken assumption keeping youngsters out of the labor market; hence they function as prisons, in that they contain an energetic population resentful of its confinement.

Yet even this fairly blunt paraphrase does not quite capture the contempt expressed toward schools and schoolteachers. One has to reread these writings to recall the tonalities (here again I think most of us suffer from some amnesia). The depiction of the ordinary school and the ordinary teacher as supercilious and at times scurrilous: these are held to be mean-spirited people servicing mean institutions. Often the writer offers himself as exemplary, though of course with the usual moues of humility or self-irony. The contrast is made with some hack or dragon or tyrant. The author's students learn more, are more creative, are suffused with the joy of learning, and love their teacher almost beyond words. These writers were generally young and viewed themselves as maverick. But we saw precisely the same attitudes in establishment figures, such as Charles Silberman, who, in an extremely influential book, *Crisis in the Classroom* (1970), takes a position that Lerner, quite correctly, characterizes as extremist in rhetoric and messianic in claims.

Nevertheless, the climate of the times was such that these diagnoses of education proved to be persuasive to elite opinion, soon found their way into the mass media, became conventional wisdom, and ultimately were enshrined in the teaching of the education schools. There was little countervailing argument. If you look through the holdings of a good public library, or a good used-book store, you will find, abundantly, the books by Silberman, Holt,

Kohl, Kozol, Friedenberg, Goodman, Herndon, Lennard. You will find hardly anything from that era by writers representing a contrary position. If you survey the journals of opinion of that time, you will find little attention given to problems of primary and secondary education, and what little there is, sympathetic to the reform outlook. Most such journals limited their attention to the universities, or to the political problems in the primary and secondary schools, especially integration and busing.[4]

This disdainful depiction of the schoolteacher did grievous damage to the self-esteem of a group many of whom were already uncertain about themselves and their value—a group that was not seen as "professional," nor as "intellectual," nor as successful in worldly terms. That loss of self-regard made it especially difficult for them to demand a disciplined effort from their students. Having been portrayed as either drones or jailers made many of them yearn to be seen as the very opposite, as charismatic teachers or as laid-back adolescents, neither role requiring or inspiring self-discipline on the part of the students. Young teachers in particular were tempted to embrace and exemplify the new values, and to serve as role models for advanced thinking. Here is Fred Bloom (1978), a brilliant young psychiatrist living in rural Maine:

> A teacher, a woman with twenty years teaching experience, resigned recently from the new community school in our town because she was expected to go on the "team" weekend encounter of the social-studies faculty. On the weekend, she told me, the faculty members play therapy games. Among other games, they lie on the ground and roll back and forth over one anothers' bodies to develop "closeness" and "trust" among the team. "I went on it last year," she said, "and besides, I can't see why, after twenty years, I have to be shown how to get along. But really, you can't get along at that school unless you go in for that kind of thing."

The liberationist school has lost influence, at least for the moment. One suspects its success would not be repeated today—not only because of obvious changes in the political climate but also because we would not insist that some evidence be provided. If such bold claims were made today, we would surely ask: "Is that so? Who said so? Do you have findings? Please show them to me." During the past decade no serious discussion of educational policy has proceeded very far without some genuflection to the facts—even when we recognize that most of the time the facts are used to justify positions already taken. Nevertheless, the appeal to findings, though it has its limits and corruptions, makes it difficult to keep discourse at an entirely sentimental level.

What the new empirical literature has shown is in a sense startling, in that it has confirmed many banal, commonsense, and traditional beliefs about the sources of effective teaching: that learning tends to flourish in schools governed by a strong and unified leadership (Rutter 1979); that it requires an orderly environment (Coleman et al. 1982); that mastery of a subject is in large part a function of the time spent in learning it (Walberg 1982); and that homework is therefore important (Keith 1982, and many others).

All of the findings cited are new, in that they are quite recent, but curiously enough they are not at all new, in that similar findings have been in the literature for some time now, ready and awaiting a readership. In an excellent review of many of these Herbert Walberg (1982) departs from an otherwise straightforward discussion of the data on teaching effectiveness to say with some justifiable exasperation: "The impressive accumulation of these scientific results in the last decade seems to have gone unnoticed by many researchers, educators, and the general public. It might indeed be concluded from widely publicized reports that schools are pathological institutions and that neither educators nor research workers know how to cure their problems and increase their productivity."

As it happens, we did know and do know many of the answers, within limits, although it remains unclear whether we will be able to put into practice what we know. And as it happens, many of the things that we know are embarrassingly obvious: intellectual achievement requires intellectual seriousness, the willingness to take pains, earnestness, motivation. But we were led away from these rather trite truths by the dominant intellectual writings of the 1960s. The liberationists did not see the school for what it was, or what it might realistically become; they saw it as a simulacrum of a society they despised, which they saw as oppressive and racist. They saw themselves as guerrillas in the service of human freedom. To liberate the student from the teacher symbolized larger and more splendid liberations that were to take place throughout the world. The other dominant movement of reform was, as we have argued, overly preoccupied with technique. It believed that schooling could be improved by the use of modern devices, or of new information on the rationalization of learning.

Both these approaches elided what we now see as central to sustained academic achievement: the internal morale marked by effort, drive, and persistence supported by purposeful leadership in the schools. The liberationist theorists either ignored those elements altogether, or assumed that sustained academic achievement would be evoked by the unbinding of a thwarted inner goodness. The technological theorists also ignored it, at least much of the time, or assumed it would be evoked by the right machine, or an up-to-date syllabus, or by scientifically devised methods of learning. Neither of these positions is altogether false, yet we can see how illusory they were. Although both positions are now in some decline, they are by no means eclipsed. They draw upon two of the deepest and most enduring themes in American thinking—the idea of perfectibility, and the love of technique—and one can expect that sooner or later, in one form or another, and for better or worse, these ideas will once again be felt in the American theory of education.

Merit and Equality

During the second half of the quarter-century our conception of equality began to be transformed in ways that were to be merely important for education. That idea has had, needless to say, a long provenance in U.S. political history, indeed so long and complex and tortuous as to discourage any effort here to trace it, even summarily. The interested reader may want to consult Lakoff's *Equality in Political Philosophy* (1964) for an extensive discussion of the history of the idea, or Eastland and Bennett's *Counting by Race* (1979) for a cogent analysis of equality in relation to racial preference.

"Equality" has been so obsessive a theme during the postwar era that we are liable to think of it as a permanent feature of our political landscape. Yet it has been a central issue, politically and intellectually, only at certain moments of our history. It gained vigor and attention in the 1950s, with the explosive growth of the civil rights movement. During that period, equality came to mean racial equality—to end systematic discrimination against Blacks, particularly the denial of electoral rights and the sanctioned pattern of segregation in schools and public facilities. These struggles won, indeed with surprising ease, the quest for equality moved ahead, toward the achievement of equal opportunity in such areas as schooling, housing, and work, and to the extension of equality to other putatively disadvantaged groups, primarily women.

These extensions of equality enjoyed widespread and enthusiastic assent, certainly among the educated and among political liberals. But in the late 1960s we began to see not so much an extension as a transformation of the earlier idea of equality. Though that transformation drew upon some of the most ancient utopian ideals (see Cohn, *Pursuit of the Millennium* [1961], and Manuel and Manuel, *Utopian Thought in the Western World* [1979]), it represented a startling new departure in the U.S. political context and, as we will see, generated a bitter and continuing struggle among intellectuals. The notion of equality of opportunity involved what the late Charles Frankel (1973) termed "corrective egalitarianism": the idea that a primary aim of social policy is to remove or modify those circumstances that disadvantage some classes of citizens. One might, for example, provide financial subsidies so that poor but able youngsters could attend college. One might even strive to eliminate poverty altogether, by income guarantees for the poorest members of the nation, so as to reduce those economic inequities that hobble the latent talents of those born to impoverished families. That mode gave way to what Frankel termed "redemptive egalitarianism." Whereas in the earlier understanding one sought to give each player a more or less equal chance to succeed, in the newer conception the fact of inequality itself was seen as unjust, in that it derived from external circumstances that favored one player over another, or from the presence of internal qualities—intelligence and drive— that the player had not "earned," or because it was itself capricious, the result of good luck and little more. That being the case, one could not say that a given person was morally more deserving of good fortune than another; and that being the case, the aim of social policy is to minimize differences in fortune or privilege stemming from differences in achievement. The short-hand formula is now familiar: from equality of opportunity to equality of result.

The new position on equality was stated elegantly in one of the few philosophical books in our era to become famous: John Rawls's *A Theory of Justice* (1971), which was—as all commentators have agreed—a book of remarkable originality. As Frankel said, the author's purpose—"which is nothing less than to overturn two centuries of empirical, utilitarian, and positivistic philosophies"—is "breath-taking." Yet the popularity of the book among the educated, the quickness with which it seized the attention of intellectuals, had less to do with its originality than with the way it centered upon the ideal of equality. In a long, brilliant, and withering critique of the book, Robert Nisbet (1974) argued that the "passion for equality, first vivid at the time of the Puritan revolution, has been the essential mark of every major revolution in the West" and has in particular been the "mainspring of radicalism." Hence in an era such as the late 1960s, in which a great many intellectuals deemed themselves revolutionary, one would expect to find the wish to celebrate a book of great intellectual power itself celebrating a revolutionary idea of equality.

Rawls's doctrine did not long escape scrutiny. By drawing such considerable attention, it evoked almost immediately some brilliant displays of contraegalitarian writing, the most famous being Robert Nozick's prize-winning *Anarchy, State, and Utopia* (1974), which, roughly speaking, did for libertarianism what Rawls had done for egalitarianism. However, the main thrust of the response to Rawls came not from the libertarian movement but from the intellectuals commonly categorized as neoconservative, those associated with *Commentary* and *Public Interest*—Daniel Bell (1972), Irving Kristol (1978), Daniel Patrick Moynihan (1972), Charles Frankel (1973), and Robert Nisbet (1974), to mention only a few. The major intellectual debate of the early 1970s pitted these writers against the egalitarians. The issues debated were pivotal in the fission between intellectuals in the postwar era, entirely comparable in gravity and scope to the debate about the Cold War in the late 1940s. As we might expect, the debate about equality involved, as a leading issue, a fierce argument about education.

In the traditional understanding of equality, it was posited that economic and other disadvantages acted to constrain the appearance and expression of talent. Jefferson's "natural aristocrats," ordinarily lost to the world by the accidents of privation, were to be uncovered by universal education. Schooling for all was to serve two aims: raising the level of literacy and competence in the general population; and bringing into cultivation those talents that would otherwise have lain fallow. The infusion of federal money into higher education after World War II has served both goals: college training was made available to large numbers of young men; and an elite education was offered to those who qualified by virtue of intellectual merit.

Soon after the war ended, the prestigious private colleges and universities began to give up the exclusion of students by religion, ethnicity, and social background. Much the same happened at the graduate and professional level and in the recruitment of college faculty. That change took place quickly and for the most part silently—without litigation, protest, or government intervention, as though an agreement had been arrived at tacitly, based on a sense of social justice, and a reckoning of the nation's needs. The example of Nazi Germany was a sufficient warning of the long-range effects of social bigotry. And beyond that, the country became aware—as did other nations—that its technical progress would depend upon the cultivation of intelligence, and that the great universities could no longer be enclaves restricted by class and caste.

The effect of that tacit decision was to open the great universities to groups previously excluded or restricted—the Jews most visibly, but also that majority of the population that had not been so much excluded as discouraged. Access was determined by accomplishment rather than by membership in favored social groups; and accomplishment (or its potential) was determined by objective and universalistic means.

That was the onset of an era of merit. One can find it taking place in almost all industrialized countries. That evolution—from ascription to achievement, and from particularism to universalism—is a fundamental tenet in this sociological theory of modernity (see Bell 1972, inter alia). One might even want to argue that in some ways the U.S. system has been more or less meritocratic than most, and that there are far more openings available in higher education than in any other country, and that the culling takes place late and is less rigorous. We have had no equivalent of the British 11-plus examinations, nor have we had anything to approach in rigor the Japanese and French examinations for entrance to the university. But the opening of our universities proved to be a major reason for the extraordinary vitality that marked our national intellectual, scientific, and artistic life during the postwar period. This country achieved leadership in many of the arts and humanities, and in almost all of the natural and social sciences, and did so much of the time by a seemingly effortless succession of European emigres by native talent. And if one looks closely at our indigenous "second generation" of extraordinary achievement—Nobel laureates, for example—we find that it is made up in significant degree of the previously excluded and discouraged, the ethnics and provincials.

Nevertheless, the hegemony of merit proved to be surprisingly brief. Not that it was abandoned—it is hard to imagine that happening entirely in any technological society, nor for any length of time. Yet it did lose its primacy, that unspoken assent previously given by all significant strata of the society. The term *meritocracy* soon came into use among the adversary elites, that term used pejoratively, or dismissively, certainly without much loving kindness. The meritocracy, it was implied, was composed not of the meritorious but of those who had the knack of taking tests, or making the right moves in school, or ingratiating themselves with selection committees. Furthermore, the tests themselves were suspect, in that there was said to be no clear relationship between doing well on them and doing well later in life. Nor was there much relationship between doing well in school and later success. Perhaps success was a matter of luck, no more than a roll of the dice. That idea, that social mobility was fortuitous, was the theme of one of the most influential books of the period, Christopher Jencks's *Inequality* (1973), based upon his analysis of the first Coleman study.

These critiques might not have had so powerful an influence had it not been for race, which proved once again to make the U.S. case different from those of comparable countries. What would otherwise have remained an argument about social class and social mobility became an argument about race, and in so doing inherited our country's complex historical legacy of racial division and bitterness. The conflation of race and class produced, among many other things, a fierce attack on intelligence testing, largely because of the false assumption that most psychometricians held Blacks to be genetically inferior in intelligence. Hostility to IQ testing—much of it ignorant, or uninformed, or based on the inflation of half-truths—was then generalized to other forms of aptitude and achievement testing. That hostility soon extended to the very idea of intelligence as a measurable attribute. A dogmatic environmentalism came to dominate most discourse on these matters among social scientists, and among much of the educated public. Differences among individuals, especially in capacity, were held to be due to socialization alone unless proved otherwise—and the conditions for proving otherwise were essentially impossible to meet. With the passage of time, the rhetorical ante was raised, in that the arguments for equality became ever more shrill. The elegant moral reasoning of a Rawls and the intricate analyses of a Jencks gave way to the vulgarity of William Ryan's *Equality* (1981), which holds that measured variations in intelligence are a scam devised by the "very rich" to swindle the rest of us.

It was a climate in which the idea of merit could not survive, at least not the belief that native gifts, cultivated by learning and effort, would produce achievement and reward, the fruits of which would ultimately add to the common good. Instead, the following propositions became commonplace: Achievement has little to do with talent, nor with effort, nor with schooling. Differences in ability are a fiction, or are not measurable, or are a kind of confidence trick. The ruling class makes sure that the system is rigged to protect its own kind. The gifted can take care of themselves, or are the products of special privilege, or are in any case not worthy of admiration or special attention. There is no reason to stress cognitive skills over all others; to do so is a bourgeois prejudice because it takes as much intelligence to survive on the street as to solve quadratic equations.

These propositions were not often stated quite so crudely, but stated they were, and they helped establish a moral and intellectual ambience in which striving, self-discipline, and the intellectual life itself came to be devalued. That in turn produced a loss of morale that was to diminish the moral energy of the public schools.

Values

Beginning in the middle 1960s, a great many parents became aware that something was going awry in the schools. Those with children in the middle or high schools could recognize symptoms of demoralization and loss of purpose: drugs were sold openly and school authorities were not doing much about it; courses in math, science, and languages were disappearing; students were rarely asked to write, and were given little work to bring home. Parents also began to believe that they could not get their concerns acted upon. On issues of discipline, school principals might say that their hands were tied because of new developments in the law, or because the schools were wary of litigation. On the issue of a softened curriculum, they might point to changes in college entrance requirements, or utter pieties about bringing education up to date and keeping it in tune with the times, leading the parents to think of themselves as back numbers. Or principals might agree, wholeheartedly, then go on to say that things were not what they once were, that students were less manageable, less motivated, and that many families had become indifferent to the academic progress of their children.

That parents, and the general public, were becoming disenchanted with the quality of public education is evident from trend statistics collected by the Roper Organization during the past quarter-century.[5] These show a striking loss of confidence in the local schools during the period we are considering: in 1959, 64 percent of Americans believed that public education was doing an excellent or good job; that figure declined to 48 percent by 1978; most of the drop took place between 1967 and 1971, when the proportion giving a favorable rating declined by eleven points, from 61 to 50 percent. We can infer what may have been involved in that loss of confidence from the Gallup figures on discipline in the schools. Those believing that the schools are too lax jumps from 39 percent in 1969 to an extraordinary 84 percent in 1978, about as close to unanimity as anyone ever achieves in opinion polling. That conclusion receives distinct support from the potential targets of disciplinary toughness—the high school students themselves, a majority of whom report as "big problems" the following: classroom disturbances (64 percent), marijuana use (60 percent), theft (56 percent), and vandalism (52 percent).

The remedies proposed for the schools also show some startling changes. There is a sharp increase in sentiment for a greater amount of homework for high school students, from 39 percent in 1965 to 63 percent in 1978. Many students themselves agree: 48 percent think the work is not hard enough, contrasted with 23 percent who believe it is too hard. Finally, there is a striking jump in the number favoring competence testing: from 50 percent of the general public in 1965 to 82 percent in 1978. Once again, the students agree: in 1977, 65 percent favored a standard examination to earn the diploma, as against 35 percent who were opposed.

These findings offer some compelling testimony: the public disaffection about the schools has been felt for well over a decade; and there is nothing whimsical about it, it has been responsive to the actual vicissitudes of U.S. schooling, specifically the easing of both academic and disciplinary demands. But what is most striking is the extraordinary cleavage it reveals between public and elite opinion on the schools. It is during the late 1960s where we begin to see a sharp decline in public confidence, and that is precisely when the liberationist writing of a few years earlier had come to dominate elite attitudes and then the media and ultimately educational practice. By the early 1970s the public attitude had become cynical when not altogether hostile— the schools had been turned into a playpen, at times a dangerous one, where little serious learning took place. Yet these perceptions were either ignored or rejected by vanguard opinion, which found itself drawn to the views of Silberman or Friedenberg to the effect that the public schools were at best stultifying or at worst the moral equivalent of Orwell's Room 101. Though it was rarely put this way, the schools were held to be havens of rather dreary lower-middle-class sensibility, lacking the presumed spontaneity and freedom of lower-class life, or the sensitivity and sophistication to be found in upper-middle-class milieux.

In one form or another that cleavage continues—it is one of the most striking aspects of U.S. education today that there is so little agreement on what is wrong with the schools, how it came about, and what if anything ought to be done about it. The public's sourness about local schooling—now beginning to change, though rather slowly—is simply not shared by a great many experts in education, who may agree that there has been a decline in quality but take it in stride, seeing it as the price to be paid for universal education. The effort to raise the level of achievement by a more focused means of instruction will produce complaints about "repression." The second Coleman report, which was greeted by many with a shrug of the shoulders, as involving little more than a demonstration of the obvious, generated a savage response from many in the education establishment, in part because of the ostensibly hard line it implied about discipline. Nor is it the question of quality alone that divides opinion. Shall we teach morality in the schools, and if so, how? The struggle on "values clarification" between some teachers and some parents has turned on the claim of the latter that under the pretext of teaching children *how* to think about moral issues, a program of moral relativism has in fact been inserted into the curriculum. The occasional disputes about sex education provide another example: though the opinion polls show that most people—even those calling themselves conservative—approve of the idea of teaching youngsters about sexuality, a great many parents become uneasy or oppositional if they come to believe that more than information is being conveyed, that social attitudes they find offensive are being taught as well.

These disputes are by no means new to the schools, which have always been an arena for the playing out of arguments about values and ideologies. Nevertheless, these quarrels now seem more intense than before, and seem to involve a larger range of issues. We may well have seen, since the middle 1960s, some loss of consensus as to the functions of the schools, and on the values they are meant to embody and teach. If so, that loss of consensus would have to do with a widespread shift in values among the population at large, from "materialist" to "postmaterialist" values. Portents of that change were pointed to by social theorists for many years, and the early appearances were noted by some of our keenest social scientists, in David Riesman's *The Lonely Crowd* (1950), in Daniel Bell's writings on the postindustrial society (1973), and in the work of the psychologist Abraham Maslow (1962). These early observations have more recently been supported in a variety of studies, most significantly in Ronald Inglehart's *The Silent Revolution* (1977), which presents data from most of the industrialized countries of the West. As these nations advance into a more affluent, postindustrial society, one less dominated by economic survival and fears of scarcity, material values lose their hold over large segments of the citizenry—especially those cohorts that are young and have enjoyed higher education—and are replaced by a greater emphasis upon aesthetic, intellectual, and communitarian values. It is a trend visible in all developed societies, and most striking in the most prosperous of them—Belgium, the United States, and Switzerland—and much less so

in poorer countries like Italy and Ireland. Certain political movements—
environmentalism, for example, both here and abroad—can be understood
fully only if we keep in mind the more general changes in sensibility they
rest upon.

Of course it is not at all clear whether this shift in values will survive the
moment, or more precisely, will survive the current worldwide economic
recession. Certainly some of the more flamboyant claims made for a new
level of consciousness, as by Herbert Marcuse and Charles Reich, now seem—
to put it generously—overstated. Nevertheless, it seems quite evident that
the emergence of these new values—transient or not, deeply rooted or not—
had some considerable consequences for U.S. education, not merely because
new values always tend to jostle the status quo but even more so because in
this case they provided the agenda for a new and assertive constituency in
our national life.

The new constituency is made up of a significant social cadre, often called
the New Class—occupationally centered in government, education, journalism, and higher education; of extremely high educational attainment; and
usually from affluent and highly educated families. It considers itself to be
a part of or at the least allied to the intelligentsia. The growth and evolution
of this cadre was sensed, with an uncanny prescience, by a number of astute
observers—Joseph Schumpeter and George Orwell, for example, but most
strikingly in some early essays by Lionel Trilling, who noted its adversarial
tendencies, its sense of affiliation with those elements in the literary and
political culture that were hostile to the given order, which in American terms
meant the business culture.

These intuitions about the New Class, which have often been dismissed as
either speculative or tendentious, have now been confirmed in some remarkable social research by Robert Lichter and Stanley Rothman (1981) comparing
the views of the media elite (journalists working for prestigious newspapers,
magazines, and television networks) with a group of high-level corporate
executives. As we might expect, the former are more liberal on political and
economic issues, and show more cynical attitudes toward American institutions. But the most substantial differences, by far, are to be found in relation
to moral questions—homosexuality, abortion, adultery—where the journalists give ''liberal'' responses three to four times as often as do the business
executives.

Each group takes an adversary stance toward the other. Each sees the other
as too influential, and itself as having too little, so each would like to replace
the other in influence. That competition involves more than pride of place.
Though it is an argument about politics and economics, it is also a struggle
as to which values will be ascendant—the ideal of self-restraint on the one
hand, and of individualism on the other.

These differences, so strongly separating two segments of the upper bourgeoisie, are important to us not merely because these are strong and willful elites but even more so because they reflect a far more general dispute about values, and because that dispute has taken place, partially, in and about the schools. The mainstream culture fears the schools may be captured by those who, out of a misguided sense of compassion, are unwilling to make those demands necessary for the child's intellectual and moral growth. The modernist culture fears the schools are and will remain academies that sustain the mercenary, authoritarian aims of the heartless elements of our society.

Notes

1. Lerner seems to believe, as I do, that the authors of these studies have gone out of their way to make it difficult to make comparisons, presumably to spare national sensitivities. This fear of invidiousness, though in some ways admirable, should caution us not to take at face value occasional soothing words on the relative quality of U.S. achievement.
2. Among the attractions of this hypothesis is that it tests itself. This is the time we should be seeing a decline in some of these indices. Has it happened? It is too early to know, but on the whole the hypothesis is proving out: there is a distinct decline in drug use, an apparent plateau in the suicide rate, a slowing down in the growth rate for youth crime. On the other hand, illegitimate births continue to rise.
3. Interviewed in 1970, shortly before his death, the great U.S. historian Richard Hofstadter said that we were living in an "age of rubbish," and it is easy to see what he had in mind as one rereads much of the mawkish, vulgar, and self-serving commentary of that period. On the other hand, the crisis also produced some remarkably fine writing, as for example, many of the essays published by *Daedalus* in a vast two-volume survey of U.S. academic thought published 1974 to 1975.
4. *Daedalus*, for example, published over a hundred articles on higher education during the quarter-century but until last year only a handful about the schools. The shining exception is *Public Interest*, which has published a steady stream of excellent articles by the most distinguished U.S. writers on education.
5. The statistics that follow are taken from the invaluable summaries published by *Public Opinion* magazine. (Aug./Sept. 1979, Feb./Mar. 1980, and Oct./Nov. 1981)

References

Adelson, J. "What Happened to the Schools?" *Commentary* (March 1981): 36–41.
Barzun, J. *Teacher in America*. 3d ed. Indianapolis: Liberty Press, 1980.
Bloom, A. "Our Listless Universities." *National Review* 34 (1982): 1537–48.
Bloom, F. "Escape from Suffering." *Social Research* 45 (1978): 467–77.

Bell, D. *The Coming of Post-Industrial Society*. New York: Basic Books, 1973.

————."Meritocracy and Equality." *Public Interest* 29 (1972): 29–68.

Cohn, N. *Pursuit of the Millennium*. 2d ed. New York: Harper, 1961.

Coleman, J. S., Hoffer, T., and Kilgore, S. *High-School Achievement: Public, Catholic, and Private Schools Compared*. New York: Basic Books, 1982.

Easterlin, R. *Birth and Fortune*. New York: Basic Books, 1980.

Eastland, T., and Bennett, W. J. *Counting by Race*. New York: Basic Books, 1979.

Frankel, C. "The New Egalitarianism and the Old." *Commentary* 56, no. 3 (1973): 54–61.

Grant, G. "Children's Rights and Adult Confusions." *Public Interest* 69 (1982): 83–99.

Inglehart, R. *The Silent Revolution*. Princeton: Princeton University Press, 1977.

Jencks, C. *Inequality*. New York: Harper & Row, 1973.

Keith, T. Z. "Time Spent on Homework and High-School Grades: A Large-Sample Path Analysis." *Journal of Educational Psychology* 74 (1982): 246–53.

Kristol, I. "About Equality." In *Two Cheers for Capitalism*. New York: Basic Books, 1978.

Lakoff, S. *Equality in Political Philosophy*. Cambridge: Harvard University Press, 1964.

Lerner, B. "The War on Testing: David, Goliath, and Gallup." *Public Interest* 60 (1980): 119–47.

————. "American Education: How Are We Doing?" *Public Interest* 69 (1982): 59–82.

Lichter, S. R., and Rothman, S. "Media and Business Elites." *Public Opinion* 4, no. 5 (1981): 42–46.

Lippmann, W. *The Phantom Public*. New York: Harcourt, Brace, 1925.

————. "Education vs. Western Civilization." *American Scholar* 10 (1941).

Manuel, F. E., and Manuel, F. P. *Utopian Thought in the Western World*. Cambridge: Harvard University Press, 1979.

Maslow, A. *Toward a Psychology of Being*. Princeton: Van Nostrand, 1962.

Moynihan, D. P. "Equalizing Education—In Whose Benefit?" *Public Interest* 29 (1972): 69–89.

Nisbet, R. *The Degradation of the Academic Dogma*. New York: Basic Books, 1971.

————. "The Pursuit of Equality." *Public Interest* 35 (1974): 103–20.

Nozick, R. *Anarchy, State, and Utopia*. New York: Basic Books, 1974.

Ravitch, D. "Forgetting the Questions: The Problem of Educational Reform." *American Scholar* 50 (1981): 329–40.

Rawls, J. *A Theory of Justice*. Cambridge: Harvard University Press, 1971.

Riesman, D. *The Lonely Crowd*. New Haven: Yale University Press, 1950.

Rutter, M. *Fifteen-thousand Hours*. Cambridge: Harvard University Press, 1979.

Ryan, W. *Equality*. New York: Pantheon, 1981.

Seabury, P. "The Idea of Merit." *Commentary* 54, no. 6 (1972): 41–46.

Sewall, G. T. "American Secondary Education" (radio broadcast). *Soundings* (National Humanities Center), 1982.

Silberman, C. *Crisis in the Classroom*. New York: Random House, 1970.

Toby, J. "Crime in American Public Schools." *Public Interest* 58 (1980): 18–42.

Trilling, L. *The Liberal Imagination*. New York: Viking Press, 1950.

Walberg, H. J. "What Makes Schooling Effective? A Synthesis and Critique of Three National Studies." *Contemporary Education Review* 1 (1982): 23–24.

3

Why the Schools May Not Improve

The report of the National Commission on Excellence in Education, *A Nation at Risk*, has become so familiar that it is hard to remember how surprised we were when it appeared. Most of us interested in education were entirely unprepared for its tone and emphasis. It had been assumed we would get a characteristic product of the committee process—a report temperate and evenhanded, which might well mean, in practice, an exercise in the vacuous, the sententious, and the banal.

From what one could learn of the commission at work, there was little reason to hope otherwise. As it happens, I had been asked to write a position paper for the commission, hence was able to meet with its members formally and informally, and watch them take testimony, hear reports, and question witnesses and one another. During a long afternoon one could see few signs of fire in anyone's belly. To the contrary, they appeared so diverse in background and disparate in views that an essentially political document, marked by restraint and compromise, seemed to be required if a report was to be issued at all. The commission's able staff had been assiduous in providing the widest possible variety of data and opinion: work showing that American youngsters were doing very poorly in international comparisons was balanced by arguments that those findings were weak, misleading, and not to be taken too seriously. A pessimistic paper on U.S. education, such as my own, would be offset by an exceedingly optimistic one. All in all, it seemed likely that the struggle to strengthen the schools would not gain much from the commission, that its report would, at best, provoke the usual one-day Washington flurry and then be forgotten.

The first surprise, then, was that the commission somehow managed to transcend those inclinations toward caution, to write a report that was straightforward, outspoken, at moments nearly fierce. The second surprise was the acclaim it received, and the—continuing—attention it gained for the problems of U.S. education. Why a chronic crisis is suddenly perceived to be acute, why one event strikes a nerve while another, similar event does not, why we unexpectedly develop the collective conviction that *something must be done*—those are the mysteries of the *Zeitgeist*, penetrable only by hindsight, if then.

It is important to bear in mind that the report made no new discoveries. The sorry state of the schools had been evident for many years. If there was a true mystery, it was not that the report said what it did, or attracted attention, but why it had taken so long, why enlightened opinion had not previously been fully engaged. One could hear a good deal about the problems privately— parents retelling some of the hair-raising stories brought home by their children, or college teachers reporting the most recent solecisms encountered in student composition. There is a local teacher who compiles a catalogue of the worst howlers he has come across in papers graded during the past year; he distributes it to colleagues, to their vast amusement; and one senses they laugh to keep from crying, there being nothing quite so frustrating as the semiliteracy they confront almost daily.

Nor was the plight of the schools known only privately, not at all. A number of journalists—notably Gilbert Sewall of *Newsweek* and Gene Maeroff of the *New York Times*—had been writing trenchant stories (later books) on the problems of education and what might be done about them. There had even come to be an annual ritual: a story reporting the latest decline in SAT scores. Another annual event was the Gallup poll of public opinion about the schools, sometimes slightly up, sometimes down, but on the whole bleak. In a number of state legislatures, plans for the competence testing of high school seniors were being debated, at times carried out. Looking back, we can now see that by the late 1970s, a critical mass of writers, intellectuals, and academics—few of them deeply within the education establishment—were beginning to be heard on the failures of the schools: Diane Ravitch, Chester Finn, Dennis Doyle, Tommy Tomlinson. And at the very end of that decade one was aware that a number of large studies of high schools were underway— by James Coleman, Gerald Grant, John Goodlad, Ernest Boyer, Theodore Sizer—these initiated by a mounting uneasiness about the condition of secondary education.

So there were many straws in the wind, but then there always are. At the time it took great optimism to believe that we would soon see fundamental changes in thinking about the schools, let alone changes in practice. There were bureaucracies to be found at all levels of the education system, from the local to the national, and they tended to be sluggish, defensive, unwilling to undertake change, unable to grasp the nature of the complaints being made, or too preoccupied with finances and housekeeping to give more than cursory attention to issues of pedagogy.

If the bureaucrats of education were generally inert, the *soi-disant* intellectuals—scholars and theorists—were likely to be testy and aggressive. The disinterested observer could sense in them an emotional raggedness, a quick-on-the-trigger sensitivity to criticism. They often saw themselves as samurai who had been given the task of defending the system that had emerged during the 1960s. That system, one would be told, might have its faults but never-theless represented a triumph of human values and democratic ideals. Threats to the system were seen to be political in inspiration. In private conversation one would sometimes hear amazing things said: that there was an orgy of book-burning in the schools set in motion by the Moral Majority; or that the high schools had no function except to keep youngsters out of the labor market, so as to maximize corporate profits. Public discourse was generally more guarded, but even there it was not difficult to perceive an embittered ideo-logical animus, two noteworthy examples being the efforts to discredit Marva Collins's work in her Chicago school, and the innuendo and obloquy that greeted the important Coleman, Hoffer, and Kilgore research on high school achievement. By hindsight, once again, it might appear that so much touchiness bespoke a dwindling sense of inner confidence, but the more common reaction was to despair for the immediate future of education, dom-inated as it appeared to be by a curious mixture of mediocrity (in personnel, techniques, and ideas) and ideology (egalitarian, individualistic, utopian).

Another reason for pessimism was that many defenders of education would hint that the critics were actuated not by politics alone but also by a covert racism. To worry openly about the collapse of cognitive skills was taken to be a surreptitious way of questioning the competence of Blacks. To be sure, there were enough instances of the poor performance of Blacks to warrant alarm about their schooling, but the general level of intellectual quality was at least equally worrisome. A university professor might, for example, read a term paper containing serious grammatical errors in almost every sentence, then learn that the writer was a college senior with a high grade point average, who was preparing to attend graduate school, the child of a successful profes-sional, and a graduate of a fast-track suburban high school. Or be asked to sign a permission slip drafted by another college senior (white, middle-class) containing three spelling mistakes in two sentences ("herby," "permision," "signiture"). In fact, the problem of Black achievement is less troubling because it is less puzzling. But how is one to understand a youngster who has had the best of everything, yet after sixteen years of schooling is unable to write a comprehensible sentence? And how is one to understand an edu-cational system that passes that youngster through a competitive high school, a selective university, and into a good graduate program? Race was only one of the many questions troubling the critics, yet the conversation on educational quality was conducted so allusively and so euphemistically that it often proved difficult to make that plain.

A final reason for pessimism: the critics of the schools were not themselves powerfully situated, and, looking about them, did not see the prospect of strong institutional support. Above all, they found themselves thwarted and puzzled by the indifference of the universities. After all, it was higher education that felt most directly the failings of the schools, yet those failings did not become a matter of institutional concern. It was not hard to see why: the universities believed that the schools—and even more, their ecology, the schools of education, and the teacher-training apparatuses, and the accreditation procedures—were a briar patch of ineptitude, stubbornness, and entrenched interests, unreformable, hopeless, best left alone. So there would be little help from higher education.

Then *A Nation at Risk* took the nation by storm. Against all expectations, the nerve had been struck. A public long unhappy about the schools but held at bay by bureaucratic inertia, intimidated by expert opinion, kept in check by a solipsistic legal system, had at long last found its own interests voiced, and by the most unlikely agent of redemption, the federal government. Other reports were to appear in the following months—Goodlad, Boyer, Sizer—but the commission, in preceding them, also adumbrated them, or seemed to, so that these later works were accommodated into the "paradigm" already established. A bandwagon was soon rolling: the pundits and politicians who had shown no previous interest in education, let alone its quality, quickly added their voices. So did, *mirabile dictu*, the National Education Association, until that moment noted only for a fastidious distaste for the idea of excellence, thought to be elitist, perhaps illiberal. Yet these elements, the opportunistic and the merely fashionable, were only the smallest part of the reaction. What seemed far more important were the actions taken locally or at the state level to revamp curricula and to increase requirements for graduation. Even these actions, important as they were, were understood be to surrogates for those changes of the spirit believed to be really needed. They were to serve to signal parents and teachers and the young themselves of the communal wish to be—once again—serious about schooling. There was to be more time devoted to academic subjects, there was to be more homework given, and done. When feasible economically, the school year and school day were to be lengthened. There were to be orderly classrooms, and more systematic, focused, attentive instruction.

The tide had turned. Perhaps there would be further struggles, even some minor setbacks, but now it seemed clear to all that corrupt progressivism, the dominating mode in U.S. education, had had its moment, had failed wretchedly, had been seen to fail, and knew itself to have failed. What many parents suspected, and what many teachers knew in their bones, was confirmed each time new findings appeared. For example: The number of American youngsters scoring over 650 on the verbal portion of the SAT declined 45 percent in the ten-year period 1972 to 1982.

In the most meticulous cross-national research yet carried out, comparing American, Japanese and Taiwanese children, Stevenson found that in mathematics "only one American child appeared among the top one hundred fifth graders,'' and ''among the twenty American fifth-grade classrooms, in not one classroom was the average score on the mathematics test equivalent to that of the children in the worst-performing Japanese classroom.''

Stevenson's prose is unemotional, yet even so he terms these (and similar) findings ''devastating,'' as indeed they are, made the more so by the fact that the U.S. children were more advantaged than their Asian counterparts, coming from well-educated families, and attending much smaller classes. Still, one felt that the pain occasioned by these findings could be borne, given the belief that reform was at hand.

The third surprise—a most unpleasant one—was the slowly dawning recognition that the tide may not have turned after all, that despite the reports and the resolve the movement for reform might well be blunted, that the disarray of its opponents, though real enough, had been only momentary, that the forces against reform were unpersuaded and unchastened. It is that supposition, that sad possibility, that this paper will examine.

As soon as the reform of education became a public issue, one began to notice efforts, witting or not, to change the subject, to divert the discussion to other questions. The most obvious form this took was political: each presidential candidate, declared and undeclared, rushed into speech. Planks were drafted, platforms rewritten. The true course of education had been subverted/had been enhanced/would be moved forward by the new/old administration. New programs were needed. New programs were not needed. More money was needed. More money was not needed. In other instances the discussion was moved to issues closer to education, yet secondary in importance. Merit pay for teachers: it may or may not be a good idea, but it is hard to see its importance. It is hard to see how, even over time, it would produce a significant improvement in teaching and learning, yet the issue of merit pay, pro and con, absorbed a considerable amount of discussion and debate. Another example was the controversy about the competence testing of current teachers. It is hard to see what effect it would have beyond harassing an already beleaguered group.

Another diversion was that many of those strongly in favor of academic reform also favored, quite as strongly, some other purpose for the schools, usually moralistic: prayer; monitoring the school libraries; scrutinizing the curriculum in sex education, or getting rid of it altogether; getting rid of the relativistic approach to moral education; teaching values through literature or philosophy; and so on. Most of us will find some of these proposals lamentable and others laudable; the problem was that their being linked to academic reform tended to confound separate domains, and much of the time tended to alienate one or another type of parent, e.g. those who might favor intellectual achievement yet were modernist (or traditionalist) in moral outlook.

These diversions and confoundings were more annoying than disturbing, were disturbing only insofar as they suggested an increasing diffusion of purpose. What was troubling, and unexpected, was the appearance of rhetorical strategies that seemed to aim at denying the very existence of problems in education. In various ways, these problems were said to have never existed, to have been trumped up, to have been trivial, to have been distorted, to have been misunderstood, to be only a small part of the total picture, to be a thing of the past, and so on. To a clinician these devices seemed eerily familiar: denial, negation, splitting, externalization, displacement. For the past few months I have been noting examples of these defensive tactics as they appear in the press. Here are the major themes:

"Things really aren't so bad." Stories reporting that though there may be minor problems in the schools, these have "been blown out of proportion."

"Some things may not be good, but other things are first-rate." Upbeat accounts of successful ventures, aiming to provide "a balanced picture."

"Those who criticize the schools do so out of base motives." These stories personalize, drawing attention away from the problem itself and toward the personality of the critic. A choice example is this statement from a press release: "A large part of the public's confusion [i.e. why the public mistakenly believes there are problems in the schools] comes from university scholars trying to attract attention to themselves." The speaker is President Derek Bok of Harvard, the celebrated shrinking violet.

"Perhaps things were bad at one time, but that was long ago." Stories that historicize the schools' problems, suggesting they are safely in the past, and long since resolved. This motif usually accompanies enthusiastic accounts of new approaches to familiar difficulties. A recent example can be found in *Time*'s account of the Reagan administration's calling attention to discipline problems in the schools. The story stresses the "dismay" of educators at the president's initiative, argues that the administration's data are dated, and offers in rebuttal several heartwarming anecdotes about chaotic schools now become pacific. In fact, the data are not all that dated, and are the most recent findings available; the story offers no new evidence, aside from those anecdotes and some indignant opinions. The thrust of the story is to suggest, quite incorrectly, that discipline is no longer a problem in the schools.

Finally, and above all: "Those who criticize the schools have a political end in mind. They are trying to turn back the clock." This last theme, openly ideological, deserves our close attention. Some of the motifs mentioned earlier seem to have little behind them; they are efforts at amnesia, or simple outbursts of pollyannaism. But the ideological strategy is another matter entirely. It is principled; it is determined; it is intelligent; it is adversarial. It takes the view that reform is reaction, that the pursuit of excellence will endanger worthier ideals, that the movement for reform is a stalking horse for the recrudescence of dangerous values. The reform proposals are seen not as merely misguided but illegitimate, a subversion of the proper ideals of education in this country. The position taken is *revanchiste*: the new era must be resisted, then overturned.

In the softer, attenuated version, the *revanchiste* idea is not taken to its limits; changes must be made, yet without giving up the accomplishments of the past. We see its quintessential expression in the press release mentioned earlier, chronicling the outcome of a summit meeting of thirty-nine university presidents who, prompted by the public concern about education, convened and considered and conceived ten recommendations for the universities, each and every one vapid, self-important, and condescending: "Providing opportunities for the continued professional development of superintendents, principals, and other school leaders"; "Strengthening existing affiliations with elementary and secondary schools or initiating new ones"; "Serving, where needed as sources of advice in the shaping of public policies affecting education." And so on.

One would not expect much bite or penetration from a summit-level communique, and certainly not one issued by university presidents. Still, one had hoped for a bit more than these fatuities. No institution is more grievously harmed by the erosion of talent this nation is witnessing, and one might presume the universities would see it as their duty to preserve and support that talent. Yet we find that the presidents give almost no attention to what caused the fuss in the first place. The concern rather is to allay anxiety because "too uniformly gloomy" a picture has been painted for the public. We are reminded that the "significant achievements" of the recent past must not be forgotten; these consist of improving achievement in younger children (in fact, an arguable conclusion), and "improving access" to the schools.

Anyone steeped in current commentary in education is soon aware of the word *access*—generally preceded by "providing" or "improving"—part buzzword, part codeword, and a delicate way of adverting to universal secondary education, and more particularly the presence of Blacks and other minorities in the senior grades of high school and the colleges. It is the succinct expression of a somewhat more complicated idea: that there is an implacable trade-off between excellence and equality (now more commonly called "equity") so that encouraging a democratic school system produces a decline in achievement. Equality means leveling, which in turn means intellectual mediocrity (of course, it is not put so crudely); mediocrity is the price we pay for universal education. That is by no means a new idea; to the contrary, it is a very old, conservative idea, albeit with a somewhat different moral emphasis. It has now become the conventional establishment-liberal idea.

One can understand its appeal. It is centrist, moderate, enlightened, above all symmetrical: excellence and equity in balance, on a seesaw, so that a rise in one virtue induces a fall in the other.

It is also a comforting idea, permitting one to take long views, and to look well past today's troubles. Unfortunately, it is more appealing than useful as an explanation of intellectual decline. Even if we limit ourselves to the two findings mentioned above, it is plain enough that widened access has little to do with it. The U.S. portion of the cross-national study was conducted in Minneapolis, which has few minority families. The sharp decline in top SAT scores cannot have been much affected by universal secondary schooling. For some years now, poor U.S. performance in international comparisons has been explained by the high retention rates in our secondary schools, but other countries—Japan notably—now show similar rates while maintaining much higher standards of achievement.

Nevertheless, the fear of excellence is real enough when the case can be made that the disadvantaged are at risk. Here, for example, is the story of a contretemps now taking place in my own community, as reported by one of the local newspapers; it tells us a great deal about what can intervene between intention and outcome when higher standards are sought. The school administration had proposed some modest increases in high school graduation requirements, essentially along the lines suggested by the various commission reports. No matter that they were modest; there was an immediate uproar. The plan agitated "angry teachers" who were said to consider it "simplistic." It was also deemed reactionary: a high school principal is reported to say that it reminds him of the curriculum twenty years ago. The new plan would require three years of math and science, so that "even marginal students would have to pass basic chemistry, physics, algebra, geometry, and logic to gain their diplomas." That might well raise the dropout rate, now very low. Mandating courses may mean eliminating electives, which students are said to like. "Electives have pizzazz," a teacher is said to have said. Besides, college-bound students already take many courses in science and math, so why have requirements? Besides, the teachers are angry because they were not adequately consulted. Besides, the community is angry because it was not adequately consulted. Besides, the administration's proposal evades the real issue, which is the presence among students of "passivity, apathy, linear thinking, and dependence on authority." A local professor of education is quoted to this effect, along with the observation that what is really needed, before we rush into things is—more research, to tell us how to "involve students more deeply in learning." The story concludes with an attack upon A Nation at Risk, depicted as fons et origo of the nation's descent into pedagogical darkness.

One finds it hard to imagine that such arguments could delay change. Given the national climate of opinion, who would not support so slight an elevation in requirements? Yet, the school administration surrendered immediately, putting up no resistance. It appointed a forty-person committee, representing teachers, students, and "the community," deputed to draft a new curriculum. That committee would in turn break up into smaller groups to hold public meetings, hear witnesses, draft reports, etc., etc., until ultimately changes would—or perhaps would not—emerge.

One also finds it hard to imagine that this farrago of shopworn and discredited ideas retains the power to compel belief. Yet the ideology persists, undaunted. In one of its major variations, liberationist, it holds that traditional schooling enslaves the spirit. Though we may achieve a rapid acquisition of skills, we do so at a terrible cost in creativity, independence of mind, joy in learning. The criticisms commonly directed against liberationist practice, that it encourages ignorance and intellectual incapacity, are treated disdainfully, it being the view that objective methods of assessment are both invalid and morally meretricious. Traditional schooling is seen to reflect an unwholesome devotion to such values as "cognitivism" and social Darwinism. The critic, in short, is seen to be a fusion of Gradgrind and Snopes.

In the Left variations, class or ethnicity outweigh all else. Here is a capsule summary of the position: "The schools are one way the privileged have chosen to intimidate, humiliate, emasculate the poor and the Blacks. Tests, grades, and the like are of no moment because they do not relate to the actual conditions these youngsters will confront: unemployment or a continuing economic degradation. Tests are little more than a means of oppressing the victims, then blaming them. All the talk about discipline is a smokescreen. It is based on straight racial bias, and is subterfuge for getting rid of the Blacks. If there are real problems, which is doubtful, they developed because the true needs of disadvantaged youngsters are not being met."

The two variations are united in a disdain for the idea of merit. In the liberationist view, the striving for merit is seen to diminish any love for the activity itself. In the Left view, that striving produces differences in rank, distasteful and unjustly achieved, with those beginning behind destined to remain behind. The use of *merit* as a *Schimpfwort* now extends to *excellence* itself, to judge by the scorn conveyed by Irving Howe and others at a recent conference of intellectuals; and it should be no surprise to us that at least one speaker at that meeting singled out the commission's report as an example of a deplorable drift in our national life.

"Given the willpower, we have the knowledge to increase school learning, and raise our national achievement standards." Reading that sentence prompted a moment of surprise. It is from congressional testimony given by H. J. Walberg, a leading researcher on classroom learning. What surprised me is not the statement itself, which is unquestionably correct, as Walberg's excellent review of the literature has shown; it was the phrase *willpower*, a term so old-fashioned, so nearly anachronistic that one rarely sees it used, not by an academician. Yet, when that brief instant of surprise had passed, it struck me that *willpower* or some equivalent—*effort, drive, energy, commitment*—some word connoting intention and purpose, would indeed be needed in discussing both the immediate past and the probable future of U.S. education.

We are of course more comfortable in discussing these matters by reference to tangibles: the economy, the labor market, demographics, and so on. What will the supply of teachers look like in the next decade, and what incentives will be available to increase it? Are there changes in prospect for school financing? What would be the impact of tuition tax credits in states willing to adopt them? These "realities" are or will be of vital importance in understanding the present and future of schooling. Who can doubt that the outflow of talented women to other professions has had—and will continue to have—a profound effect on teaching quality? Who can deny that many of the problems of the schools have been due to the population anomalies of the last generation, larger families, and crowded age cohorts, which contribute in the first case to lowered intellectual capacity, and in the second to a staggering increase in such pathologies as drug use, criminal violence, and illegitimate births, all of these having the deepest impact on the climate of schooling? It is perhaps worth mentioning here that the lowering of family size and birth rates, though little noted by writers on education up until now, will likely be the single most important benign influence on schooling in the next decade.

Nevertheless, there seems to be no calculus of tangibles that allows us to comprehend fully the debacle of U.S. schooling in the recent past. It is the underlying argument of this paper that it is far more important to understand those ideas, true ones or false ones, that allow us either to overcome or to succumb to the hard facts of life—above all the ideologies and illusions, the illusions fed by ideologies, and the ideologies fed by illusions.

At almost every moment during the last two decades, the schools and the young have been held hostage to our fantasies. Why in the world did so many university professors allow themselves to believe that the college students of the 1970s were so remarkably gifted? They were not, yet that illusion contributed to grade inflation at the universities, which led in turn to the despoliation of the high school curriculum. Why did so many social scientists—many of them familiar with the psychometric literature—allow themselves to believe that minority students functioning two standard deviations below the mean in aptitude and achievement would nevertheless do successful work in the most competitive graduate and professional programs? Why did we believe that schools incapable of teaching correct spelling would nevertheless be able to convey the highest degree of moral, psychological, and social insight? Why were we unable to perceive and reflect upon the uncertain relationship between schooling and later achievement—why it is that a James Joyce could be delivered out of the most rigid Jesuitical circumstances, whereas a hundred Summerhills have yet to deliver a James Joyce? Why did it require an accumulation of empirical work to confirm the obvious, that learning is best achieved, given enough time and enough effort, in an orderly milieu; and why has that simple finding met such outrage and condemnation?

A final question: why did some of us develop the illusion that these and like illusions would be easy to overcome? Why did we assume that the exposure of false doctrine to experience, or to careful empirical test, would be sufficient to change belief? I would guess we assumed so out of innocence and wishful thinking, almost as a counterpart to the innocence and wishful thinking in the utopian ideas we ourselves sought to correct and overcome. We were also too drawn to the metaphor of the pendulum, the view that cultural and intellectual life moves regularly from one pole to another. Although that view is by no means entirely false, our error was in failing to grasp the many ways in which ideologies are embodied in human lives. They provide a career, or a personal identity, or a badge of status, or a measure of religious faith. We did not anticipate how much would be at stake, hence how bitter the struggle would be.

Part II
Current and Recurrent Problems of American Education

Part I
Current and Recent Conditions of
American Education

4

The Social Sciences versus the Humanities

I strongly suspect that many social scientists, perhaps all of them, think of the humanities as a mode of secular uplift. The humanities! Ah, yes, the humanities! Very nice, very good for all of us, very important for the young, keeps them from being barbarians, don't you know. My more rigorous colleagues, appraising applicants for our graduate program, find it quite acceptable if the candidate's record shows some exposure to the humanities, but become quite uneasy if there is too much of it, as though that might bespeak a certain mental or emotional weakness. Needless to say, I have never heard that uneasiness about applicants whose records show a heavy concentration in science. Several years ago I was offered a fellowship at the National Humanities Center, and on telling these colleagues about it, the common reaction was a sort of uncertain grin, followed by vague murmurs of very vague approval, mixed with some disbelief, much as though I had announced I was leaving to attend a school of divinity. "Oh, how interesting," is what they said; "is he having a midlife crisis?" is what they were thinking.

To put it another way, the common attitude among social scientists, even friendly ones, is condescending. The humanities are all right in their place, but our ultimate allegiance is to science, and if you should forget that, you will quickly be reminded. Through the wonders of serendipity, on the day I wrote that sentence, I came across an illustrative letter in the *Wall Street Journal*. In the course of an editorial on the "yellow-rain" controversy, the *Journal* had been dismissive about the credentials of some of its opponents, and had termed anthropology and sociology "sort of second-cousins to science." There was a quick response from the president of the American Anthropological Association, reminding the editors quite firmly that it *was* a science, that it had been recognized as such by the AAAS as far back as 1882, and that the National Science Foundation had given it two hundred grants the year before. The letter concludes: "Some of us are admittedly kissin' cousins to the humanities, but the discipline of anthropology is firmly based in the biological and social sciences." An equivalent response would no doubt be given by the president of any other social science association. It is quite obvious why. The sciences are prestigious, indeed awesome; they are powerful both intellectually and in worldly influence; and as that letter tells us by indirection, they have the money, so much so that their leftovers are sufficient to keep many social scientists fed.

There is of course another reason for distancing the humanities, in that during the nineteenth century most of the social sciences evolved from humanistic disciplines—psychology from moral philosophy, political science from political philosophy, sociology in part from history. There is another derivation, from the sciences, psychology from physiology, the other social sciences not so much from particular disciplines as from the general growth of quantitative and empirical methods during that century. It was indeed the collision of scientific and humanistic modes of thinking that was central to the thought of many of the early masters of social science. The great example is the great work by William James, the *Principles of Psychology*; much the same is true, though perhaps less obviously, in Freud's earliest and most seminal psychoanalytic writings; and some of the same tensions can be seen elsewhere, as in Durkheim's *Suicide*, which merges statistical and historical analysis.

It is interesting to note that both James and Freud in time turned away from their scientific origins. James began as a physician, drifted into physiological psychology, then into larger psychological questions, ultimately to philosophy. Freud's early training was in science, then in medicine. His earliest efforts as psychology were highly physicalistic; he moved gradually toward a more psychological approach, and ultimately toward humanistic questions— indeed, the fullest range of those, to history, religion, literature, the arts, theology, philosophy. In both cases we sense, reading their lives, that the movement to the humanities was accompanied or occasioned by impatience with the constraints of conventional science. Think of the ever-amiable James poking fun at the tedium and the ultimate irrelevance of German psychophysical research; or think of Freud's ill-concealed disdain toward those who would limit analytic training to physicians, thus depriving psychoanalysis of that animation brought to it by, above all, the humanities.

There is one more career that may be instructive to us, in that it shows much the same evolution and many of the same tensions. Henry Murray is for all intents and purposes the inventor of modern personality psychology, a feat he accomplished during the 1930s. Murray, too, began in the natural sciences, initially as a physician and embryologist, then had a genuinely transforming encounter with Carl Jung which persuaded him to turn to psychoanalysis and psychology. Eventually he gave himself over almost fully to humanistic studies, above all to a series of works on Herman Melville. Once again we note the evolution from the natural sciences to the social sciences to the humanities. And in Murray's case, too, we note how a restless mind finds it cannot be peacefully contained by the limits set by conventional science and seeks to rise above them. (It is of some interest to note here that one of

Murray's most important psychological papers is on the myth of Icarus.) Murray's disaffection was quite open, indeed outspoken, so much so as to have played a role in alienating his colleagues and in leading to a long delay in being awarded tenure. He makes his complaint most forcefully in a controversial paper written about fifty years ago—still quite applicable today— that examines the state of research, theory, and teaching in psychology. After reviewing sardonically a series of topics of interest to some hypothetical psychologist, all of these picayune or irrelevant, he concludes that "academic psychology has contributed practically nothing to the knowledge of human nature. It has not only failed to bring light to the great, hauntingly recurrent problems, but it has no intention, one is shocked to realize, of attempting to investigate them."

What Murray is saying is that he, and social scientists like him, are problem-driven, whereas most others are method-driven, or perhaps method-limited. Murray's first question is: What are the important—or interesting—problems? And only after that is determined does he ask the second: Is there a way to study them, and if not, can we invent a way? The more common approach, Murray might tell us, is to work within a tradition dominated by certain tried-and-true methods, and to seek new discoveries within that tradition. In looking for new problems, one first scans, perhaps unconsciously, the range of acceptable or perhaps tolerable techniques, and exercises a silent, reflexive veto over those approaches that are felt to be beyond the parameters. There is a well-known joke about this, about the drunk who is found looking for his car keys under the lamppost, not because he lost them there but because that is where the light is. Let me say here that I have told that joke myself, because temperamentally I share Murray's inclinations; yet I now believe that Murray vastly understated the problems involved in studying the great, hauntingly recurrent questions. Since Murray's time, a great many people have been doing it, or trying to, and we have begun to understand how extraordinarily difficult it can be. I will return to that matter a bit later.

The movement we see in these three towering figures—James, Freud, and Murray—from the sciences to the humanities, is the reverse of what we have seen in the social sciences as a whole. Although most of them begin closely allied with the humanities, they moved—perhaps it is better to say that they were moved, gravitationally—toward the quantitative, or toward experimentation, so that they seem to be dominated by science, or the scientific ethos, or, quite commonly, by scientism. If the social sciences are in their foreign policy, so to speak, awed and at times obsequious toward the sciences while patronizing toward the humanities, those attitudes are amplified on the domestic front. Most of the social sciences have been marked, some continue to be, by bitter schisms between scientific or quantitative approaches on one hand and nonquantitative approaches on the other, these being termed variously idiographic, or clinical, or interpretive. There may be exceptions here and there, but so far as I can tell the quantitative approach is dominant over the long run, though it remains arguable whether that is due to merit or simply to the temper of the times.

That long run can take a long time, and until hegemony is attained, conflicts can be fought out with a fratricidal intensity, so much so that it can be hard to convey to an outsider the lunatic rages that can sometimes overcome the participants. The outsider is liable to find these disputes strange indeed, filled with arguments about matters entirely incorporeal, not necessarily about divergent findings as about differences in research strategy, or the proper way to give credence to different classes of evidence. When I was in graduate school I had one teacher, a very famous man given to violent opinions, who absolutely hated psychoanalysis. During the course of a graduate seminar, one of his students rather saucily pointed out to him a passage from the writings of an analyst who had many years before anticipated a theoretical breakthrough lately proposed by our teacher. He responded that it would make no difference if *everything* psychoanalysis propounded should turn out to be true, it would still be false because it had not been earned honestly, that is, discovered through the proper procedures. In his view, however wrong he was, psychoanalysis employed largely solipsistic methods, which *eo ipso* were not the rational methods required by science.

This example is an extreme one, yet it tells us something about the nature of the schisms within the social sciences. They have to do with profoundly different epistemologies. Isaiah Berlin, possibly the leading humanistic thinker of our time, has traced the conflict between the sciences and humanities back as far as the eighteenth century, where we see the final triumph of an attitude toward knowledge deeply rooted in Western thought. Berlin tells us that this attitude, or tradition, in its many forms, rests on three basic assumptions: (1) every genuine question has one true answer and one only, all others being false; (2) the methods leading to correct solutions are in essence identical, and rational in nature; and (3) the solutions achieved are "true universally, eternally and immutably" for all times, places, and people.

A lustrous vision, yet also alas a Lorelei for those wanting to believe that the social sciences already have or will sometime soon provide such questions, methods, and solutions. Most of those lured to shipwreck have been social scientists themselves, so often consumed by illusions of an imminent "breakthrough" that will allow law-like generalizations meeting Berlin's criteria. To be sure, steady disconfirmation has produced some tempering of our millennial zeal, has even produced heretics who no longer believe that the social sciences can ever become "scientific." Yet the old faith does linger on, and remains strong enough to persuade others—certainly those in the schools—that in teaching social sciences we are offering empirical rigor and theoretical elegance as applied to a subject matter enjoying wide general interest.

The Weakness of the Social Sciences

It is fairly clear that in the competition for time and attention in the high school curriculum, the humanities have suffered losses during the last two decades or so, the winner much of the time being one or another of the social sciences, or what purports to be social science—that is, courses in self-improvement or mental hygiene, or family harmony, and the like, or courses that draw heavily on the jargon or data of the social science disciplines, most commonly a watered-down psychology or sociology.

When we ponder these changes, we lament what has been lost: that knowledge of history or literature or languages or the classics or political theory which we believe to make up an important part of what it is to be educated. That emphasis, on what is being lost, is quite understandable; it startles us when we observe how little of our cultural legacy is being passed on. But there is another side to the matter one finds rarely addressed: the character and quality of that which replaces what is no longer taught. We tell ourselves that while we might prefer our youngsters to be taught literature or history, the psychology or sociology they are getting instead is, after all, quite satisfactory in their own way, and probably more interesting to most students. The question is: Are they in fact satisfactory?

I believe not. The social sciences are far weaker than is commonly realized. They are especially weak in those areas likely to be of interest to a general audience, most frequently taught in high school courses, and for that matter in introductory undergraduate courses. I will argue that these deficiencies are extensive enough and deep enough to warrant a reconsideration of the place of the social sciences in the curriculum. Let me first set limits and offer some clarifications.

What I will say does not apply to all of the social sciences, but on the other hand it is meant to apply to those with which I am acquainted: such fields and topics as clinical psychology and psychiatry, many parts of child and adolescent psychology, personality theory and research, and portions of social psychology and sociology. Further, the more deeply one penetrates into the literature of a given topic, the more one is likely to entertain doubts— grave doubts—about the adequacy of our knowledge. Let me stress that I do not have in mind exalted standards, the stringent criteria a philosopher of science might bring to bear in judging the strength of a discipline, but weaknesses that would be plain to any educated person instructed in a discipline's languages and techniques. Finally, the problems I will be discussing are not the result of incompetence or lack of talent, insight, or diligence. Almost all social scientists actively engaged in research are intelligent, most are re-sourceful, and many are brilliant, quite the equal in capacity, mutatis mu-tandis, of scholars and scientists in other disciplines.

The difficulties lie deeper. They derive from the fact that human nature and social existence are stubbornly, irreducibly complex, so that the problems of studying them are maddeningly refractory, often insoluble, except in a long run that never seems to arrive. Easy problems turn out to be hard, hard problems turn out to be close to impossible. Problems that were thought to be long solved turn out never to have been solved at all. I sometimes believe that the myth of Sisyphus was written with a social scientist in mind.

As an example, here is an easy problem: some years ago I was asked whether educating secondary school students to the hazards of drug use would prove to be effective. I said that I did not know but would try to find out. I discovered that there was a substantial literature, many studies having already been done. I also discovered that the question remained unanswered. Some of the time drug education reduced use, some of the time it increased use. So far as I could tell, there seemed to be no relationship between type of outcome and the apparent quality of the research, that is, the more carefully controlled studies did not seem to produce different types of results from others. This was some years ago, as I said, and it may well be that a pattern has begun to emerge. A mystery—no doubt soluble, given enough time and effort, but bear in mind that the question posed could not have been more straightforward, and the design necessary to answer it easier to implement.

It is not an odd or anomalous example; to the contrary, one can find dozens—no, hundreds—of other questions where research findings point in no particular direction. After much earnest and ingenious effort, we still have no clear idea as to whether and when and how viewing television violence induces aggressive behavior. Nor do we know whether or when or how early experience affects the development of personality. Or whether and when and how emotional disorders are consequent to trauma. Or just why it is that boys are more able in mathematical and girls in verbal skills. These four examples come from the top of my head, without searching memory. Just why is our level of achievement so low? Here are a few reasons.

Some Reasons for Low Achievement Level

Thinness

It is not usually recognized by the general public—or, for that matter, by specialists in adjoining areas—how skimpy our knowledge really is on many important topics. Several years ago I edited a handbook of adolescent psy-chology designed to be a definitive reference work, aimed at scholars and graduate students. The most unsettling effect of this task was to become aware of how little is known on some very vital matters. For example, two distinguished experts separately refused my request to prepare a chapter on female adolescent psychology, on the grounds that there was too little solid information at hand to warrant it. I had the same experience in casting about for a treatment of adolescent family relations; here again those I consulted argued that although there was a great deal of writing on the topic, it was on the whole anecdotal, little of it informed empirically. I discovered we have only recently begun to study the effect of part-time work on the lives of adolescents, despite its being a major social and economic phenomenon. We know little about normal personality development, nor much about the growth of adolescent thinking. And so on.

Now one may suspect that for various reasons adolescence is an underfunded and understudied topic within developmental psychology, just as developmental studies in general are underfunded compared with many others. Be that as it may, there are a great many other topics within the social sciences where we have the sense of knowing much more than in fact we do. There are many reasons. We quite naturally tend to study what is or seems easiest to study, or what seems feasible. As a result, we have many more studies of children's thinking, a fairly accessible topic, than of children's personality, which offers formidable difficulties; for the same reasons, we have more studies of children's thinking on mathematical and scientific tasks than on how they deal with problems in such areas as literature and history. We also tend to study what is being funded, and funding is often a response to political pressures or to the crises of the moment. Or we study what is in fashion to study, which may or may not prove to be of enduring value—examine any ten-year-old journal in the social sciences. The reasons are many, and the usual result is a relative surfeit of work on some topics and a remarkable barrenness elsewhere.

Unless one is deeply expert in a topic, and beyond that, given to a certain mordancy in the appraisal of others, one is not apt to become fully aware of these deficiencies. There is that tendency to strive for closure, to achieve narrative consistency and completeness, so that we find ourselves, unwittingly, filling in what we do not know by reference to what seems plausible, or intuitively correct, or the current conventional wisdom. We find ourselves offering our students (or the press) a portrait of our knowledge that unwittingly covers over its limitations. It is not unusual to find our assumptions not merely shaken but entirely overturned by the appearance of one or two new studies, a state of affairs we would simply not find were our data base more substantial to begin with.

Complexity

Even in areas where we have an apparent abundance of evidence, we soon find that it adds up to much less than we thought; it merely instructs us that the topic is far more convoluted than we imagined. The deeper we penetrate, the more information we amass, the more confused and uncertain we become. Consider that question the clinical psychologist is so often asked: Does psychotherapy work? As it happens, we have had a vast number of studies carried out on the question, in fact, over a thousand. Through a statistical tour de force called meta-analysis, this plethora of investigations has now been reduced and analyzed, so that we may conclude that it does indeed work. Yet having discovered that, over the years and painfully, we now find that we can say little more. We do not know whether any given form of therapy is more effective than any other, or which therapists do good work and which do not—that is, whether it is the training that counts, or the theory, or the personality, or the experience, or the mode of treatment, or whatever. We cannot tell with any degree of confidence which patients are likely to get better, and which are not.

Now, one may reply that even these questions have been posed too broadly, that if one were to ask more focused questions about psychotherapy and its effects, one might well come up with satisfying answers. Yet here is what one finds in a quick survey of two recent volumes of *Psychological Bulletin*, a magisterial journal specializing in literature reviews. There are six articles in very specific areas of psychotherapy. Here is a sampling: an article on desensitization procedures in the treatment of childhood disorders; sixty-six studies are reviewed. The conclusion is "clear evidence for the effectiveness of any variant of desensitization with children is limited." Here is another on the effect of therapists' interpersonal skills. It reviews ninety-one studies and concludes that "the efficacy of popular interpersonal skills models has not been demonstrated." Finally, a review on a very narrow topic indeed, the effects of disconfirmed client role expectations in psychotherapy. There were seventy-two researches available for review, the idea tested being that it will have a negative effect on the therapy if something happens that the patient did not look forward to. The conclusion: "The empirical studies are evenly divided in supporting this hypothesis." In the two-year period surveyed, in no instance do we find unequivocal support for any given hypothesis or expectation.

Bias

A third source of weakness is the unrecognized influence of ideology, such that the results achieved confirm the sentiments or attitudes or presuppositions of the investigator. One senses that although the problem is recognized, its full dimensions are not. For one thing, social scientists are extremely homogeneous in politics and social outlook; for another it is infra dig to raise that kind of objection to any line of research, except when the position being criticized has acquired pariah status, as in studies of race and intelligence.

Yet whether or not social scientists are ready to face up to it, unrecognized ideological bias exercises a corrosive effect on the probity of the work. There is a strong and persistent bias against nativist explanations with respect to personality, psychopathology, competence, and so on. There is a strong tendency to write glowingly of those groups that share the modernist-liberal outlook common to most social scientists, and to patronize those groups that do not: studies of the "authoritarian personality" are one example, studies of "radical youth" are another. Research on sex differences has recently become so politicized that one cannot accept findings before giving them the most careful scrutiny. And much the same is true of many topics within such domains as sexuality, child care, marital conflict, and the like.

These weaknesses—and others—are most evident in those areas likely to be of widespread general interest: the family, politics, morality, and so on. And it is also worth noting that many of these topics are also the concern of the humanities.

The social sciences are attractive to us through the promise—sometimes made openly, sometimes merely implied—that they will provide a scientific answer to age-old questions the humanities have handled through mere assertion, or by Jesuitical disputation, or by a stubborn reliance on tradition. For example, how can we decide about right and wrong, without relying entirely on the dogmatic asseverations to be found in most Western religions, or becoming lost in the linguistic tangles of analytic philosophy? How do we choose, let us say, between a doctrine treating morality as a commitment to the social order, and one that stresses a universally valid sense of inner conscience? How appealing it would be to learn that there is a scientific theory, supported by hard empirical findings, meeting those difficult positivist criteria specified by Isaiah Berlin, that will bring us to the solution of those presumably insoluble questions.

The example given is by no means hypothetical. Our most widely known theory of moral psychology, proposed and elaborated by Lawrence Kohlberg, makes just that claim. By analyzing the responses to a rather limited set of moral dilemmas (involving distributive justice) he is able, Kohlberg says, to establish a level of moral maturity, and place the respondent on a six-step scale ranging from a brutish *Macht-ist-Recht* primitivism at the bottom to a sort of Kantian nimbus of principled morality at the top. This is not the place to examine the system and its claims in detail; nevertheless, it should be said that most other scholars of moral psychology hold it to be deeply flawed technically and empirically, and most moral philosophers interested in psychological questions view it as both naive and mistaken. Even those writers who honor Kohlberg's effort, or find some merit in parts of his work, see the system as grandiose and simpleminded, promising more than it can possibly deliver, and delivering a highly reduced version of the realm of moral experience. Yet these grave reservations have not so far hindered a general acceptance of Kohlberg's system as a path-breaking discovery. It is treated in a variety of college-level texts as though it were among the established truths of contemporary psychology. Why should that be? Because its very deficiency, its reductiveness, is taken to be, mistakenly, the concision characteristic of the natural sciences. It is a six-rung ladder of virtue, easily remembered, easily understood, yet with enough apparent complexity to suggest that the social sciences are fully up to the large, eternal questions.

If that is the moral theory we provide for undergraduates, it is not hard to imagine the further reductiveness required to accommodate the high school student's far more limited background. Inevitably, the stages of moral development would become fixed truths, hence facts to be memorized, like the table of elements or the Watson-Crick model of DNA. What is most troubling is that the conversion of a humanistic issue to a "scientific" one will almost certainly inhibit the discussion of those moral questions we would address more fruitfully in the study of history, philosophy and literature—such questions of moral relativism and absolutism, or the relation between moral belief and moral action, or the nature of free will in moral choice.

The case of moral psychology is in no way unique. To the contrary, it is difficult to think of instances where social science—particularly through its quantitatively derived findings—genuinely enhances our grasp of the humanities, or of those haunting, recurrent issues Henry Murray wrote about. Up to this point the social sciences have been most fruitful as a new and alternative mode of humanistic discovery and interpretation. In psychology Freud is the most obvious example, but our other great men—James, Piaget, even Skinner—will survive not through their findings but as humanistic visionaries.

If the social sciences were taught in that fashion one would have few qualms about social science in the secondary schools. Yet the social sciences are taught in entirely different ways and for entirely different reasons: because they are topical, or because students find them relevant personally. One teacher told me that the social science curriculum could not be displaced because students found the courses enjoyable and because they believed, however erroneously, that they were learning matters of great value to them. If that is so, and I fear it is, so be it, but we ought to recognize that what is taught most of the time is a gussied-up version of the human-interest social science we find in newspapers, midcult magazines, and television docudramas. These bring us breathless news about solutions to "important social problems" provided by "recent studies." There is a good chance that the account provided will be of that new journalistic genre called "faction," that is, not quite fiction yet not quite hard fact either. It is, rather, a melange of studies with varying and unknown degrees of reliability, varying and unknown degrees of validity, varying and unknown degrees of generalizability. If the social sciences were taught honestly, with their defects fully visible, as an example of the pain and patience required to secure a few truths, then and only then would they merit a place in the schools.

Even then, they could not provide that amplitude of knowledge and mind we gain from the humanities taught earnestly and well. It cannot be put better than it was by John Stuart Mill, a century and a half ago, in the great essay on civilization. Discussing the study of history, he wrote that it must occupy an important place in education

> partly because it is the record of all the great things which have been achieved by mankind, and partly because when philosophically studied it gives a certain largeness of conception to the student, and familiarizes him with the action of great causes. . . . Nowhere else will the infinite varieties of human nature be so vividly brought home to him, and anything cramped or one-sided in his own standard of it so effectually corrected, and nowhere else will he behold as strongly exemplified the astonishing pliability of our nature, and the vast effects which may under good guidance be produced upon it by honest endeavour.

What Mill wrote would be true as well for other humanistic disciplines, certainly literature and philosophy, the exacting study of which can stimulate other largeness of conception, and offer other exposures to the variety and pliability of the human spirit. How much we have lost through the eclipse of the humanities is evident each time we read, say, the documents of the American Revolution, above all the *Federalist Papers*, and remember that the writers were on the whole ordinary citizens of the educated class, their collective genius formed by the classics and literature and philosophy. Or in reading the letters of William James, and finding much the same command of language and ideas among so many of his correspondents, not themselves great men, but educated to the standard of the times. Regaining that standard is almost certainly beyond our means, yet some effort must be made in the schools to restore some of the common culture. Otherwise, the citizen becomes, as Mill said in another compelling essay, "a poor, maimed, lopsided fragment of humanity."

5

Terrorizing Children

(with Chester E. Finn, Jr.)

For Sir Francis Bacon, the child was hostage to Fortune; today the child is far more often hostage to ideology, and to the fears it can induce: "I think about the bomb just about every day now. It makes me feel sad and depressed when I think about a bomb being dropped. I hope I'm with my family. I don't want to die alone." Or a hostage to ideology, and to the sanctimoniousness it can also induce:

> I assume you are all sensible people, since it requires great intelligence to be elected to a highly important part of our nation. Other nations have their intelligent people. I'm sure Yuri Andropov is intelligent. Ronald Reagan, our President, is intelligent.
>
> But why, instead of using our intelligence for good uses, like peace, for example, do we use our intelligence for war? Is it right to call having missiles in Europe peace? Is it right to call a nuclear missile "peace keeper"?
>
> This is a waste of intelligence. We are criminalizing Newton, Dalton, Einstein, Lucretius, and Democritus, great pioneers of the atom. What would Einstein have thought of this?

These anxious, earnest voices belong, respectively, to a sixteen-year-old girl and a twelve-year-old boy, brought to Washington to instruct Congress and the nation about their fears, and about the epidemic of nuclear anxiety said to be overwhelming the young. These youngsters are described as representative—perhaps a bit more outspoken than most, yet typical in their being tormented by a vision of atomic apocalypse.

Their public appearance on September 20, 1983 was hosted by the House Select Committee on Children, Youth, and Families, and sponsored by a group of psychiatrists and psychologists often thought to embody the "mental-health community." The presentation to Congress was one of a number of like events beginning in the autumn of 1983 and continuing for about a year after that. The American Orthopsychiatric Association offered several programs at its 1984 convention purporting to document the mental-health crisis being endured by children because of nuclear anxiety. Similar programs were presented at meetings of the American Psychological Association. That group's newly acquired magazine, *Psychology Today*, published a cover story on children's nuclear fears. There were any number of press releases, television appearances, and the like, all designed to alert the country to the terror produced in the young by the prospect of a nuclear war, said to be viewed by children as a clear and present danger.

These events have had some influence. There are many efforts to introduce "nuclear education" into the primary and secondary curriculum, in order to allay the panic—overt and covert—experienced by the young. During the 1984 presidential campaign, Walter Mondale said—as though it were settled fact—that American children are experiencing "nuclear nightmares." And why should he not believe so? We are told there is "research evidence," it is provided by famous names from famous universities, and presented at scientific meetings.

Yet things are not what they seem. Once we look at it closely, the "evidence" is suspect in various ways. Much of it is amateurish (one cited study was carried out by a high-school student); most of it is unacceptably soft, consisting of anecdotes rather than data; almost none of it has appeared in respectable journals; most of the "scientists" are in truth not scientists at all. Nor should we be impressed by the fact that the findings were presented at presumably scholarly meetings. The American Orthopsychiatric Association has for some years been devoted, in much of its programming, to agitprop pure and simple. The meetings of the American Psychological Association, once quite sober, are now a fifty-ring circus, some of it still given to scholarship but much of it to commerce and entertainment and politics, the last usually featuring such luminaries of the Left as Ed Asner, Ralph Nader, Bella Abzug, and Benjamin Spock.

Yet little of this is known generally. Those few social scientists with a strong interest in the matter are likely to have other fires to fight. Others are indifferent, or discouraged. In the absence of opposing critical voices, we will soon come to accept as proved the idea of nuclear anxiety among the young. So it may be time to look carefully at the issues, and at the evidence.

The recent election campaign has made it clearer than ever how fallible surveys can be in helping us assess seemingly simple questions. Throughout the campaign, the major presidential polls were far apart; less than two weeks before the election, at a time when attitudes presumably had stabilized, there were differences as large as sixteen percentage points between major surveys. If a straightforward question—whom would you vote for?—can produce such extraordinary variations from poll to poll, it does not require much imagination to understand how elusive findings will be when the questions are more difficult or ambiguous.

How in the world *do* we appraise the degree of anxiety in a population? The most direct and efficient method would appear to be self-report—that is, asking people what worries them, or makes them anxious or fearful. But the problems are visible immediately; it is likely that the specific word chosen will produce significant variations in the answers evoked. "Worry" will call to mind certain feelings, "anxiety" another group of feelings, "fear" still another, and so on. Yet that aside, it is evident that in dealing with so subjective a matter as a person's emotional state, responses will be conditioned by his vocabulary of self-report, and even more by his sense of what the questioner is up to, what *kind* of answer the interviewer has in mind. Thus, if you were to ask two citizens what makes them anxious these days, and one tells you he worries about Paul Volcker's monetary policy, and the other about the moisture that has begun to appear on his basement walls, you can be fairly sure that the two understand the questioner's intentions rather differently. (The example is not far-fetched, as we will see in a moment.)

The point is that interviewers ordinarily establish a context which influences and at times governs the answers given, and until that context is understood, we will not grasp the meaning, if any, of those answers. In short, the responses to questions on mood or state of mind or inner feelings simply cannot be taken at face value.

To do so is to commit the sin of literalism, a sin rarely practiced nowadays except by uninstructed undergraduates in their first attempts at social research, or by pop psychologists writing on such topics as the sexual revolution. Yet the evidence to support the idea of a widespread nuclear anxiety is being adduced, precisely, by just such a literalist use of self-report data. Children are asked to list their worries and (so we are told) report increasingly a concern about nuclear war, which now ranks number three in frequency. That seems impressive, until we discover that number two is . . . getting poor grades. The witness communicating these statistics to the Select Committee did not seem at all troubled by this; it was left to a Republican Congressman to point out to the assembled savants that findings so peculiar suggest some deep flaw in the study itself.

That may be putting it mildly. The survey evidence cited to the Committee is essentially worthless—not surprisingly, since the studies were carried out by persons without apparent background in survey work with children or adolescents, and giving few signs of familiarity with the appropriate scientific literature, or with the excruciatingly difficult technical problems inherent in research with the young. The contingent before the Committee was led by Harvard's John Mack and Yale's Robert Jay Lifton, both psychoanalysts, neither trained in empirical research, both nevertheless trading on the credentials of "doctor" and "professor," on that sense of the sacred we now give over to science, and on the gullibility and good faith of their listeners, all to the end of making an argument unabashedly political.

Poor as they are, the survey data are nevertheless rather more solid than the other findings adduced, which are drawn from "clinical interviews," workshops, and the like, all conducted by zealous partisans of a nuclear freeze, using as respondents youngsters drawn from New Class milieux. If the survey findings are amateurish, the interview data are corrupt, confounding amateurism and deliberate political purpose. That comes through clearly enough in the congressional transcript.

The survey findings were presented to the Committee by John Goldenring, M.D., M.P.H., F.A.A.P., S.A.M., who is a pediatrician, and in water well over his head, to judge both by the technical ineptness of his study and by his failure to recognize it. Dr. Goldenring went into great detail to tell how he drew an absolutely representative sampling of California adolescents; but a moment's inspection of his tables suggests what a more careful perusal will confirm, that his sample is by no means representative. He also argued that his findings reveal a terrible fear of nuclear war among the young, though as we have already seen, considerably more children seem to worry about getting bad grades, and an equal percentage worry about crime and about being unable to get a job one day.

The transcript next brings us the words of the Committee chairman, George Miller of California. Miller had been under great pressure from the Republican minority members, who had been arguing, justifiably, that the Committee's function—to study such matters as divorce, broken families, child abuse, illegitimacy—was being perverted by these hearings, which had nothing to do with its mandate.

Miller, determined to justify the session, now throws this very fat pitch to the witness: "Does the research show, or does it suggest, that fear of war is a significant driving force on the acting out of children, whether it is drug-seeking or suicide or bad grades or what have you, recognizing that our childhood is a mosaic made up of many, many experiences and pressures?" (There is nothing more infectious than shrink-talk.) Dr. Goldenring answers:

> I would like to say that how we tried to get at that was with a couple of questions I mentioned that were very imperfect. It looked to us, this is just preliminary data, and very difficult to analyze, that some 5 to 15 percent of the kids may at least be thinking about nuclear war to a degree that might affect their behavior. Whether it actually affects their behavior or not we really can't say at this point. . . .

Imperfect, preliminary, difficult to analyze, 5 to 15 percent, may, might, cannot really say: Dr. Goldenring, to his credit, has been overcome by a sudden seizure of scientific caution; but what has happened to the nuclear nightmare, and what is the point of the hearings?

Needing some help, chairman Miller asks for further comments, and Dr. Lifton rushes in to fill the breach:

> We have certain parts of the puzzle—that is, we know that suicide in young people, or in older people, too, for that matter, occurs with despair even more than with depression, they are not quite the same thing. Despair involves the loss of larger human connectiveness. We know that the nuclear threat impairs that sense of larger human connectiveness. We don't have hard evidence that the nuclear threat as such has increased youth suicide or other forms of suicide, but we have lots of reasons to be worried about that combination, that interaction, and the research is needed, but we have something very suggestive and worrisome.

It would take a great deal of space to give this self-assured pronouncement the careful gloss it deserves. Let us just note that "we" do not in fact "know" any of the things said to be known—that suicide occurs more often with despair than depression (themselves not so easily distinguished); the link between despair and "human connectiveness"; the effect of nuclear threat upon that "connectiveness." The statement is not quite cant, since we must assume its sincerity; but it certainly is fancy invention, every bit of it, including the nonexistent word "connectiveness."

There is a steady streak of what can only be called intellectual bad faith running through much of the expert testimony. Drs. Lifton and Mack, in particular, want us to believe that they are scientific, hence disinterested, that they—speaking for the collective body of scholars—"know" things of import to the citizenry, and that their "findings" are indeed findings and not mere solipsism. So they discourse solemnly about tentative results and methodological problems and further studies needed, at the same time telling us of "research" whose trashiness defies belief.

Here is Dr. Mack reporting to the Committee on the "interview study" he and some colleagues carried out, wherein thirty-one Boston-area adolescents—"located" by teachers, students, and counselors—were questioned about the nuclear threat. What he reports about these youngsters is odd, yet strangely familiar. Each and every one expects a nuclear war in his lifetime. Dr. Mack tells us that "some" resist any "stereotyping" of the Soviet Union, and are skeptical about its reported enmity to the United States. They believe that the Soviet and U.S. governments are equally responsible for the arms race. Dr. Mack goes on to say that "many" want to know more about the Soviet Union, and want to "participate in the decision-making process, which is also seen as a way of overcoming the sense of terror and helplessness.'' Curious. All those teachers and students and counselors, scouting the entire Boston metropolitan area, were able to locate only mini-Macks for Dr. Mack to interview.

Having provided us with these research findings, he then moves to a different level of science, clinical impressions: an eleven-year-old asking her parents if she would have time to commit suicide before the bombs fell; five- and six-year-olds fearing they will not grow up; children who play video games in order to master their nuclear fears. And even youngsters seemingly without nuclear anxieties in fact suffer from them, since they may be ''defending themselves.''

This last idea is an important part of the gospel of nuclear terror. Children who talk about their fear prove the case, and children who do not talk about it also prove the case, since they suffer from ''psychic numbing.'' The heads-I-win-tails-you-lose mode of analysis is conspicuous throughout the testimony. The young are depicted as overcome with despair, futurelessness, anomie; even when they seem not to be, they really are, really. To the question of how today's youngsters—despite their constant gazing into the abyss— nevertheless remain conscientious about their studies, Dr. Mack answers by quoting a sociologist who quotes a student who says: ''It's the only alternative to despair when the world can blow up at any moment.''

The inventor of the term ''psychic numbing,'' Robert J. Lifton, then adds his own testimony. After much talk, again, of research demonstrating the universal sense of doom now found among the young, he tells us of another finding, the rage that the young feel toward the old:

> I have been able to confirm this anger in workshops I have done with young people. Strong rage toward the older generation, toward political leaders who have so much control as the kids say, over our lives and our deaths.

We now know that American ''kids,'' despite their ''strong rage,'' gave their support in the November election overwhelmingly to Ronald Reagan, that avatar of ''nuclear lunacy,'' and rejected a Democratic ticket endorsing a nuclear freeze. No doubt Lifton and Mack, if called upon, could provide some fine phrases and fancy inventions to explain this phenomenon, along with a new collection of heartrending excerpts from interviews conducted with youngsters drawn from the better neighborhoods of suburban Boston. There will always be a fresh supply of ''kids'' to tell us those amazing truths no one else seems to grasp—for example, that a nuclear war would be terrible. But as the repetitive use of the pseudo-chummy ''kids'' itself suggests, Lifton and Mack are adrift in the past. What they have done is to reinvent the young of the 1960s, the young seen as suffering seers, or as generational Jeremiahs, now adding a new dimension, the young utterly lost to terror and hopelessness.

Those young were fictive in the 1960s, and they are, if anything, more fictive today.

We remain with the question: speaking realistically, how anxious are the American young about a nuclear war? We do not know. They are certainly not in a state of panic, for if they were, we would soon be aware of it, in the reports of parents and teachers, or in the course of psychotherapeutic practice. There is no reason at all to believe that acute anxiety assumes recondite forms, and there are few public signs of the so-called "nuclear nightmare." The only testimony we have comes from those engaged—deeply engaged—in the nuclear-freeze movement; there has been no spontaneous evidence of intense anxiety among children or, for that matter, among adults.

One of the authors of the present essay is a supervisor of psychotherapy, and spends part of each day reading the detailed notes taken by clinical interns. During the past year, in the course of reading well over one thousand pages of such notes, involving more than twenty adult patients, he came across only one mention of a nuclear disaster, and even here the patient was reporting not her own but a friend's anxiety—this at a time when the nuclear-freeze movement was extremely active locally, and during the period the television drama *The Day After*, depicting the effects of a nuclear attack on an American city, was shown.

Although psychotherapy patients do not usually talk much about current events, they do during periods of national anxiety, e.g., following the Kennedy assassination, and during the Cuban missile crisis. They are also—quite naturally—responsive to news which may affect their personal safety; thus, male homosexual patients became extremely anxious as news of the AIDS syndrome was brought to public attention. So it is difficult to believe that any widespread and deeply felt emotion would fail to appear in psychotherapy. Nor do we we see signs of acute nuclear anxiety among children and adolescents. A recent check of a dozen texts in clinical child psychiatry and psychology revealed no mention at all of the topic. The most recent book we have on children's conceptions of death shows them to be rarely associated with war or bombing.

Will this change? No doubt it will. No doubt it already has. The prospect and the horrors of nuclear warfare have been brought to our collective consciousness by the freeze movement; there is an earnest campaign to use the schools to "educate" children, supposedly to reassure them, but in ways that are certain to upset them; and there is, of course, the realistic apprehension all of us share. These elements have produced—and will continue to produce—concern, worry, some anxiety, in a few cases intense fear. That being so, one will be able to "prove" the existence of nuclear anxiety, since it will have become recognized as an appropriate and normal state of mind, hence a legitimate answer to survey questions addressing one's worries.

But bear in mind that at the present time a large number of adolescents also report "world overpopulation" as a significant worry. We may imagine that they think about it every now and again; but it is hard to believe that it is the source of many sleepless nights. Quite clearly, people of all ages will sometimes respond to questions about their worries by taking on the persona of the concerned citizen. That does not mean they are deeply or even moderately anxious in a personal way.

In this connection, we ought to remember that *The Day After* was expected to set off a national epidemic of nervous breakdowns, so much so that hotlines were set up by mental-health experts across the country, hotlines which quickly cooled off when the phones did not ring. That fiasco was instructive in many ways. There was, first of all, no evidence of *any* discernible increase of anxiety, or its derivatives, following the broadcast, which enjoyed the third largest audience of any dramatic program in television history. Indeed, an impact study by a faculty team at George Washington Univesity concluded that the only effect this film had on people's views was one that its producers surely did not expect: "reduced willingness to link President Reagan with nuclear war." As for the hotlines, the researchers drily noted that "psychologists and psychiatrists appear to have spent far more time talking to television-station reporters than to disturbed patients."

Yet a failure of prophecy does not necessarily dissuade belief. The *New York Times*, in a follow-up story, quoted a New York psychiatrist as saying, "We'll never know how many people sought help later." A Yale psychologist went so far as to take credit for the absence of panic: "I had a sense that if we'd done nothing, if we hadn't warned parents, that there would have been many more problems than we had." And a former president of the American Psychological Association revealed that the absence of effects showed their presence: "We are seeing the defense mechanism of denial." Heads I win, tails you lose.

What we have here is an example of the easy corruptibility of psychologists and psychiatrists when called into missionary service—a scandal that has now become commonplace. During the last generation, these disciplines have squandered much of their moral capital by lending themselves eagerly to this or that political cause. In the early years, the sins were venial, stemming from an ingenuousness which did not perceive how silently one's biases can penetrate the design and outcome of research undertaken and carried out in full sincerity. What we encounter more often today is a kind of recklessness, wherein the righteousness of the cause and the felt urgency of its success ride roughshod over any effort at scientific constraint.

The case made at the congressional hearings was thus as flagrant an abuse of scientific testimony as one can imagine, in part because most of the studies mentioned were so wretchedly done, in part because they were surely known to be poor yet were presented nevertheless, in part because the findings offered were themselves *outré*, violating both common sense and common experience, and in part because the political intent of the witnesses was so bald and unconcealed. ("We are hoping," Dr. Mack reported to the Select Committee, "that as this material, this information, comes forth . . . a dialogue about how to approach these very difficult problems such as the United States-Soviet relationship will be looked at in different, more innovative, creative ways so that children won't be troubled.")

The abuse of science goes hand in glove with another abuse, this one of the legislative process. As some members pointed out, the hearings were clearly outside the mandate given to the Select Committee. The intention of the hearings was to gain publicity for nuclear disarmament, as part of a larger campaign to influence national policy; but since that aim could not be acknowledged, the hearings were legitimated through the invention of a mental-health crisis, with experts and legislators taking turns doing variations on Uriah Heep.

To complete the scenario, one more element was needed, the testimony of the young. And this is the third and most serious abuse, the exploitation of children, both by the organizers of the congressional hearings and by the nuclear-freeze movement more generally.

Why are children brought forward to testify? Quite clearly they are meant to tug at our heartstrings, and to provide some discreetly mawkish television coverage. But there is more to it than that. The child is meant to have a role in a drama wherein head and heart play off against each other.

Nuclear strategy is considered—correctly—to require an extraordinary degree of disinterested intelligence. The prototypical strategist is a Dr. Strange-love figure, that is, a figure yoking the greatest brilliance to cold Machiavellian cunning. The very coldness of the intelligence, moreover, is believed to produce its own form of lunacy, a rationality which turns on itself to become the quintessential irrationality.

To oppose the idea of malevolent intelligence, we need a figure representing guilelessness, an innocence whose parity and perception achieve truth more closely and quickly than mere brilliance can. The child is the exemplary choice; and it is striking how frequently children and the childlike are employed as inherent arguments for nuclear amity. Consider the way President Carter adduced his daughter Amy's ideas on the nuclear-arms race during his presidential debate; or the beatification of Samantha Smith, the child from Maine who visited the Soviet Union at the invitation of Yuri Andropov; or the popularity of Dr. Seuss's children's book on nuclear warfare, *The Butter Battle Book*; or the pilgrimage to Russia undertaken by several American psychiatrists (our own Dr. Mack among them) to interview Soviet youngsters (blond, winsome, soulful) on their yearning for peace.

That we can attain truth more easily through innocence than through intelligence is a notion too sentimental to withstand scrutiny. One must therefore display innocence *an sich*, in its own self. And even then, if the audience should prove skeptical, if it should demand something beyond the iconic, the presentation will not sustain itself and may quite possibly backfire. The hearings themselves provided a telling example of this when one of the youngsters, asked to testify to her fears, revealed upon gentle questioning that her anxieties and concerns, far from being typical, had marked her as an eccentric among her peers. If the audience is more than skeptical, if it is challenging or hostile, the results can be devastating—remember the scorn which greeted Jimmy Carter's invocation of Amy's views. To accept the childlike as testimony or as argument requires a suspension of disbelief. We may be intrigued by the spectacle of a twelve-year-old lecturing U.S. Representatives on Democritus and Einstein; but if we blink once, the spell is gone.

Hence, the career of the prodigy will be vivid yet brief. The child must be forthcoming yet not brassy, bright yet not freaky, articulate yet not overbearing, sincere yet not self-righteous, consistent yet not mechanical, above all, coachable without seeming overcoached. It is not easy; few do it well; and fewer still do it well for very long. Samantha Smith, although carefully managed, soon came to seem artificial and tedious. When she testified from her experience that Soviet kids were really neat, really *peace-loving*, just like American kids, her audience may have been credulous enough for a moment to take her at her word; but as soon as she was asked to interpret her experience, to supply some context, to embellish, to defend—in short, to step out of her original role as witness and to assume another as historian or commentator or advocate—the contradictions became all too apparent.

For these reasons, the child must always be displayed narrowly, *qua* child, much as a medieval morality tableau shows figures representing only virtue or other single attributes. To some degree that is true of all public performance, but it is intensified when the performer's appeal rests entirely on his persona. What makes these performances abusive is that they reduce the child's individuality to that persona and in so doing exploit him, in the exact sense—use him for someone else's ends.

Who are the children so used? With few exceptions, they are the progeny of the "enlightened," from politically active families. The child's views generally reflect the parents', and at times the youngster is little more than the family mouthpiece. At the Committee hearings, one eleven-year-old girl, not far from mute, spoke barely two hundred words, whereupon her father took the stand and rambled on for several pages of transcript.

This is hardly surprising: we now have nearly two decades of good research on the acquisition of political attitudes, and it is clear that there is a strong transmission from parent to child (rather stronger than from peer to peer), especially when the issues are salient and intensely felt. There is, for example, a large parent-child concordance on the question of school prayer, and we would quite likely find a similarly strong correlation within families where there are intense feelings against, say, abortion, and also among those actively committed to the nuclear-freeze movement. As the child psychologist David Elkind has noted: "When issues like nuclear warfare worry and threaten children is when these issues worry and threaten their parents. If parents talk about the threat of war . . . their children become apprehensive."

Elkind's conclusion is supported by the observations of the Harvard psychiatrist Robert Coles, who for the past five years has conducted wideranging interviews with more than one hundred children. Among other topics bearing on moral and political belief, he has been probing their thoughts and feelings about the possibility of a nuclear war. Reports the *Harvard Gazette*:

> In the children of the upper-middle class, liberally inclined parents, he found concern, but not the kind of fear "that would get in the way of a generally flourishing life." Among working-class white and black children . . . he found the fear to be practically nonexistent.

To judge by the examples he has provided in a recent manuscript, Cole's interviews promise to be remarkable, ranging as they do from children genuinely haunted by a sort of nuclear nihilism to those voicing an intelligent and forceful patriotism. Coles is clear-headed throughout, never losing sight of the traps lying in wait for the zealous or simpleminded researcher. He reports what a teacher told him about a student of hers whom he had interviewed:

> I heard him at lunch laughing and telling his best friend . . . that he convinced you "the world is coming to an end." . . . Then the friend asked how he knew he had persuaded you. He said he knew because he had met people like you, friends of his parents, and "if you cry they cry" were his words.

Coles lives in the belly of the beast—he is an Ivy League psychiatrist, a colleague of John Mack and others, and himself a supporter of the nuclear-freeze movement. Nevertheless he has been able to separate his observations from his politics. It is quite plain to him that "the purported fears of American children have been used in a political way.'' And he warns his colleagues: ''If we in the freeze movement continue to assume [these fears] as fact, we have to make sure our facts are in order. If they're not, we're politically and morally on thin ice.''

The most serious abuse of children may lie ahead, in the campaigns now being planned to introduce thermonuclear education into the schools. To judge by the curricula so far developed, what lies before us will be perversely iatrogenic, a treatment producing the very disease it is designed to cure, and a course of instruction generating or increasing the anxiety it is allegedly trying to allay.

The parent who places a child hostage to these curricula can expect him to be subjected to a heavy dosage of what can only be called gratuitous sadism. The child (according to the curricular units that have been prepared) will be shown close-up photographs of Hiroshima victims, and given detailed contemporary accounts of that grim event: ''A mother driven half-mad while looking for her child was calling his name. At last she found him. His head looked like a boiled octupus''; or, ''I was horrified, indeed, at the sight of a stark naked man, standing in the rain with his eyeball in his palm.''

If those accents seem vaguely familiar, it is because they recall a classic passage of this century's literature: ''The blood seethes and boils in the veins, the brains are boiling in the skull, the heart in the breast glowing and burning, the bowels a red-hot mass of burning pulp, the tender eyes flaming like molten balls''—it is the preacher recounting the torments of hell in James Joyce's *Portrait of the Artist as a Young Man*, and doing so (as he might tell us) not because he enjoys it but only to instruct the young and to assist in their salvation. And just as the preacher insists that the terrible fires will soon become his listeners' own destiny, so do these curricula strive to bring the nuclear horrors home. The youngster will be taught to ''empathize'' with the Hiroshima survivors. He will be given a map showing the effects of a megaton bomb in his own community. In some units, children are encouraged to confess their secret fears to the group at large, a tactic almost certain to produce anxiety *de novo*.

Treating the nuclear peril as a discrete curriculum unit in its own right, something to be dropped into place in the social-studies, health, or English class at almost any grade level, means that gross simplifications and omissions inevitably appear. Children are asked to engage in wildly unrealistic intellectual exercises, mostly involving the simulation of analyses of exceedingly complicated matters that even experts find difficult.

These exercises, moreover, are conveniently rendered for classroom use by snatching them from historical context. Thus, a New York City social-studies unit has students appraise the wisdom and morality of Truman's decision to drop the bomb—after admonishing teachers that this decision "was an important step in the arms race which continues to threaten the very survival of mankind.'' Later, the youngsters are invited to "analyze the relative nuclear strength of the United States and the Soviet Union,'' to "assess the legality of using nuclear weapons,'' to "analyze the psychological changes caused by the bomb and its after-effects,'' and to "assess the health risks inherent in using nuclear energy.''

The didactic parts of these units provide lessons in geopolitics and world history—at about the level of Dr. Seuss's *Butter Battle Book. Choices*, the much-publicized contribution of the National Education Association (NEA), to give but one example, looks blandly past any differences between the superpowers. Its one-page "fact sheet" on the U.S.S.R. simply summarizes population, land area, and military resources. The geopolitical situation of the Soviet Union is captured in an extraordinary sentence: "The Soviet Union is bordered by many countries, including some unfriendly countries and others that are part of the Warsaw Pact, which includes countries that are friendly to the Soviet Union.'' The beleaguered Soviets are tacitly compared to the United States, which is bordered (we are told) only by "friendly countries.'' The youngster is thus plainly led to conclude that the Russians have rather more reason to be fearful than the Americans and that the relationship between Washington and Ottawa is indistinguishable from the ties between Moscow and "friendly" Warsaw or Kabul.

As one might expect, the student is told nothing by the NEA "fact sheet" about the two political systems—nothing about the Gulag or the KGB, nothing about internal passports or the control of emigration, nothing about Poland or Afghanistan. It is Dr. Seuss's Yooks against Zooks, two systems morally equivalent, sharing similar goals and policies and strategies, much the same in their domestic and economic priorities.

One curious feature of these curricula is that they encourage youngsters to be passive about their own survival; games and exercises are intended to teach the necessity of nonresistance. But another curious feature moves in the opposite direction altogether. Although it is an axiom of today's educational ethos that on any remotely controversial topic, such as deviant sexuality, schools are to maintain a pose of exquisite neutrality, these curricula openly encourage children to engage in political action. In one instance it is recommended that letters be sent to elected officials and local newspapers; in another, teachers are urged to influence parents "by sharing what we as teachers have discovered about peace and peacemaking.'' A New York City unit concludes with an "action collage" of bumper stickers, antiwar headlines, "peace walks,'' and disarmament rallies. Another recommends seven separate projects, one of which is to write to Congressmen about nuclear-power plants in the community.

To sum up: nuclear curricula, presumably designed to ease a child's anxiety, in fact introduce him to fears he has probably not entertained, and exacerbate any that he has. The child is provided with false or misleading political information which makes national policy seem capricious or malevolent or irrational. He is on the one hand taught the virtues of helplessness, on the other recruited to the propaganda purposes of the teacher.

Will such a curriculum find its way into the schools? It is already beginning to. The NEA has proudly sold thousands of copies of its notorious *Choices* unit, and New York City is not the only school system to be preparing its own packets for teachers. The *Washington Post* reported in mid-1984 that the three huge suburban systems of Montgomery, Prince George's, and Fairfax counties were developing, incorporating, or "piloting" such materials, that the District of Columbia schools had begun to "review and provide information on nuclear-weapons material for their teachers," and that 14,000 Washington students had viewed "*Peace Child*, a musical which raises the nuclear issue." Elsewhere, there is even greater compulsion. In Cambridge, Massachusetts, according to the *Wall Street Journal*, the "school board requires teachers to cover peace and nuclear war from kindergarten through 12th grade."

Certainly conditions are right for this pattern to widen. A number of powerful organizations are pushing hard, above all the NEA, which recently renamed its foreign-affairs staff unit the office of "peace programs and international relations." Like the rest of us, educators fear missing the boat, and they are being told that to be antinuclear in the classroom is to be with-it. "It's the issue of our time," says a New York school official, "and we have to do more about it." The head of a group called Educators for Social Responsibility echoes the sentiment: "Nuclear war is *the* hot curricular issue." Not only hot but also, *McCall's* recently informed its readers, vital to the well-being of our children: even the tiniest tots will fail to develop adequate "ego ideals" unless they "perceive life as stable and enduring," something that will be possible only if their parents become actively engaged against the nuclear menace.

The private schools have also joined the crusade. The board of the National Association of Independent Schools—it includes virtually all of the traditional prep schools—not long ago urged its members to lead students toward "informed participation as citizens in the consideration of issues of nuclear power and weapons." An article in the journal, after a ritualized caution about the dangers of indoctrination, trots out the usual studies and experts to testify to the widespread terror and mistrust all of us feel. The cover of the magazine depicts a little girl against a backdrop of destruction and death. The Catholic parochial schools are being urged by their own national organization to follow the policy lines set forth by the American bishops in their pastoral letter on war and peace. The journal of the Association is filled with lesson suggestions parallel to those offered by the NEA, and some of its leaders are reported (by *Education Week*) as having said that "Roman Catholic schools can no longer call themselves Catholic" if they fail to "infuse" the concepts of "peace and justice" into the training of their students.

More is at work here than a pedagogical passion for current events, controversial issues, or childhood anxieties. The schools obviously cannot and do not incorporate every hot topic into their curricula. If children learn anything in class about the federal budget deficit, for example, it is almost accidental. Other grave concerns, such as the deterioration of the family, are more or less taboo. Nor do instructors routinely base their content selections on pupil worries, else more of them would teach units on "how to avoid being an unpopular adolescent," "why parents sometimes abandon their children," and "what to do when a bully approaches."

Teachers have considerable leeway to pick topics that they deem important, so long as they cover the prescribed material and do not violate any of the taboos. In making these choices, the teacher may be influenced by his own politics, by the educational values he acquired in college, by the messages his union transmits, and by such mundane but consequential factors as the availability of curricular material. Over time, however, the most potent force will be the opinion elites in education, arbiters for the whole profession of what is really important and how to think about it.

In these lofty elevations, it is now assumed that schools—public and private, primary and secondary—have a solemn obligation to instruct their students about the nuclear menace. The most prestigious journals in the field— among them the *Phi Delta Kappan*, the (Columbia) *Teachers College Record*, and the *Harvard Educational Review*—have recently suspended their customary standards of balance and scholarship and have given over entire issues to advocacy of the antinuclear cause. Many of the articles published in these journals are based upon the scant data and slovenly thinking we have examined here, and some seem to slide into superstition altogether: a piece in the *Phi Delta Kappan*, for example, argued that the recent decline in SAT scores could be accounted for by radioactive fallout affecting the fetal development of those born in the 1950s and early 1960s.

In this venture the education elite is joined by the "progressive" foundations, themselves ever in search of hot new issues. Witness the president of the Rockefeller Brothers Fund: "The prevention of nuclear war is going to be to the 1980s what civil rights was to the 1960s, and foundations are increasingly concerned about . . .," etc. The MacArthur Foundation recently committed a staggering $25 million to a group of universities and think-tanks that propose through research and education to reduce the thermonuclear threat. In short, the coffers are open. And if private philanthropy cannot fully meet the demand for grants, fellowships, syllabi, workshops, conferences, what have you, we now have the U.S. government setting up its own cash window, through the United States Insititute of Peace, established by Congress this past session in its latest spasm of misguided Wilsonianism. So there will be even more millions available, now carrying a federal seal of approval, for more of the same.

The consequence of all this is easily foreseen: the politicization of education will deepen, as will the electorate's alienation from schools dominated by an ideology so distant from its own. Gazing at this prospect, one wonders, and not for the first time, whether the education elite is entirely bereft of sense— to take on a task hazardous to its students and inimical to the beliefs and values of most Americans, and to do all this just as the schools had finally begun to recover a bit of their lost standing with the public. But then one reflects that this elite helped bring the schools to ruin in the first place, and in much of the same way, through seeing them above all else as instruments of its particular idea of salvation.

6

Living with Quotas

Several months ago former President Gerald Ford spoke to a political science class at my university. During the question period that followed he was asked for his views on the *Bakke* case, and replied that he was opposed to "arbitrary numerical quotas." Thereupon the class broke into what the local newspaper termed "vociferous applause."

A few days later I was interviewed by a young journalist who thought the story might be worth pursuing. He had himself been so disbelieving of the original press account that he had sought out and listened to the tape made during the former president's appearance. Sure enough, he told me, the applause had been enthusiastic, so much so that he would describe it as turbulent. He was dumbfounded. Is that what the students really felt? At Michigan— of all places—the founding campus of SDS (Students for a Democratic Society)? What did it mean? Was I as surprised as he was? I told him I would not have expected the students to have made public their private feelings, but was not at all surprised by the direction and intensity of those feelings; that most students in my experience have come to despise "affirmative action" because of the double standards it imposed, and which victimized them; furthermore, that most of the faculty I knew were equally scornful because of the duplicities these programs have come to involve; and that to my certain knowledge many in the administration hoped, in private, that the Court would hold for Bakke and thus rescue them from their own cant. And *that*, I said, was the story he ought to write. He ought to reflect upon his own surprise, and recognize that the press had made almost no effort to discover whether racial-preference programs—after nearly a decade in place—had in fact fulfilled their promises, and what faculty and students now thought about them. Why such indifference to reality? What was at work, I suggested, was a strong wish not to know, to sustain a state of self-deception.

At this my interviewer became noticeably morose. He told me he felt very ambivalent about the problem. He had himself been in graduate school several years earlier, had been disturbed by the poor quality of minority students then enrolled; on the other hand, he could see no alternative except to admit many such students in the hope that some of them would make it. So he could not bring himself to write that story. Perhaps someone else could; perhaps I could.

And with that we returned to the story he wanted to write, a "changing-mood-of-the-campus" piece.

Note that the key term in this anecdote is *doubleness*. The journalist describes himself as ambivalent (of mixed or double feelings). The students resent the double standard, and the faculty members feel themselves forced into duplicity (double dealings). The administration is troubled by its hypocrisy (double-facedness). These and other dualities dominate the history of affirmative action and in a sense fittingly because these programs have from the beginning been haunted by an unacknowledged ambiguity or doubleness of purpose: whether to expand opportunity or to compensate for prior injustice. The major means chosen has been a double-track system of admissions. Unable to confess to these contradictions, those in charge of racial-preference programs find themselves using deception or ambiguous language, that is, of mixed or double meaning: most commonly, the word *goal* when *quota* is meant, or, as will be evident later, the word *qualified* when in fact *marginal* or *unqualified* is correct. To sustain these deceptions, or to keep them hidden, other dualities come into play: the world is divided between insiders and outsiders, those who are and are not privy to secret information; or a schism develops between public and private discourse, the first tending toward blandness and boosterism, the second toward rumor and innuendo. The ultimate effect is a corruption both of language and conduct.

Does that seem overstated? Yet consider that in a milieu like the university, where one is customarily buried in statistics, it is generally difficult to obtain accurate information on the comparative credentials of majority and minority students, or on the relative attrition rates of the two groups, or on the costs— many of them hidden—that these programs entail. Because any good news is an immediate stimulus for publicity and self-congratulation, one tends to assume, in most cases correctly, that no news is bad news. The subordinating of information to policy is something we have become accustomed to in other domains of public life, but it takes some getting used to at the university, and it has had a troubling effect on the way its members regard themselves and relate to each other.

An example: last summer a professor I know was called by a law firm and asked whether he could obtain some data on his university's medical school's admissions policies. The firm was preparing an *amicus* brief for the then-forthcoming *Bakke* hearing before the Supreme Court, and wanted to argue that objective credentials—test scores, grade point averages—were in fact valid predictors of achievement in medical school. Though it was generally held by expert sources that this was so, the law firm had been unable to find enough published evidence, despite a thorough search of the literature, and was now fairly sure it was being suppressed. Perhaps as an insider he could obtain data pertaining to his own medical school. The professor thought he could; he remembered that an old friend of his had connections there and would no doubt have the information. He called upon the friend, who first asked him, suspiciously, which side he was on, then told him, bitterly, that he did not think the data would be released, and that one ought to expect to get the runaround from the medical school. Not that one could trust the figures in any case because the admissions dean was known to put the best face on things. There were only two sure ways to get the data: to threaten to sue if they were not released, but because that would take time, a more expedient means would be to find a "Deep Throat," someone at the medical school who had access to the information and would be willing to steal it!

Finding both these alternatives too troubling to contemplate, the professor thereupon arranged an informal, off-the-record interview with the admissions dean, representing himself as sympathetic but concerned, and thus inducing the dean to unburden himself. The dean depicted himself as a beleaguered man, caught between the university administration, which kept urging him to keep the minority numbers up, and the medical-school faculty, which kept wanting him to keep the standards up. The trouble was that the administration was not being realistic about the level of intellectual quality required to complete medical school these days. He had some serious questions about many of the minority students he was admitting, perhaps as many as half. Some of them he knew would not be able to make it through, and he felt sorry for what would happen to them. But he was even more worried about those who would just manage to get through and were, as he saw it, doomed to a career of marginal competence. Medicine became every day more technical, more demanding, and he doubted that they could keep up. It was not a matter of race. During the 1950s the medical schools had so few really good applicants that they accepted and pushed through many white students of low quality. And what had happened to them? The dean was convinced that this was the group now giving medicine its rotten public image, through malpractice suits and Medicaid ripoffs. And at that point, he launched into what the professor later characterized as "lurid medical detail."

It is tempting to linger over those details because stories of incompetence—real, imagined, or prospective—form a familiar genre of academic gossip. In doing so we would be ignoring what may be far more significant, the skewed relationship among colleagues that the anecdote reveals: false assumptions, misunderstood motives, an atmosphere of mistrust and paranoia that comes to infect almost everyone involved. It is the ambience of a novel of intrigue—Eric Ambler, let us say. The professor, an innocent, embarks upon what seems to be a simple enough errand of discovery and is quickly drawn into the suspicions of the milieu. A friend, hitherto open, at first mistrusts him, then, assured of his loyalty, warns him to expect thwarting and deceit, and hence feels it legitimate to deceive in return. (The friend, it will later turn out, is deceived in another sense, in that he misunderstands the dean's public statements, thinking they reflect his actual sentiments, which turns out not to be quite the case.) The professor, in hopes of evoking honesty from the dean, engages in some deceit of his own, simulating a sympathy he does not really feel. The dean reveals himself to be a deeply divided person, seeing himself compelled to offer entirely different messages to different audiences, telling the university administration one thing, "We're doing the best we can"; the medical-school faculty another, "Do the best you can, and I'll try to limit the damages"; the outside world still another, "Standards are not going down, you can count on that"; and apparently sympathetic insiders yet another, "*Caveat emptor.*"

What are we to make of the admissions dean? We may think of him as a divided, indeed fragmented soul, but it is unlikely that he would agree. Though he sees himself as subjected to contradictory pressures, he probably does not recognize the degree of inner division he must maintain. Nor would he accept our judgment that such extraordinary differences between public and private discourse amount to a form of fraud; he would be offended, or hurt, by that charge because it does not take into account his sincere belief in racial equality. One is led ultimately to the idea that everyone is right—the dean is indeed divided, and to be so eases the practice of duplicity, itself in the service of an undeniable good.

In this sense, the dean's contradictions, internal and external, are no different from those experienced by anyone who must serve the inherently divided, confused, ambivalent aims of a racial quota system; the contradictions are merely more visible, more dramatic, because of the peculiarly salient position he occupies. What strikes me as more important is that similar divisions, similar deceptions have now become commonplace, almost a habit of mind, so taken for granted as to escape notice. Another example: we are now at the faculty dinner party and one of the guests, looking like the cat who swallowed the canary, announces that he has managed to secure from the dean of his college a "slot," that is, permission to appoint an assistant professor. It is a rare opportunity, given the privations we share. He is head of the search committee and is overwhelmed by the range and depth of talent available. There are several hundred applicants, and at least fifty seem good enough to warrant a closer look. The problem the committee will have is narrowing that number down to the handful who will be invited to visit. It is no simple task because a number of them, all younger than thirty, already have substantial bibliographies and burgeoning national reputations.

At this point another guest asks him whether there were any minority candidates, and if so what did they look like. He is startled by the question, then recovers, and says something like: "Oh yes, there was I believe—uh— one—and she was—oh—somewhere well below the midpoint." As he tells us this his face breaks into an astonishing sequence of expressions: first a slight closing of the eyes, almost a wink; then a sardonic half-smile; then the sudden assumption of the most solemn gravity. It is over in a moment, so quickly that no one else there, I suspect, caught that quick sequence, and I imagine I would not have seen it myself had I not at that time been pondering whether to write this essay. The final phase of that sequence, the solemn expression of sincerity, will be seen again, and more than once, certainly when he informs the departmental meeting of the committee's search for a candidate, of its success, and of the *earnest efforts* to find suitable minority candidates. It may also be seen in a later colloquy with the dean, wherein those efforts are again described, and in that conversation several persons will be present—my friend addressing the dean, the dean nodding gravely, my friend half-winking, half-smiling, to signal his detachment from and acceptance of the ritual, and the dean winking back. In that exchange they are signaling their submission to the improbabilities and absurdities of academic hiring in the era of affirmative action: the improbability that there is an undiscovered abundance of minority talent, that a diligent search will uncover it, that bureaucratic monitoring (carried out by failed or mediocre academics) is necessary to insure the diligence of that search because—*credo quia absurdum*—the modern university, the most liberal of U.S. institutions and, beyond that, devoted fanatically to the celebration of achievement, is nevertheless so steeped in racial bigotry that it cannot be trusted to recognize and overcome it independently.

It is the university's failure to resist that last, malicious idea, the idea of its bigotry, that is a major source of its current loss of dignity and self-respect.[1] But to return now to the professor and the dean, we may observe that the interchange between them, marked by acquiescence and inner disavowal, by a seeming acceptance of the forms and an aloof contempt for them, involves an internalization of dissent and thus its inhibition. Dissent is kept "inside," either inside the self, or inside the dialogue (as in the hinting and winking among "insiders") or within the "system," whatever that may be at the moment—the committee, the department, the college.

By keeping potential dissent confined to the family, one also keeps the secrets that occasion and sustain that dissent, in this case the illusions and falsehoods that have gathered around university quota systems. I have over time become convinced that this is not merely the effect of keeping dissent inside but its unconscious intention. One is permitted to take a critical position about affirmative action as long as this is done on the grounds of high principle, but one produces consternation and panic through a descent to mere information. Some time ago I mentioned to a colleague of mine that I had collected some data that suggested the essential futility of our own well-regarded efforts in affirmative action, and that I was planning to bring these dolorous findings to the attention of our faculty. My friend looked at me in genuine horror and urged me not to do it, saying that many of our colleagues become agitated when confronted with unpleasant facts about our quota system.

I decided not to do it, no doubt prudently, but if you think my colleague's alarm overdone, consider the truly curious case of Dr. Bernard Davis of the Harvard Medical School. Davis is a distinguished medical scientist who was one day overcome by an aberrancy of candor. It led him to write an editorial for the *New England Journal of Medicine* in which he worried about a possible erosion of standards due to affirmative action. Having read the editorial a dozen times, I can attest that there is nothing in the least provocative about it, that it is cautious and sober to a fault. But it was Davis's error to cite a specific example, involving the waiving of requirements for a minority student, and it was that concreteness, one may imagine, that led the press to pick up the story. From that moment on, all of Davis's scrupulosity of tone was of no avail, for he had "gone public" (however fortuitously) and had offered a datum. He was thereupon the object of demonstrations, denunciations, and a motion of censure brought against him by the more thuggish elements of the Harvard medical faculty, many of them no doubt life members of the ACLU.[2]

The gravamen of the charge directed against Davis is not merely that his concerns found their way into the press, but that once made known they tended to mislead the public, who would mistake the part for the whole, and would be led to distrust all minority medical students and physicians because of statements—either true or false in substance—that apply only to some. It is certainly true that the public is uneasy about possible minority incompetence, and it is also true that the competent—such as my own current group of minority students—are thereby unfairly burdened. But the distrust felt by the public is due not to the breaking of silence but to the silence itself. The unvarying diet of sanctimony and false reassurances purveyed by our educational leaders has in the end produced an almost complete cynicism, not in the university but in the public at large. Those youngsters applauding Gerald Ford have parents and friends and neighbors living in the real world, and the word gets out that the official pieties are not to be believed. What *is* believed is hard to say: it seems to be the usual mixture of truths and exaggerations and some falsehoods, but on balance—and it grieves me to say so—the uninformed gossip of the public is far closer to the truth than all the press releases issued by all the law- and medical-school deans in all of the United States.

I spoke earlier about the illusions and falsehoods that have gathered around the topic of affirmative action. The vast outpouring of writing prompted by the *Bakke* hearing has made these more evident than before, in that the arguments offered for reverse discrimination have involved the reiteration of certain ideas about the quota systems, how they work, whom they work for, and what their long-range effects have been. We find that in particular three central statements recur: (1) whatever one may feel about the moral worth of these programs, they enjoy the merit of success; (2) those being helped are the disadvantaged; and (3) those favored are fully qualified for the programs they enter and fall short only in modest and easily remedied ways. I want to take up these assumptions and show that each of them is open to serious question, that the realities are far more complex.

The Quotas Controversy

Are Quotas Successful?

In the course of arguing with any proponent of racial-preference systems, one is likely to find, sooner or later, that the trump card offered is the argument from results. Triumphantly: "Whether you like it or not, the fact is that it *works!*" Or beseechingly: "I don't see what else we can do; it's the *only* thing that will work." Here is Father Hesburgh of Notre Dame, in a letter commending an article by McGeorge Bundy, telling us that the "embryonic effort of a decade has multiplied by a factor of ten or more the number of minority students now preparing nationwide to be doctors or lawyers." That is an inflated figure, as such figures often are, but let it stand. Let us accept that there has been substantial rise in the number of minority students enrolled, from 2 to 3 percent before affirmative action to about 9 percent today.

That is indeed an impressive increase, if we can bring ourselves to believe it, that is, to believe not merely the numbers but also what they are meant to imply: that the increase in those preparing will translate into an equivalent increase in those being graduated; that those graduated are fully competent; that the rise is due to quotas themselves; and that nothing else will work.

Note first that these figures almost almost always tell us the proportions admitted or enrolled, and rarely the percentages who are graduated. We know how many are in the pipeline but not how many emerge, and it is no longer quite the secret it once was that there is often a considerable gap between those numbers. To take an example close to home: my own training program in clinical psychology adopted in the early years an ambitious one-third minority quota, and in order to meet it admitted students recklessly. The attrition rate has been extremely high: of those admitted in those early years, at most one in five will achieve the doctorate (compared with two-thirds of those admitted regularly). We brandish one statistic, the large percentage of minority students admitted and enrolled, and conceal, even from ourselves, the fairly complete failure to carry students through the doctorate. Nor do we comment on the cruel loss of time and self-esteem suffered by the students involved; all of them would have succeeded elsewhere but were misplaced in our program, drawn there only to satisfy political demands and our own moral vanity. Somewhat similar patterns have been reported for many law schools where, at least in the past, the proportion of minority students graduating is substantially lower than those enrolling, and the percentage of those who pass the state bar examinations is lower still, at times shockingly low.

Yet I would not want to lean heavily on these or other examples. To do so is only to add to the general mindlessness wherein statistics when available are torn out of context, or otherwise used to dissemble and deceive. In particular one must take skeptically the news that things are going swimmingly at Harvard Law and Stanford Medical and MIT Economics and the like. Elite schools and programs, once they put their minds to it, can command the best of everything, and their successes in minority training tell us nothing at all about what is happening elsewhere. This country's educational institutions are so diverse, and so variously organized, that it is nearly impossible to discern what any given set of figures actually means. I know of two nearby law schools: one is elite, admits selectively, and fails hardly anyone. Another is nonelite, admits more generously, yet fails a large percentage. There is no easy way one can compare their statistics of "success" or aggregate them; nor do national statistics tell us much unless we have some sense of what levels of competence those figures represent. The only thing we can say with confidence is that the statistics of "success" bandied about are inflated to an unknown degree.

What is even more troubling than the inflation is the tacit assumption that all improvements in minority enrollment are due only to the quota programs. We have here the characteristic mind-set of the New Class of foundation executives, university presidents, bureaucrats, and publicists who simply cannot bring themselves to understand that good things can happen without the benefit of their intervention. One would never suspect, in reading the reams of anti-*Bakke* writing, that minorities—and especially Blacks—have during the last generation accomplished, partly through their own exertions, an amazing series of transformations: from agrarian to urban, from poverty to the beginnings of economic stability, from dispossession to modernity. One would never imagine that these profound demographic changes may account for the largest part of the increased representation of minority students in higher education. None of this is evident in Father Hesburgh's letter, which asserts that "for only ten years now have we provided a modicum of equal educational opportunity" etc. That is *de haut en bas*, the voice of the good Father tending a mute and faithful flock, or of the foundation chief dispensing largesse to those he deems worthy. It simply does not correspond to the realities of an energetic and clamorous democratic culture, in which *we* do not provide for *them* but in which all of us strive, compete, negotiate, accommodate, succeed, fail, rise and fall and rise again.

Do Quotas Help the Disadvantaged?

One afternoon several years ago, while serving on our admissions committee, I came across the applications of two young women. One was an ambassador's daughter who had been educated in private secondary schools and was attending a most prestigious Ivy League university. The other might have stepped out of a Harriet Arnow novel. She had been born in Appalachia, the daughter of a poor farmer. The farm failed, the family moved north, her father died, the family survived on welfare and odd jobs, she married young, bore a child, was divorced, began attending a municipal university, and ultimately was graduated with an excellent record. With respect to objective measurements—test scores the like—these two young women were more or less evenly matched. It was the ambassador's daughter who, being black, was offered an invitation (which she did not ultimately accept, having a surfeit to choose from); the welfare child, being white, was not admitted, did not come close.

This anecdote has been chosen to illustrate as succinctly as possible the moral problems inherent in any system that provides privileges by race alone, and that will not recognize other bases of disadvantage. Either one must argue that race is the only stigmatizing condition in the United States, an argument sometimes made but not commonly accepted; or else one must assume that race and class are essentially identical, which is simply not the case. And it is least likely to be the case at the higher reaches of higher education, given the strong association between social class and scholastic competence, an association that seems to be universal. This past year our admissions committee decided to give some attention to the socioeconomic status of all plausible candidates. What we found was startling: of the five minority "finalists," three were attending elite private colleges, and two were at selective state universities. Only one had received scholarship help. Three of the five came from affluent—not merely comfortable—families, and one of these gave every evidence of being rich. The committee member who interviewed most of them reported back to our faculty, somewhat ruefully, that their average family income was considerably higher than that enjoyed by the faculty itself.

The luck of the draw that year may have given us an unusually well-to-do group—I suspect it did—but the fact remains that during the past few years almost all of the minority students in our program have appeared to be of middle-class background, to judge by dress, speech, and quality of sensibility. They are talented and likable and interesting; they are well-schooled; they will succeed in getting their degrees. But it is pointless to pretend that they are disadvantaged, or that their presence introduces any diversity to our program except in the most superficial fashion. Nor does one find them all that interested, as a group, in specifically minority problems (nor do I think they ought to be), especially after they have been admitted to graduate training, and can relax and discover what really interests them.

The interaction between class and race is an issue that has yet to be addressed seriously by most commentators on affirmative action, not to mention its bureaucrats. Any intelligent analysis of the issue will have to begin by recognizing the aforementioned relationship between being middle class and being competent scholastically. Hence a policy of preferential admissions that favors the disadvantaged—of any race or ethnic group—will involve a high rate of failure; conversely, any attempt to choose minority students likely to succeed means a preference for the middle class among them. What has happened, I think, is that the strong departments and schools—such as my own—having viewed the wreckage of their earlier efforts to favor the economically deprived, have now decided to recruit those more likely to succeed, which in practice means middle-class minority students. Hence a program that began as an effort to remedy disadvantage has become increasingly a program that most helps those minority youngsters who least need help.

Are the Students Qualified?

I have kept for last the most difficult question of all, the meaning and use of the term *qualified*. The question is so difficult emotionally that only a genuinely self-confident minority scholar, like Thomas Sowell, can deal with it in a straightforward way. It is also difficult conceptually because the term is intrinsically a matter of context; when we use the word we ordinarily specify when and how and for what purposes and compared to whom. Given these sources of ambiguity, it makes one uneasy to observe the shrillness with which the idea is advanced that minority students chosen for professional training are "entirely qualified." A few nights ago I watched a television debate on the *Bakke* case in which an old war horse of the old liberalism insisted that the minority students chosen ahead of Bakke were *qualified*; he stressed the word, almost shouted it. What made him think so, he was asked. Well, the doctors who chose them thought so, otherwise they would not have been chosen. And having uttered that tautology, be broke into a smile of seraphic self-satisfaction.

What lies behind all this blustering, all this shrillness, is an intention to rewrite the common understanding of what it means to possess adequate academic qualifications. A subsidiary intention is to depict academics as rigid, hard-hearted pedants who for the sake of a few measly points on this or that meaningless test refuse to offer a helping hand to deserving minority students. Yet the differences are not trivial. Were they trivial, there would be no issue because it is hard to imagine many teachers or students becoming indignant or concerned about the difference between an A − or a B + level of achievement, or between a Graduate Record Examination score of 650 as against 600. The differences we worry about are large and at times enormous, so much as to raise issues that go beyond the issue of fairness to the larger question of whether the public is being responsibly served. It is rather ironic to note that the more sophisticated moral arguments in favor of reverse discrimination have emphasized "the common good," yet it is precisely that common good that a feckless reliance upon quotas is liable to injure.

One of the unexpected by-products of the *Bakke* case is that it liberated data on medical-school admissions held closely or concealed. These findings are especially important in that they refer to the medical school Bakke sued— the University of California at Davis, a run-of-the-mill institution—rather than to Harvard or Johns Hopkins and the like, which can choose from the very best minority applicants. The findings from the Davis medical school may in that sense be more representative, and what they tell us is simply distressing. Students admitted under a quota to the school had an undergraduate grade-point average in the B— to C range. You will not grasp what these figures say without being aware of the current level of grade inflation at U.S. universities. For example, the typical student at my university graduates with a B+ average, and a good (though not brilliant) one will graduate with an A—. The minority students admitted to the Davis medical school were at the very bottom of the grade distribution; in an era of honest grading, most of them would have been at the D level or below. A friend of mine, deeply sympathetic to affirmative action, looked over the table of grades and test scores I provided for him, groaned, and said, "My Lord. If that's who they let in, whom do they keep out?"

These are painful matters to read and write about, yet anyone confronting the Davis medical statistics for the first time, as I myself did a few weeks ago, and can construe from personal experience what they mean, will likely be overcome with dismay. It is deplorable that these data have received almost no attention in this press; that the university presidents and deans who have access to this information keep silent; that students so marginal are encouraged to enter medical training; and that as a consequence the able minority student inevitably comes under suspicion.

When quota programs in higher education first went into effect, thoughtful critics warned that the logic of the situation would ultimately compel an extension of quota-mindedness into all other areas of public life, and not merely by infection and example. They reasoned that marginal students, once recruited and enrolled, would tend to be passed through educational programs—at least in many cases—and then be unable to compete equally in an open market for talent. Hence new systems of preferment would be established and sustained. That is just what has happened. The emerging solution, which we see in faculty hiring and elsewhere, is to set aside, tacitly, certain positions as "minority" slots. Thus we reach the final and most wretched duality of all: a two-tier system of categories, involving on the one hand "real jobs" for which serious candidates compete seriously, and on the other, "minority jobs" that are set aside as a sop either to conscience or, more often these days, to the demands of the government bureaucracies. The corrupt means chosen to achieve the virtuous aim of integration ends in imposing, for the first time, segregated statuses within the university.

At this writing, the ultimate fate of racial preference systems remains unclear, pending the Court's decision on *Bakke*. Most lawyers I speak to believe the Court will rule as narrowly as possible, and if it does we can expect the struggle to continue, even to intensify, and to be fought via legislation and popular initiative. On the other hand, the Court may hold for Bakke on broad constitutional grounds, and the quota issue will fade away, to be remembered only as one of the many unpleasant episodes of the 1970s. Yet even so we would be left with the most disturbing questions about how social policy is made in this country.

The rapid conversion of "affirmative action" to bureaucratically mandated quotas has taken place despite specific congressional intentions to the contrary, despite its overwhelming rejection in public opinion polls, despite the solemn disavowals of President Carter both before and after his election, and despite a body of legal doctrine presumably removing race as an acceptable criterion for preferment. None of this has made the slightest difference. Congress is paralyzed. The president, characteristically, waffles and then yields. Some of our most prominent legal theorists promptly discover that, on second thought, a little racial discrimination is just what the country needs, as long as it is understood to be for our own good, and carried out by high-minded folk. Those folk turn out to be revenants from the Great Society—McGeorge Bundy, Joseph Califano, and the like—who seem bent on repeating all of the errors of that era, who are still unable to grasp that sheer energy and mere good will do not in themselves accomplish wise policy, and that authoritarian means, however well meant, will not achieve democratic ends. A thwarted and resentful public seems to understand this perfectly; it is only our leadership that cannot.

Notes

1. What is worse, the university masochistically subsidizes its own defamation, in its sponsorship of affirmative-action *apparatchiks* whose sole metier is the propagation of witless charges of racism and the like. Here is one of our own, addressing the multitudes: "There is no way a white male professor will bring a minority person into his clan." Here is another: "The old-boy network has always worked—there is really no affirmative-action program." All of this, mind, you, at a university that submits—meekly, obsequiously—to the most outrageous demands made upon

it in the name of affirmative action. We still await the day when the leadership of a major university defends itself or its faculty against such derogation. The failure to do so both reflects and contributes to the university's loss of self-confidence.

2. There is an excellent account of the Davis incident, by J. W. Foster, in the *New Republic*, 17 July 1976.

7

Looking Back

In preparing to write this essay I thought to reread as much as I could of the vast literature on the university written during the past fifteen years. In one way that proved to be a terrible mistake, in that the hope of saying something new simply shrivels. All positions have been occupied, all explanatory strategies explored, or so it seems; to strive for novelty is to court eccentricity. In another way the exercise, though hardly inspiring, is at least instructive, in demonstrating the short half-life of rhetorical fashion. Much of the writing now seems mawkish beyond belief; one watches the life cycle of a genre—what someone has termed The Beatification of The Young— one watches it germinate, grow, thrive, flower, and then, relentlessly, wither and die. One reads this journalism in a state of numb amazement; how could there have been so widespread a belief, only five or six or seven years ago, that the young were the builders of a New Jerusalem? And what do the believers believe now? Are they disenchanted, or have they moved to new enthusiasms, or have they simply forgotten?

It is certainly tempting to forget, if only because remembering reminds us of our continuing failure in prophecy. There are some notable exceptions, but by and large informed commentary has been spectacularly wrong in its apprehension of the future. I have in my possession a letter, dated 1959, from a most distinguished educator, in which he laments the death of student idealism, suggesting that it is a permanent casualty of the technocratic state. I also have in my possession a manuscript of my own, written in 1965, happily never completed and thus happily never published, wherein I argue that the recent troubles at Berkeley are purely a response to local conditions and tell us nothing of the future of the university. I do not have in my possession, though I wish I did, transcripts of a number of conversations, circa 1969–70, wherein some of my colleagues were imagining (rather zestfully, I thought) an imminent political revolution that would begin on the campuses.

The published literature is, of course, rather more circumspect but no more prescient. At the threshold of the 1960s all we hear about is a future given over to apathy, conformity, suburbanization, and the like. The mid-1960s celebrate idealism regained; few discern the totalitarian spirit that will soon become evident. The late 1960s are apocalyptic, both pro and con; only a few writers sense that the era is coming to an end, and no one quite foresees the peculiar mood of the moment, made up of careerism, artificial nostalgia, determined sensuality, and diffuse self-righteousness.

All of the above is an oblique way of resisting the editor's invitation to speculate on the future of the university, but it points to another possibility: it may be useful to look to the writing of the immediate past to see why our collective record of analysis and (often tacit) prophecy was so often mistaken. The observations that follow are by no means exhaustive, nor are they meant to be original, far from it. They are, I hope, offered without the condescension allowed by hindsight; indeed, given my own indifferent success in understanding and forecasting of the events of the sixties, they are written in the spirit of a chastened self-instruction.

The sad examples I began with point to what was perhaps the most common error, which was to see the future as a mere extension or exacerbation of the present. The tendencies of the moment are predicted to persist, though they may gain in force or may weaken, but it is the categories of the present that command attention. The present dominates our consciousness in part because we can so easily find its apparent precursors; thus the momentary tendency seems to have the sweep of history behind it: it was, it is, and therefore it will most certainly continue to be. The dialectical mode, the idea that the existent generates its opposition, seems to be difficult to put into practice, whatever lip service we may occasionally give it. Hence social forecasting tends to be conservative, in that it is based upon the extrapolation and generalization of current analytic frameworks. It may well be that we have here an implacable habit of the mind as it dwells upon the future, perhaps not. In either case the writing of the sixties, much of it, now seems to have been possessed by an almost reckless self-confidence in the validity of current categories.

In many cases commentary on the university and on the college young was a displaced or disguised mode of commentary on our national life in general. The part was taken for the whole; the university became a surrogate for the quality of U.S. institutions; the college student came to be seen as the vessel of this or that side of the American spirit. The tendency was most visible in that abundant critical literature animated by the adversary temper but it was evident elsewhere as well. In all such instances there was a significant loss in particularity, and with it a loss in precision, and in the complexity of analysis. Let me grant that the matter is complicated, in that the university and the national polity are so interpenetrated as to be mutually influential at all times. In particular, the mood and morale of national life is quickly felt in the mood and morale of the university; thus, the brief euphoria of the Kennedy presidency corresponded to a sense of potency and purpose on the campuses. Despite these (and many other) common reverberations, the two systems are best held apart analytically, as was not the case in the grander writing of the sixties.

Some of the decade's best writing, and some of the worst, concentrates upon the university as an institution, its structure, governance, curriculum, and the like; and most of that writing is dominated by a single assumption—in Kenneth Burke's terminology, it imputes to the scene of action motives that belong properly to the agents of action. To be concrete: the hurly-burly of the 1960s inspired a great many studies of putative academic malfeasance, informed by the conviction that trouble *in* the universities was somehow caused *by* the universities. There ensued a flurry of reform, in curriculum, in governance, and so on, some of which has since fallen by the wayside, some of which hangs on. Both the writing and the reform it initiated are now to be seen, I would argue, as forms of propitiatory magic, for as the decade ended, it had begun to seem suspect that there was any clear articulation between a university's structure and spirit, and the difficulties it contained. The troubles began to seem like a plague, which capriciously strikes innocent and guilty alike. By the end of the decade, there was a general but often silent recognition that the troubles had had their origins elsewhere—in the times, in the war, in the demographic bulge, in the upper-middle-class sensibility—but not necessarily in the university itself, in that neither the most stubborn complacency nor the most zealous reform had much to do with either the onset or the termination of student uproar.

Only belatedly, and even then fitfully, did we give attention to the force of the nonrational. I include in that category such phenomena as the following: the religious and spiritual hungers that were at work, often in distorted form, behind the youth movements of the sixties; the yearning for communalism; the violence, irrationalism, and anti-intellectualism that were so conspicuous throughout the period; and what may be the most important, though the least visible, the struggle for moral purity that, having become secularized, expresses itself in political moralism and indignation. Somehow our categories were out to touch. Had we been Jungian enough, we would have anticipated some of these developments; had we been Freudian enough, we would have sensed others. Perhaps it would be more precise to say that though some writers recognized the presence of the nonrational, very few imagined that it would not be contained by the stabilizing structures of the personality, or expressed adequately through prevailing social institutions. The psychodynamic theory of the early sixties emphasized the integrating, conflict-mediating sides of the personality; the sociology of the time stressed the integrating, tension-reducing functions of social institutions. Both were subtle and powerful theories, far more so to my mind than the vulgar, ideologized doctrines since risen to prominence, yet they now seem to have shown a certain fatal innocence.

Until fairly recently, and even today, there was, and is, a tendency to treat both the college-student cohort and the university as homogeneous. The extraordinary diversity within both groups was ignored to allow large, oracular statements about the university and the young. What was meant, almost all of the time, were liberal arts students in the elite universities. This bias, when recognized, was sometimes justified on the grounds that these students were, in their values and outlooks, the heralds of things to come, but that assumption was itself unexamined, and simpleminded. Thus an initial failure to make appropriate differentiations was rationalized by a leap into instant futurology. One obvious source of this constant error is the specialization of knowledge, wherein commentary on the university is drawn almost exclusively from scholars in the social sciences and humanities and rarely from the ranks of natural scientists, engineers, and the professional faculties. One obvious result is that certain vital disciplines, and the teachers and students who occupy them, remain nearly invisible; it produced a considerable skew in the common view of the young, their teachers, and the colleges at large. For example, the symptoms of malaise and self-doubt presumably prepotent among the students in the sixties were, I suspect, felt far less strongly in the scientific, technical, and professional departments and schools, where we found, and continue to find, an emphasis upon merit and achievement, a more complete immersion in work, and a more highly focused sense of vocation.

Finally, many writers were simply too close to the subject matter, and thus too identified, too involved. There was a loss of scholarly distance, at first largely unwitting. An example: the extensive though highly redundant body of scholarship on the young activist tended toward a single discovery, that the students studied were oriented toward "modernist" and against "traditionalist" values and attitudes. Because the investigators themselves shared those perspectives, the writing on the topic was tacitly partisan. Nonetheless much of this writing intends toward detached scholarship; its error lay in the failure to scrutinize unconscious bias. But as the decade wore on there was an increasing, willful abandonment of scholarly distance. The ideals of disinterestedness, of restraint, were set aside, the argument being that all knowledge is, in its origins and function, political. That attitude is now respectable, and widespread; research and theory in social sciences have become increasingly tendentious, and deliberately so. For the university, that may yet turn out to be the most sorrowful legacy of the sixties.

8

The Teacher as a Model

There are any number of difficulties that beset us when we try to treat this topic. We find it hard to keep ourselves dispassionate; this theme, the teacher as model, is peculiarly likely to engage our capacities for self-deception. When we think of ourselves as we once were, as students, we tend to reconstruct ourselves at the feet of a great teacher—some great man, or perhaps only a kindly and devoted one—someone who infused in us whatever modest claim to merit we possess. Now this may indeed have happened to us but I have come to feel that whether or not it has, we will rearrange the past to imagine that it has. There is something in us, something almost archetypal, that makes us feel that we achieved our maturity only by taking over the strength and wisdom of our teachers.

Then there is the other side to it, the teacher's perspective on himself as a model. I imagine that we vary greatly in the degree to which we recognize and accept this aspect of the career. For some of us, some few of us, to serve as a model is at the very heart of teaching; our self-esteem may demand it, and even more the need to give meaning to our lives. We have here a mystique of the vocation, and its dangers to self-understanding are all too evident. When we so define ourselves, we end by overestimating our value: we collect testimonials to our influence; we mistake being tolerated for being liked, being liked for being admired, and being admired for being taken as a model. But this form of self-deception is, I would guess, fairly uncommon. The more usual reaction of the teacher nowadays is to deny or to make light of his potential as a model. Perhaps we, as Americans, are too diffident about exercising authority to accept this part of the role easily. A model to youth— so to think of ourselves is to seem fatuous, narcissistic, even undemocratic. We permit ourselves the fancy only in our more elated or depressed moments, and even then not too openly. The most we will allow is to see ourselves taken as a model not for what we are but for what we represent: the self as a delegate from, let us say, the humanistic spirit or the scientific tradition. In defining ourselves so modestly, we may imagine that we are being matter-of-fact, down-to-earth, hard-headed, but I would argue that this view, which prefers to ignore or underestimate this side of teaching, is as fanciful, as mistily romantic as the earlier one.

These are some of the sentimental barriers to an understanding of the topic; there are substantive ones as well. One of these is that our knowledge of personality change in adolescence is still sketchy and uncertain. Another and related difficulty is that we have no theory of modeling. Assume that the student does (or can) become in some degree like his teacher. How does it happen? Is it a learning process or does it go deeper than that? In any case, what do we mean by ''become like''? The student does not become exactly like his teacher; he chooses and rejects, and what determines that? Does he take over the teacher's ego qualities? Does he set him up as an ego ideal? Or does the teacher become a superego figure? And what is the teacher's part in all of this? How does his activity influence the process? It is rather startling to recognize how little we really know about these and other fundamental problems, the more so because theories of education require a theory of modeling; in fact, they often contain such a theory, implicit, unacknowledged, unexamined.

When I first began thinking about this paper I made the bland assumption— rather thoughtlessly, it now appears—that the intellectual demands of the topic would easily be met by the concept of identification. The student identifies with his teacher and, to the extent that he does, is changed. There is an elaborate literature on identification (so elaborate as to be ornate; there is a literature that categorizes the literature), and my task would involve simply applying our documented knowledge of the identification process to the specific problem at hand. A moment's reflection suggests how much more complicated the matter really is.

One trouble with identification, as the psychologist Nevitt Sanford pointed out several years ago, is that it has become so fashionable, and thus so ubiquitously used, that it has lost the precision it once had. Not that it had much to begin with. It is an unusually docile and elastic concept, one that gives way easily to whatever stretching we want to impose on it. Because it serves us so well in elucidating many psychic phenomena, we tended to stretch it to include more and more instances of behavior and experience. We find it used in discussions of hysteria and of depression, in descriptions of normal personality development, in the psychology of creativity, and so on almost endlessly. Sanford suggests that there is not much similarity among the various appearances of identification. The processes are, to be sure, vaguely analogous, but is that enough? Do we gain any deeper understanding through the total embrace of the identification concept? Are we not better served by a more limited use of the term?

The amorphousness of the identification concept is one problem; there is an even more serious one. When we review our experiences we are likely to come up with some dramatic examples of the effects of identification, cases where the student's life was changed, decisively, by the choice of model.

These instances are likely to be highly persuasive, so much so that they may mislead us into feeling that identification is the critical process in personality change, that more moderate changes in the student simply involve a more moderate degree of identification. Let me illustrate what I mean through a pair of examples.

The first of these concerns what is probably the most striking example of character change I have ever seen. In college I had a friend who was an amiable, somewhat cynical, rather aimless sort of boy—pleasant enough, something of a buffoon in fact, and without much drive or conviction. He decided to go on to graduate school, not because he had received any inner call but largely because many of his friends were doing so and because there seemed to be no viable alternative except to go to work. He made plans to study with a famous social psychologist, an ebullient, restless, imaginative man. When my friend arrived at the university he discovered that this professor had suddenly departed. There seemed to be nothing else to do than to study with another dominant figure in that department, a brilliant man, at his best willful and forceful, and at his usual worst arbitrary and authoritarian to the point of being vicious. I next saw my friend a year later; he had become this man's disciple. This was surprising; what was unnerving was the change in manner and behavior that had taken place in him. He had been transformed from a rather affable, indolent boy, a kind of academic Good Soldier Schweik, to an academic tiger, disputatious, ill-tempered, mean-spirited, believing firmly that the world's salvation depended on its adopting his master's views on learning theory.

Here is another instance, this time taken from psychotherapeutic work. The patient was a physicist whose career, after an extremely promising start, had petered out into haplessness. We soon learned that his career was from the beginning based on identifications: he chose physics largely because it was his older brother's field; he chose his specialty through an identification with an important teacher. For several years into his postdoctoral career things went fairly well for him. His research during this period, while decidedly his own, followed a path that had been pioneered by his teacher. Then suddenly he found it impossible to work. Two coinciding events seemed to play a part: he had exhausted the line of research begun in graduate school and he had received a promotion in rank. Work was possible for him only so long as he defined himself as acolyte, apprentice, lieutenant. The change in rank, together with the need to find his own research interest, endangered the state of discipleship that was necessary for him to function intellectually.

Now what shall we make of these two accounts? We have in the first a rather plain example of "identification with the aggressor." My friend found himself in a situation that he took to involve the choice "identify or else," and more deeply, "submit or be killed." He had taken this awesome, frightening teacher into himself and with a convert's zeal had transformed himself. The second case is rather more complex (I have given only part of the relevant information). Essentially, the patient found it necessary to contain a profound hatred of men in authority through fairly elaborate maneuvers; these involved splitting academic fathers into good and bad ones, pitting them against each other and ending up as the favorite son, heir apparent, and junior partner to the idealized teacher, after whom he modeled himself to the point of parody.

It would not be hard to find further examples in this vein. When you quiz people about their thoughts and experiences on the topic of modeling, you find that almost everyone can contribute a bit of folklore. A dentist told me about one of his teachers at dental school: a pipe smoker, he had had a golden palate plate made up for himself to reduce the chances of cancer. His two junior associates had taken up pipe smoking, had had plates made for themselves. When they met together at conference, all three would take out their plates, insert them, then light up their pipes—an unforgettable image. Almost all of us, I am sure, can chip in with similar anecdotes, where the disciples of an impressive teacher—the kind word is *dynamic*—took over his mannerisms, speech habits, tastes, interests, eccentricities, and what have you.

But this anecdotage, although seductive, is in the end deceiving. We remember these instances because they are vivid or amusing. Are they paradigmatic? Do they represent the extreme end of the continuum of modeling, the "far-out" instances that display, in an exaggerated way, the normal processes of modeling? Or are they discontinuous, qualitatively different from the mundane forms of modeling? I would say the latter. This is not to minimize the importance of dramatic identification phenomena in the educational process; to the contrary. One can argue that we gain much in our understanding of teacher-student patterns if we take account of such phenomena. But first we will have to put identification in its place, so to speak, not permitting it to dominate our thinking.

Sanford argues very effectively that the identification processes we know from clinical work—mainly introjection and identification with the aggressor—are defensive maneuvers designed to keep the personality intact and functioning in situations that threaten its integrity. The changes we see are brittle: they remain in effect only so long as the person is under duress; they then vanish. Genuine changes in personality are brought about not by unconscious defenses but by processes, such as learning, where the ego's role is not entirely passive or regressive.

If we review our own experiences with students, review them in totality as against singling out impressive exceptions, we are likely to find that what the student takes from the teacher is swiftly and silently synthesized into the existing personality. We may have here one criterion for appraising the quality of modeling: the ego's success in synthesizing the "introject." Whenever we see a radical alteration of the student's behavior (as in the student's adoption of the teacher's pet mannerisms), we have some reason to be wary both of the genuineness and of the permanence of the "modeling." Under these circumstances we are probably right to suspect that the student is moved not by his best long-range interests but by infantile or conflict-ridden feelings toward the teacher or the teaching situation, by anxiety, or ambivalence or one of the many counterfeits of "love." We ought to be as mordantly skeptical of change in our students—especially when it seems too good to be true—as the psychotherapist is when appraising the vicissitudes of behavior in a patient.

Up to this point I have followed Sanford's argument closely, but I have some disagreements with it. For one thing, I feel he gives too short shrift to the identification processes. They do have their uses. Granted that in the long run they tend to inhibit or distort the best development of the personality, yet that is sometimes a very long run indeed. Consider the two cases mentioned earlier. In my college friend we saw the emergence of initiative and purposefulness, of a sense of mission, that had been conspicuously absent before. The identification provided a momentum that carried him through graduate school and into a respectable, although lackluster, career. Something of the same was true of the physicist. To be sure, the identification failed him in the end; it depended on conditions that could not be met indefinitely. But we must remember that in this case we had a seriously flawed personality; the infantile attachment to his teacher did at least allow him to be launched into his career. I very much doubt that this would have happened otherwise. These are, of course, Pyrrhic victories. When the modeling is as deep and thoroughgoing as it was in these instances, the person is generally incapable of original or individual work. The master, now within, retains his influence beyond the point where he is needed. New ideas are likely to be subject to criticism by the internalized presence of the teacher; the result is a blight on thought outside doctrine.

Identifications are useful in other and more benign ways. In adolescence especially they sometimes seem to provide the means through which needed restructurings or crystallizations of personality take place. In some cases, the student can become himself only by first becoming someone else. He may find it difficult to acquire new and complex skills unless he protects himself psychically by borrowing, through identification, the teacher's power. Or he may use the identification as a mask, as a form of camouflage: while he pretends, to himself and to others, that he is being a certain someone, achieving this or that identity, he is actually accomplishing the inner changes that will allow him to achieve an identity closer to his own talents and dispositions. In all of these uses the identification is shallow and temporary; it is used as a prop, a crutch, a smokescreen, or a shield, and once it has served its purpose it is dissolved. The identification serves as the means of achieving a new and necessary identity.

What we have to do is to turn our attention from identification to identity. If we are to comprehend the variations in students' relations to their teachers as models, we shall have to do so by understanding often subtle and elusive differences in identity commitment. Consider that large group of students who are pleasant and polite enough but carefully keep themselves remote from modeling. In most cases, I suppose, we would find that they already feel themselves committed to life goals and styles to which the teacher cannot really contribute. But there are some interesting variations. For example, the student may actively resist the teacher's influence because the teacher is, in fact, too tempting as a potential model. We can see this quite clearly in some premed and prelaw students. The premed is astute enough to recognize that he must manage a certain detachment from his physiology or biochemistry courses and teachers; to become too interested, or too involved, may divert him from the long-range goal of medicine. The student who may seem to us to be invulnerable to modeling may simply be waiting until it is safe.

In other cases the student who seems untouched and untouchable is in a state of limbo—in a *moratorium,* to use Erikson's term—waiting for the proper time to commit himself. He does not feel ready to find a personal identity; he is, in fact, actively *not* looking for it, shielding himself from influence, keeping himself ''loose'' and unattached; committed, so to speak, to the bachelorhood of preidentity. He is not really waiting for the right model to come along; he is waiting for something to happen inside of him. Then he will make his move.

At the other extreme we have those students who actively, even frenetically, shop around for models. Just as some students will spend the first weeks of a semester auditing different courses, so will some (often the same ones) spend their college careers auditing different identities. In this group of model-seeking students, we again find revealing variations. The youngster may come to college with some idea of what he wants to become; what he is looking for is the external embodiment of a predetermined identity, some teacher who will personify an image of the self that the student has imagined. At a state university we see some intriguing examples: the young man from the provinces who, out of his own resources, assisted only by his reading or by the mass media, has imagined himself into the role of scholar, poet, painter. He needs only the living instance—in the form and presence of the teacher—to complete what the imagination has begun.

These variations in the identity-needs of students are also of some importance in influencing the teacher's qualities they are interested in acquiring. I was made acutely aware of this not long ago while interviewing some graduate students about to receive doctorates in the social sciences. I was interested, among other things, in the roles teachers had played in the choice of under-graduate majors. One student I talked to told me at great length about a professor who had been, he said, of central importance to him. This man had been a real influence, had taught him much of what he knew; the student had, in fact, been this man's undergraduate teaching assistant. What was his name? I asked. There was an embarrassed silence; he could not remember it. He could, however, remember his professor's research, accurately and in detail. We might consider this curious lapse of memory to be unconsciously motivated, but I think not altogether; it fitted perfectly well with this young man's general lack of interest in his teachers as personalities. He struck most of his graduate instructors as unusually detached and independent, so much so as to affront some of them. He was brisk, brusque, business-like. (He had, in fact, come from a business family, and it seemed to be a case where you might take the boy out of the business, but not the business out of the boy.) He looked to his teachers, one felt, more for what they knew and could teach him, for their skills, than for what they were as individuals.

Compare him with another young man, of the same age, training, and apparent ambitions. His manner was gentle and sensitive; he gave the impression of being somewhat ineffectual. At the beginning of a professional career, he was still uncertain that he had made the right choice. This uncertainty and lack of conviction, the air of doubt and restlessness he conveyed, all of these suggested at least a mild case of identity diffusion. As a boy he had been raised in a middle-class family and milieu that existed quite apart from the world of intellectual concerns. He was bright and received a scholarship to an Ivy League college. He was overwhelmed by what he discovered there, overwhelmed on a number of counts but most of all by the range and intensity of the intellectual life as it was felt there. The young man I spoke of previously could not remember his teachers; this young man could remember little else. He dwelt on them lovingly, still filled with awe and childlike wonder at their flair and potency. That was the trouble; he could not get over it. Perhaps we can put this down, ultimately, to the Oedipus complex. But the point that concerns us here is that he looked to his teachers not for what they could teach him visibly and tangibly, not for skills or techniques, but for what as exemplars of an elusive and desired life-style they could offer him.

This distinction—between skill and style—is of course a rough one, but it may help give us some sense of the differing modalities of the modeling process. Sometimes style—in the sense, now, of the professional identity—emerges or evolves out of the acquisition of skills. We may speak of a *progression* from skill to style. The student is changed gradually and by accretion; as he acquires skills, these become part of the ego repertoire and, finally, of the ego identity. The professional style—manner, attitude, and so on—is likely to be both role-syntonic and ego-syntonic.

At other times we see a *retreat* from skill acquisition to style acquisition. This may happen out of purely intrapsychic motives (for example, the student mentioned above), but we may also find it occurring when the skills to be learned are in their nature difficult to master. In his despair or frustration the student may turn his interest from the achievement of craft to the premature absorption of the professional style or manner. We see this quite frequently in the teaching of psychotherapy. The skills here are complex and ephemeral. The student, feeling himself overwhelmed by the task, is tempted to retreat to the therapeutic persona. We sometimes find a kind of ersatz identity, the student in the guise of therapist, much given to a sonorous and sententious profundity of manner, or to overly brilliant formulations of psychodynamics. In most cases, I should say, these outbreaks of "modeling" are transient and soon disappear. But when they persist, it may signal an end to learning; the "role" is a retreat from the oppressive demands of the apprenticeship.

Generally speaking, we have every reason to feel troubled when we observe the student to be overly eager to acquire the professional style at the expense of skill. In most cases he does so when he feels himself marginal or over-whelmed, either because of personal shortcomings or because the educational circumstances are such as to make him helpless or infantilized. We must recognize that some educational situations produce this effect in their very nature, and not because of the obtuseness or bad intentions of the educators. In some fields—especially the technical and "practical" ones—the student's performance can be judged objectively and unambiguously. The student has no trouble discovering how well he is doing; his competence and relative standing can be appraised by visible, concrete criteria of proficiency. In these circumstances he is not so dependent on the teacher's opinion and gives his attention to the acquisition of skill. But in other fields the criteria of good performance are intrinsically ambiguous and depend upon a subjective as-sessment by the teacher; indeed this is the case in any discipline at its higher levels, where good performance demands creative or synthetic capacities. Here the student cannot easily tell how well he is doing, nor can the teacher do more than measure him subjectively, or even intuitively. Furthermore, the teacher often cannot coach the student properly; he can say what the student is doing poorly but not tell him how to perform well. How do we tell someone to write a better poem or for that matter to think of a better research idea, or design a more interesting experiment, or write a more penetrating paper? The more demanding the work, the more ambiguous both the procedures and criteria of good performance, and the more the student is tempted to rely on hollow style modeling. He may take over the peripheral or irrelevant qualities of the teacher or of the professional role, or he may ape his teacher's man-nerisms and tricks; in either case, he abandons his own resources to incorporate the teacher's, no matter how poorly they suit him.

Discussions of the good teacher are likely to leave us more uplifted than enlightened. The descriptions we read generally amount to little more than an assemblage of virtues; we miss in them a sense of the complexity and ambiguity that we know to characterize the teachers's work. Here are some paradoxes to help us get going: a teacher may be a good teacher yet not serve as a model to any of his students; he may inspire his students and yet fail to influence them; he may influence them without inspiring them; he may be a model for them and yet not be an effective teacher; and so on. To say all of this is to make the point—an obvious one but generally overlooked in the more solemn and global discussions of the teacher—that charisma, competence, and influence do not necessarily go hand in hand. A great many college teachers, perhaps most of them, are "good" teachers—good in the sense that they are conscientious and devoted, that they are lucid, articulate, and fair-minded lecturers, and that more often than not they succeed in illuminating the subject matter. Their students learn from them, often learn very much, yet these teachers ultimately do not make much of a difference in their students' lives beyond the learning they impart. At another extreme we have those rare teachers who stir and enchant their students, and yet who may be spectacularly inept in teaching subject matter. I think now of a former colleague of mine, in some ways a truly great man, who is so ebullient, erratic, and distractable, so easily carried away by the rocketing course of his thought, that his students—even the bright ones—just sit there, benumbed, bewildered, and finally enthralled. They know themselves to be close to a presence and are willing to suffer incoherence to join vicariously in that demonic enthusiasm.

What we must do, plainly, is to recognize the pluralism in teaching: the many styles of influence, the many modes of connection that bind student and teacher to each other. Teaching styles are so diverse that they can be categorized in a great many different ways. The grouping I want to try out was suggested by the yet unpublished work of Merrill Jackson, an anthropologist who has been doing a cross-cultural study of the healer's role. He has isolated five distinct modes of healing: shamanism, magic, religion, mysticism, and naturalism. Here is an abbreviated description of these types: the shaman heals through the use of personal power, using craft, charm, and cunning; the magician heals through knowledge of arcane and complex rules, and the ability to follow ritual precisely; the priest claims no personal power but achieves his healing capacity as an agent or vessel of an omnipotent authority; the mystic healer relies on insight, vision, and wisdom, through which he cures the sick soul; the naturalist (the present-day physician) is impersonal, empirical, task-oriented.

You may be struck, as I was, by the reflection that these separate modes of healing in some sense persist to this day. While the present-day type of medicine is naturalistic (and in fact it is a common complaint that medical specialists are *too* impersonal, and do not give enough attention to the patient as a human being), we nevertheless find that the physician's relation to the patient is often patterned on an older style. Thus we have those physicians who follow the shamanistic mode, in that they implicitly define healing as a struggle between disease on the one hand and their own cunning and power on the other; or those for whom medicine involves a ritualistic following of rules; or those who claim no personal charisma but define themselves to the patient as humble servants of a godhead, in this case modern medical science. This typology may be a useful one for treating other forms of interaction, such as those that obtain between teacher and student. For example, those teachers who define themselves primarily as experts in subject matter are roughly equivalent to naturalistic healers, in that the relationship to the client is in both cases impersonal and task-oriented. In any case, it is worth trying; I want to use Jackson's schema to consider in detail three types of teachers.

The Many Faces of the Teacher

The Teacher as Shaman

Here the teacher's orientation is narcissistic. The public manner does not matter; this type of teacher is not necessarily vain or exhibitionistic; he may in fact appear to be withdrawn, diffident, even humble. Essentially, however, he keeps the audience's attention focused on himself. He invites us to observe the personality in its encounter with the subject matter. He stresses charm, skill, *mana* in the self's entanglement with ideas. When this orientation is combined with unusual gifts, we have a *charismatic* teacher, one of those outstanding and memorable personalities who seem more than life size. The charismatic teacher is marked by power, energy, and commitment. By *power* we mean sheer intellectual strength or uncommon perceptiveness and origi-nality; by *energy* we mean an unusual force or vivacity of personality; and by *commitment*, a deep absorption in the self and its work. Generally, all of these qualities are present to some degree; energy without power turns out to be mere flamboyance; power without energy or commitment is likely to be bloodless, arid, enervating.

This tells us only part of the story. In that group of teachers whom we term narcissistic we find considerable variation in the degree of impact on the student. In some cases the narcissistic teacher's impression on us is strong but transient; he moves us but the spell does not survive the moment. We admire him as we admire a great performer; in his presence we dream of doing as well ourselves. But when the occasion is past we return to our mundane selves, out of the spell, unchanged, uninfluenced. In other instances, we may find the teacher's narcissism at the least distasteful and at times repelling. Something in it warns us to keep our distance, to remain wary and uncommitted.

What makes the difference? I am not sure that we know, but I think we will understand it better when we know more about variations in narcissism. There is a narcissism that makes a hidden plea to the audience; it cries out, "Look how wonderful I am! Admire me! Love me!" There is also a narcissism that is vindictive and vengeful; it says, "I love myself. Who needs you?" In either case the audience, or at least a good share of it, seems to sense the infantile source and quality of the teacher's narcissism, senses the petulance or anxiety that informs the teacher's manner, and keeps itself from becoming involved.

There is another and rarer form of narcissism that affects us quite differently from these. It is directed neither toward nor against the audience; it is autonomous, internally fed, sustaining itself beyond the observer's response to it. The best description of its appeal remains Freud's:

> It seems very evident that one person's narcissism has a great attraction for those others who have renounced part of their own narcissism and are seeking after object-love; the charm of a child lies to a great extent in his narcissism, his self-sufficiency and inaccessibility, just as does the charm of certain animals which seem not to concern themselves about us, such as cats and the large beasts of prey. . . . It is as if we envied them their power of retaining a blissful state of mind—an unassailable libido-position which we ourselves have since abandoned.

It is this form of narcissism—ingenuous, autonomous—that, when it is joined to other qualities, makes the teacher memorable. This orientation invites us to identification, to share in its bounty, to seek its protection and care, or to join its omnipotence. Yet teachers of this kind are most problematic. They tempt us into regressions. We may come to feel them to be too exalted to serve as models for us. Or we may feel defeated by them before we begin, thinking that anything we achieve will be only second-rate, that we can never grow up enough to equal them.

The Teacher as Priest

The priestly healer claims his power not through personal endowment but through his office: he is the agent of an omnipotent authority. Do we have a parallel to this in teaching? I would say it is the teacher who stresses not his personal virtues but his membership in a powerful or admirable collectivity, for example, physics, psychoanalysis, classical scholarship. The narcissistic teacher to some degree stands apart from his discipline and seems to say, "I am valuable in myself." The priestly teacher says, "I am valuable for what I belong to. I represent and personify a collective identity."

It is difficult to generalize about this mode of teaching because the teacher's behavior toward the student varies so much with the nature of the collectivity. It is one thing when the collectivity is coterminous with a subject matter, and another when it is an enclosed or beleaguered sect within a discipline (for example, the various "schools" within sociology and psychology). Collectivities differ in their openness, their degree of organization, their status vis-à-vis other groups. Some are easy to enter, others are closed; some are loose and informal, bound by common interest and camaraderie, others are stratified and formal; some are marginal in status, others are secure, entrenched elites. Other differences involve the teacher's status in the collectivity: the undergraduate teacher may proselytize, seeking recruits among the promising students; the graduate-professional school teacher will first indoctrinate, then examine, and finally ordain the recruit.

To illustrate the teacher's activity in the priestly mode, I will refer to the more enclosed and differentiated collectivities. We generally find the following elements.

Continuity. The collectivity defines itself along a temporal dimension. It has itself along a temporal dimension. It has a version of the past and a vision of the future. In the past there were great ancestors whose qualities and trials established the collective identity. There is a program for the immediate future as well as a prophecy of the distant future. One of the teacher's tasks is to help the student absorb the sense of the collective past and accept the common blueprint for the future.

Hierarchy. Generally (although not always) the collectivity is stratified in prestige and authority. The teacher's personal authority depends in some part on his position on the ladder of authority. The teacher is superordinate to the student, but in turn is subordinate to more elevated figures. The student internalizes the group's system of hierarchy, and learns that he is beholden not only to his teacher but to other members of the hierarchy. One of the distinctive features of this mode of teaching is that both teacher and student may share a common model or group of models, either exalted contemporaries or great ancestors.

Election. When the group is an elite, when membership in it is desirable and hard to achieve, we generally find that emphasis is placed on discipline, the enduring of trials and self-transformation. The educational process is in some degree an extended rite of passage; the teacher's role is to prepare the student for the trials he will endure, and to administer the tests that will initiate him.

Mission. The collectivity often offers a utopian view of the future (especially when it is powerless and competitive) as well as a program for achieving dominance and instituting reforms. In these cases, the teacher's work is informed by missionary zeal; the student is expected to absorb the group's sense of mission and in turn to recruit and socialize others once he himself has achieved office.

There is no question of the potency of the priestly mode of teaching. It achieves its effectiveness for a great many different reasons. Teacher and student are generally in a close relationship to each other. The student is encouraged to model his *activity* after the teacher's, very much as in those charming experiments on imprinting, where the baby duck follows the decoy. We also find a good deal of close coaching, both of behavior and ideology. In most cases the teaching is both positive and negative, that is, the student not only is trained to develop new behaviors but also is required to eliminate competing or discordant responses. Generally the student is given an un-ambiguous ideal of character and behavior (he may be allowed, as part of the strategy of training, to feel uncertain whether he is meeting this ideal, but the ideal itself is usually clear-cut enough). In some instances the collectivity offers an encompassing doctrine, and the student is exhorted to reinterpret his experiences in the vocabulary of the doctrine; when this is not the case, the training itself demands so complete a commitment of time and energy that the student's ideational world narrows to include only the collectivity and its concerns. The teacher customarily enjoys a great deal of power in relation to the student, which reinforces the latter's dependency. The student's tie to the collectivity is further reinforced by his close association with peers—rivals, fellow aspirants, fellow sufferers—who share his trials, sustain him in moments of doubt, restore his flagging spirits, and keep alive his competitive drive. Finally, this mode of teaching is effective because it offers to the student a stake in a collective, utopian purpose, and also a promise of such tangible rewards as power, position, money, intellectual exclusiveness.

Less obviously, but quite as important, the collectivity makes its appeal to the student in helping him to resolve internal confusions. His participation allows a distinct identity choice; it supports that choice by collective approval; it reduces intellectual and moral ambiguity. A great many advantages also accrue to the collectivity; over the short run, at least, it is helped in achieving its aims by its capacity to recruit a cadre of devoted, disciplined believers. (The history of my own field, psychology, has been decisively influenced by the ability of certain schools to select and organize students in the "priestly" framework, an ability that has very little to do with intellectual merit.) But we also must recognize that this mode of education possesses some deadly disadvantages, both to the student and the group. The student purchases direction, force, and clarity, but does so by sacrificing some share of his own development; in some important ways he is no longer his own man. For the collectivity the danger is in a loss of flexibility and innovation. (We have a perfect example in the history of the psychoanalytic movement. Through the 1930s it was, in its policies of recruitment and training, the most cosmopolitan of groups, a circumstance that produced an extraordinary boldness and vivacity of thought. Since its capture by U.S. psychiatry it has developed a priestly mode of education, the result being a severe loss in intellectual scope and energy. It has not settled into its own Alexandrian age, repeating itself endlessly, living off its intellectual capital, affluent yet flatulent, an ironic example of the failure of success.)

The dominance of this mode of teaching in the graduate and professional schools, while regrettable, is probably inevitable. It is more disturbing to note its steady encroachment in undergraduate education. For many college teachers the introductory courses have less value in themselves than as a net in which to trap the bright undergraduate, and the advanced courses increasingly serve only to screen and socialize students for what the faculty deems "the great good place," namely, the graduate school. Furthermore, academic counseling at the freshman and sophomore level frequently produces a guerrilla warfare among disciplines, each seeking to capture the promising talents for itself, and without too much regard for the student's needs and interests. If matters are not worse than they already are, it is not because the disciplines have any genuine concern for the undergraduate or for liberal ideals of education but because the leviathans have managed to neutralize one another's demands. Even so, the pressure of required courses and prerequisites serves to force the student into premature career commitment, while the onerous demands on his time (especially in the laboratory sciences but also and increasingly in other fields) keep him from trying anything else.

The Teacher as Mystic Healer

The mystic healer finds the source of illness in the patient's personality. He rids his patient of disease by helping him to correct an inner flaw or to realize a hidden strength. The analogy here—perhaps it is a remote one—is to the teacher I will term *altruistic*. He concentrates neither on himself, nor the subject matter, nor the discipline, but on the student, saying, "I will help you become what you are." We may recall Michelangelo's approach to sculpture: looking at the raw block of marble, he tried to uncover the statue within it. So does the altruistic teacher regard his unformed student; this type of teacher keeps his own achievement and personality secondary; he works to help the student find what is best and most essential within himself.

At this point we are uncomfortably close to the rhetoric of the college brochure. This is what the colleges tell us they do, and yet we know how very rarely we find altruistic teaching. Why is it so rare? For one thing, it is a model-less approach to teaching; the teacher points neither to himself nor to some immediately visible figure but chooses to work with his students' potential and toward an intrinsically abstract or remote ideal. For another, this mode of teaching demands great acumen, great sensitivity—the ability to vary one's attack according to the phase of teaching and to the student— now lenient, now stern, now encouraging, now critical.

But the reason that the altruistic mode is so rarely successful lies deeper than these. The mode is selfless; it demands that the teacher set aside, for the moment at least, his own desires and concerns to devote himself without hidden ambivalence to the needs of another. In short, the teacher's altruism must be genuine; and altruism, as we know, is a fragile and unsteady trait, all too frequently reactive, born out of its opposite. If the teacher's selflessness is false, expedient, or mechanical, if it comes out of a failure in self-esteem, or if it gives way to an underlying envy—and, in the nature of things, these are real and ever-present possibilities—then the teaching at best will not come off and at the worst may end in damaging the student.

Some years ago I taught at an excellent progressive college that, quite unwillingly, induced some of its younger faculty to opt for a pseudoaltruistic mode of teaching. The college was committed to the ideal of student self-realization, and this was not, I should say, the usual pious cant but a conscious, deliberate aim that showed itself in day-to-day planning and policy. In pursuit of this ideal, the college authorities stressed altruistic teaching; it was held that talent, productivity, and eminence were of only secondary importance in the hiring and firing of faculty, that teaching talent per se was primary. Here things went seriously awry; for a variety of reasons, the college managed to attract an astonishing proportion of charismatic teachers: either men of established reputation, or ambitious and talented young men on the way up, but in either case men of great vitality, self-confidence, and self-absorption. The presence of these teachers produced a star system: the students, quite naturally, adored them; and they gave the college its distinctive tone, febrile, impassioned.

When a young teacher was hired by the college it was quite natural for him to gravitate to the charismatic mode of teaching. But sometimes it did not work out for him; he did not have, or felt that he did not have, the necessary resources of talent, drive, and "personality." If he wanted to survive at the college (or so he believed) he had to carve out a niche for himself, or even better, make himself indispensable. He had to find a new style, and he was likely to choose altruism, whether or not it really suited him. He played the role of the teacher who had given up his own ambitions to put himself at the service of youth. In some cases, I suspect, this role was chosen coolly and cynically, the teacher reasoning, quite correctly, that the college authorities would find it embarrassing to fire someone who was so true a believer in the college's ideology; in other cases the teacher adopted this role gradually and without deliberation, waking up one morning, so to speak, to discover that this had been his metier all along.

Expedient altruism very rarely came off, either for the teacher or his students. The latter sometimes showed an uncanny, although largely unconscious, sensitivity in these matters; they could sense that the pseudoaltruist was somehow not quite the real thing. They might deem him "nice," "friendly," and "very helpful," but they said so in a forced or lukewarm way that often concealed a polite disdain. The teacher's manner was often so artificial and oversolicitous that students, I think, were made uneasy by it, believing that they did not really merit all that elaborate concern. This type of teacher tended to attract the marginal and unmotivated students, primarily because he was reputed to be soft. The more serious students continued to prefer the charismatic teacher, however difficult and demanding he might occasionally be; and this was so, I think, not only because of his greater gifts but also because such students would cleave only to someone who showed them that he loved himself.

Expedient altruism produced most of the time a kind of dead-level mediocrity in teaching; students were not much influenced but neither were they damaged. It was a very different matter when this mode was chosen not as a survival technique but to perform some obscure personal restitution, when the teacher loved his students to avoid hating them, helped them to avoid harming them. As I suggested before, this equilibrium is ordinarily too delicate to sustain, and in fact I know of no examples where the students of the reactively altruistic teacher did not in some way suffer from a breakthrough of envy or sadism on the teacher's part. I remember one man, widely known to be lovable, who was warm and encouraging to his students and who, when their backs were turned, would write the most damning letters of recommendation for them. In another more spectacular instance a particularly sanctimonious advocate of good teaching was fired when his own major students petitioned the college to do so. It turned out that he had the habit of helping his students by being "sincerely frank" with them, expositing their "weak points" at great length and in excruciating detail, and so managing to wound and humiliate them deeply.

The last anecdote reminds us of what might otherwise escape our attention, that the teacher may sometimes serve as a negative or *antimodel*. Here student uses teacher as a lodestar, from which he sails away as rapidly as he can, seeming to say: Whatever he is, I will not be; whatever he is for, I will be against. Teachers who exercise the power of revulsion are, in their own way, charismatic types; indeed, the teacher who is charismatically positive for some will be negative for others. He breeds disciples or enemies; few remain unmoved. If we follow a student's development closely enough we generally discover both positive and negative models; the decision to be or become like someone goes hand in hand with a negative choice of identity and ideal.

An even more important topic on the negative side of modeling concerns the teacher whose value changes, the *disappointing* model. I would not have thought this to be so important—it does not come up in casual conversations on modeling—but close interviewing frequently brings to light examples of disappointments in the model.

Let me suggest why this may be so. It may be trite and facile to say so, but we are led again to the importance of the oedipal motif, especially where we find a close relationship between teacher and student. These apprenticeships tend to be colored by the student's earlier tie to the father; they repeat or complete the oedipal interaction. For most of us—and for some of us acutely—one outcome of the oedipal situation was our coming to feel disappointed by the father. When we were very young, we thought him to be grand and omnipotent; then we learned better, and for some this was a galling discovery. In these cases the close tie to an esteemed teacher has the meaning of a second chance, an opportunity to relive and master that early disenchantment. The attempt to cure disappointment, however, generally leads to its repetition. The student must keep up the fiction of his teacher's perfection; any flaw, any failing in the teacher, must be denied out of existence. It is too hard a position to maintain, and sooner or later the discovery of some defect in the now idealized teacher will send the student into a state of acute disappointment.

When the student uses his relation to the teacher in this repetitive way, he is especially vulnerable to any failure in the teacher's work or character. In the main, students are not so vulnerable; they learn to be realistic about their teachers, enough so that they are spared any strong sense of disappointment. Indeed, they manage it so well that we are likely to remain unaware that it is a problem, that even the "normal" student undergoes at some time some crises, however minor, concerning the clay feet of an intellectual idol. I remember a poignant moment when talking to a young man who was telling me of his admiration for a brilliant teacher. After working for this man for some time, it dawned on him that the teacher was in some respects petty, petulant, and vain. At first, he told me, he had a hard time reconciling these traits with the man's great intellectual gifts, but then he was able to recognize that the two really had nothing to do with each other. What was poignant—painful in fact—was that the student told me this in a strained, bluff, overly hearty manner that spoke tellingly of the struggle it had been to accept it.

The student's response to disappointment depends not only on his susceptibility but also on the type of flaw he discovers in the teacher. It makes a difference whether or not the failing is role-relevant. It puts a greater strain on the student when the model's fault involves role performance than when it is unrelated to how the teacher does his work. In the latter instance the student can more easily compartmentalize his view of the teacher.

Probably the most difficult type of failure for the student to accept is a moral one. By "moral" I do not mean, primarily, the teacher's living up to conventional standards in pleasure-seeking; rather, I mean such qualities as integrity, fairness, ethical sensitivity, courage. The student is not overly demoralized to discover that his model's ego qualities are not quite what he thought or hoped they were, that his teacher is not as intelligent, penetrating, or perceptive as he first appeared to be. It is, indeed, part of the student's maturation that he learn to tolerate this fact, just as the child in growing up learns to give up his belief that the parents are omnicompetent. But a moral failure is not so easily accepted and, if it is serious enough in nature, is likely to be a disheartening or even a shattering experience. When we think of the teacher as a model, we think naturally of the teacher as an ego-ideal—an avatar of virtue—and take for granted, and thus ignore, the superego aspects. Yet some teachers influence us primarily because they embody the moral ideals of the role, or because they represent the unpleasant necessities of work, duty, or intellectual honesty. Edward Tolman played such a role for graduate students (and faculty too, I imagine) at Berkeley; many of us were not deeply influenced by him intellectually, but all of us were profoundly touched by his integrity and humility. And Freud has told us how, many years later, he could still recall an incident of his student days when, arriving late to work, he was "overwhelmed by the terrible gaze of his [Brucke's] eyes." Most of us do our work in the silent presence of some such gaze, terrible or (nowadays) merely reproachful.

The teacher's life is as filled with moral tension and ambiguity as any other, but the moral dimension is most visibly operative in areas that do not affect the student (such as departmental politics); consequently, moral issues do not ordinarily become problematic in the teacher-student relationship. But when they do, we become intensely aware of their tacit importance. I know of only one clear-cut occurrence of this kind: a group of students in one of the sciences discovered that their teacher, who was ordinarily full of pieties about the holy obligations of the scientist, was not entirely responsible in his handling of evidence; he was not guilty of outright fabrication but of cutting, fitting, and suppressing data to fit the needs of the study. Not all of the students were distraught by this discovery—here again vulnerability varies— but some were entirely demoralized, and in one case a student (who had been sitting on the fence) decided to give up research altogether and chose an applied career.

Those of us who were at the University of California during the loyalty-oath troubles had a unique opportunity to observe how the moral qualities of our teachers, ordinarily taken for granted and so overlooked, could assume overweening importance in a moment of moral crisis. It was an uncanny time for us: with one part of ourselves we lived in the routine of things, concerned with courses, prelims, dissertations; and all the while our inner, central attention was elsewhere, held in a fretful preoccupation with the morality play in which our teachers were involved. We wondered how things would turn out, of course, but beyond and deeper than that the intimate, compelling question was whether our models would behave honorably. Most of them did not, although for a time we kept ourselves from recognizing this, largely by allying ourselves psychically with the very few who acted heroically while ignoring the very many who did not. It taught us, on the one hand, that moral courage is possible and, on the other, that it is uncommon. All in all, it was a quick and unpleasant education. Perhaps it is just as well for all of us, teachers and students alike, that serious moral examinations occur so rarely.

Part III
Adolescence and Its Politics

9

Adolescence for Clinicians

Three major problems confront us in reporting research on adolescence to practicing clinicians. The first of these is that empirical work in most parts of the field is thin, yet widely spread. A vast number of topics have been studied, so much so that a first glance will offer the impression that we occupy a lively, bustling arena of research. But when we look more closely, we may discover that there are only a handful of studies on a given topic, that one or two of them are seriously out of date, another suffers from grievous flaws in methodology, another is simpleminded, and so on. It is not at all uncommon for the specialist in adolescent psychology to be approached by a colleague, or a journalist, with the observation that he or she has made a preliminary study of this or that topic in adolescence, and has been unable to find much. Surely there is more, and where is it to be found? More often than not, one will reply that there really is no more than that handful.

Here are some examples: We know very little about the effect of the biological changes of puberty on the child's behavior and psychological experience; as Petersen and Taylor (1980) point out in an excellent survey of the biological approach to adolescence, research "is in a preliminary stage and has not kept pace with biological studies. . . . Consequently, despite a proliferation of theoretical positions hypothesizing causal connections between physiological and psychological changes in early adolescence, much of our thinking in this area remains in the realm of assertion and belief" (p. 132). We also know surprisingly little about developmental changes in psychological testing during the course of adolescence, particularly in relation to "depth" and "personality variables." Aside from the seminal work of Greenberger and Steinberg (1981; Greenberger et al. 1981; Steinberg et al. 1982; Steinberg 1982), we know little about the effects of the work experience upon adolescent psychological development. As we will see later in this essay, our knowledge of the adolescent's family is so underdeveloped as to be unreliable. Despite generations of work on the roots of adolescent delinquency, almost all we know is sociological in nature; work on the psychological sources and functions of crime is just getting under way. And so it goes; the examples are chosen almost randomly, and the list is easily extended.

With so few studies available, we find ourselves deprived of the clamor and dissonance we expect in a thriving scientific enterprise. It is rare in social science for studies to support each other fully because even slight variations in method and population can produce significant variations in outcome. What emerges as scientific "truth" develops only gradually, from the juxtaposition and collision of findings. Deprived of that thickness of texture, the writer on adolescence soon finds himself leaning too heavily on the few empirical studies, and beefing up that knowledge by references to secondary sources (reviews, or reviews of reviews), to social commentary, to stray clinical observations, and the like. Though each of these genres is important to any intellectual endeavor, in the case of adolescent psychology we find a relative feebleness of the empirical mode, one that puts stringent limits on the confidence and scope of an essay such as this one.

A second difficulty is in the systematic underrepresentation of important populations of the young, such that general statements about adolescence or "the adolescent" are, if not entirely false, then surely misleading. The most important example of this has been the failure until recently to study adolescent girls, or to represent them equitably in studies of adolescent problems. That failure has been evident for many years—it was brought to scholarly attention in the national survey of adolescents by Douvan and Adelson (1966), which pointed out the significant disparities between their male and female samples, and suggested that the then-prevailing theories of adolescence were tacitly and no doubt unconsciously theories of male adolescence, and that such important topics as the psychology of achievement involved an unwitting imputation to girls of dynamics derived from and applicable to boys alone. In one form or another that discovery keeps being made: Recently Carol Gilligan's studies of moral development (1982) suggested that the Kohlberg scheme does not sufficiently take into account differences between the sexes in the perception of moral issues. The bias is now beginning to change, in that there are concerted efforts to study both sexes and the differences between them—one recent example is that the important longitudinal study of boys by the Offer group (Offer 1969; Offer and Offer 1975) is now being replicated on a sample of normal adolescent girls by Anne Petersen. Nevertheless, there is an androcentric bias built into most general propositions about adolescence.

Another source of bias, much harder to document, is to be found in the overrepresentation of certain social strata. An informal survey of my own suggests that "normal" samples probably overrepresent the upper middle class, probably because those groups are more available for study. In one recent volume of a journal in developmental psychology, the samples in adolescent studies were these: college students; children from a suburban school; the children of professional parents; and those attending a private camp. There is also a contrary tendency; many studies draw upon atypical populations from the other end of the status spectrum, especially youngsters in trouble with the law. One senses that there is a "silent majority" of teens, blue collar and lower middle class, not commonly represented in proportion to their numbers.

The two problems—the thin development of empirical work, and the biases in research samples—are linked to a third, perhaps the most important of all: the presence and persistence of a number of fixed, largely false ideas about adolescence, shared by much of the laity, by the media, by many social scientists, and by most clinicians. These ideas involve a profound misunderstanding of what is and what is not typical or modal or "normal" in adolescence. There is a tendency to see adolescence as a more dramatic and tempestuous period than it is, and to see intensified inner and outer conflict as normative. Consider how the fact of peer relations is understood in most accounts of adolescence, as a revolutionary event wherein the parents' authority withers, to be replaced by the enthronement of the peer group. The underlying assumptions are false, in seeing parents and peers as intrinsically oppositional, involved in a zero-sum game, wherein the achievement of influence by one produces a devaluation of the other. That way of framing the question simply does not capture a far more complex state of affairs.

The presence of these false ideas is not nearly as intriguing as their persistence. The idea of a sanguinary struggle between the adolescent and his parents has been known to be flawed for about thirty years. Yet it seems to have made no impact on the common awareness. As chance would have it, on the very day that I write these words, the *New York Times* provides a perfect example. In a feature story headlined "Youth: A Change in Values" we learn that the Gallup Youth Survey has just found that U.S. youngsters aged thirteen to eighteen report amicable ties to their parents: 60 percent say they get along very well; 82 percent think parental discipline is "about right"; 77 percent would consult parents (as against 18 percent for friends) if faced with a serious life decision. Yet the story is written entirely from the perspective of change. It assumes that the findings convey a remarkable shift in the attitudes of youngsters since the halcyon days of the youth revolution. The reporter asked a number of psychiatrists to play pundit, which they were glad to do, averring solemnly that there was indeed a return to traditionalism among the young. What no one seemed to grasp, neither the *Times* nor the experts called upon, was that the results obtained were essentially the same as in all previous research.

It is not an isolated case. Much of what clinicians believe to be true about adolescents is unsupported by research findings; what is worse, much of it is flatly contradicted by those findings. When pressed upon the clinical consciousness, the data are resisted by means ingenious and otherwise. I can remember, at a convention of psychiatrists, one panelist saying that he did not care about findings because he was a therapist and knew better. One might accept such dismissals if the data in question came from hostile theoretical positions, but as we will see, most studies have been carried out by psychodynamic psychologists and psychiatrists. One might accept such dismissals if the issues involved were trivial or peripheral, but they involve issues central to an understanding of the adolescent experience. Clearly we are dealing with something of a collective illusion, stubbornly held, and for that reason it seems best to eschew any effort at a conspectus of adolescence research and to concentrate instead upon what is at issue between common clinical belief on the one hand and the empirical canon on the other.

How Normal Is the Normal Adolescent?

Most of us, I suspect, will shy away from any precipitous diagnosis of an adolescent patient. Not at the extremes, perhaps—that is, if the youngster is in serious trouble with the police, or is severely addicted to hard drugs, or is beginning to show signs of cognitive slippage, we are prepared to see him or her as psychologically troubled. Or if he or she is entirely free of symptoms, doing well in school, dating with normal frequency, and so on, we are then prepared to judge the youngster to be well adjusted. But between these extremes we find ourselves holding back, not only because we want to avoid stigmatizing someone so young but also because we believe that adolescence is customarily marked by emotional turmoil. We may feel that psychoneurotic symptoms, let us say, may be misleading in adolescence because they may reflect only transient or evanescent conflicts. It is an era, we believe, that is "normally" marked by emotional distress, the sources of which are such stimuli as the dramatic biological changes of the period, psychosexual marginality, rapid cognitive growth, striking and at times volatile shifts in identity, the savage pressures of peer group homogeneity and exclusion, the anxiety one feels about an uncertain future, and so on.

The belief that a normal adolescence is "abnormal" can be traced as far back as G. Stanley Hall's *Adolescence* (1904). Yet the most important current expression stems from psychoanalysis, initially in the work of Anna Freud, later taken up and elaborated by Peter Blos. This view of adolescence initially focused upon a revitalized conflict between the drives, and the defensive and superego forces. Indeed, Anna Freud (1936) used what she took to be characteristic adolescent behaviors—asceticism or intense intellectualization—as a way of illustrating the operations of the ego under stress. In her later writing (1958), which is both succinct and marvelously lucid, she moves away from the ego-id conflict to the adolescent's struggle with revived infantile object attachments. It is that emphasis that is developed in Peter Blos's many writings on adolescence (1962; 1967; 1974). Blos's version of the vicissitudes of adolescence, too complex to report here, sees the youngster's progress through the period as dominated by the need to overcome a continuing series of regressive dangers involving earlier introjects. The picture we derive from these writings is of a youngster beleaguered by the recrudescence of infantile drives, primitive fears, and threatening imagos, and holding on valiantly, despite an affective volatility and a general stretching and impoverishment of ego functions. The child's relations to the "outer world," that is, peers and parents, are dominated by their status as threats and temptors, or as defensive anchors.

Most of the work in this tradition—that is, adolescence-as-pathology—derives directly from or is heavily influenced by psychoanalytic writing. The data base, so to speak, seems for the most part to be youngsters suffering from severe psychoneurotic or character-neurotic problems, or—more recently—addictive, narcissistic, and borderline states. It is assumed in these writings, as in most writings of the psychoanalytic tradition, that there is no fundamental difference in kind, though perhaps in intensity, between the states of mind uncovered in deep analytic work with these youngsters and what might be uncovered in therapy with those less disturbed.

Those working in the empirical tradition (adolescence-as-normality) have been drawn from a large number of disciplines, though primarily from the clinical fields, and have used diverse methodologies, ranging from questionnaire studies to intensive clinical interviews and projective tests. On the whole, they share a psychodynamic outlook, a great many of them having been trained in clinical psychology or psychoanalysis. Most continue to practice. Commonly they began their research as believers and became heretics in the course of doing it, that is, they began with the assumption of adolescence as a period of turmoil but were unable to find that confirmed in work with normal subjects. There is a remarkable uniformity to the findings. Every systematic study that has been published has been unable to discover a significant degree of psychopathology in the experience or history of the ordinary adolescent. Because the number of such studies is now too large to permit a complete report here, we will limit ourselves to several of the most widely known, reporting them chronologically.

Douvan and Adelson's *The Adolescent Experience* (1966) was the first national survey of adolescent boys and girls, conducting interviews with about 3,000 of them; it was also one of the first to employ projective questions as part of the survey interview. A large number of topics were covered: family, friends, attitudes toward achievement, work and family, the future, and many more. The typical youngster was found to have a fairly realistic assessment of himself, to be more or less at peace with his family on such issues as discipline and values, to have conventional and essentially realistic work and family ambitions.

J. F. Masterson's well-known study (1967) made a direct comparison between a group of adolescents seen at an outpatient psychiatric clinic and a control sample of "normal" youngsters, that is, normal in that they had not been referred for psychological help. If adolescence is a period marked by regressiveness, a weakened ego, and the like, one would expect to see a high rate of symptomatology among the presumed normals, perhaps even matching the level found in those labeled "disturbed." In fact, Masterson found substantial differences between the two samples; the disturbed adolescents had an extremely high rate of symptoms of a portentous type: disturbances in behavior, such as antisocial conduct, and disturbances in the quality of thinking. Nearly 60 percent of the adolescent patients showed these symptoms, as against fewer than 20 percent of the nonpatients.

The studies by Daniel Offer and his associates (1969; 1975) were of particular importance in filling a methodological gap; they were longitudinal, following a group of adolescent boys for eight years, from the age of fourteen to twenty-one. Beyond that, the researchers used intensive clinical methods—depth interviews, projective tests—upon a nonclinical sample. Whereas social psychological studies might be faulted for their use of survey-style questioning, hence insufficiently "deep," and whereas Masterson and similar studies could be said to focus too narrowly on clinical data, the Offer research used depth measures on a normal sample, thus finessing both objections. The findings confirm the direction of all previous (and following) work: adolescence in a nonclinical population of boys is marked by a general absence of symptoms, or other signs of intense inner conflict; by an absence of rebelliousness toward the parents; by a general mood of reason and amity in the family; and by an acceptance of the values of the larger society.

We might be willing to agree that adolescence is not quite the quagmire of psychopathology it is sometimes taken to be, yet we would still want to ask whether the level of inner turbulence is or is not equivalent to what we find among adults. In the course of a superb scholarly review of this material, Irving Weiner (1982) had the happy idea of collating the extant studies of normal adolescent populations that attempted to assess the proportion of disturbed youngsters. These researches were carried out at different times, on rather different populations, by different investigators using different measures; nevertheless, one finds a strong central tendency in the data, a clustering of "disturbance" at the 20 percent range, the range itself extending from 16 percent to 25 percent (see table 1). As Weiner points out, that 20 percent figure is about the same level we find in the more reliable studies of disturbed behavior in the population at large. One can only be suggestive here, but we may be willing to infer that about one in five persons in the general population shows symptoms of emotional disturbance, as adolescents do, and that the latter group is neither more nor less disturbed than others.

TABLE 1
Incidence of Psychological Disorder among Samples
of "Normal" (Nonpsychiatric) Adolescents

Study	Subjects	Percentage with Psychological Disorder
Hudgens, 1974	110 12- to 19-year-olds	23.0
Kysar et al., 1969	77 college freshmen	22.1
Leslie, 1974	150 13- to 14-year-olds	17.2
Masterson, 1967	101 12- to 18-year-olds	20.0
Offer and Offer, 1975	73 male high school students	21.0
Rimmer et al., 1978	153 college sophomores	15.3
Rimmer et al., 1976	200 14- to 15-year-olds	16.3
Smith et al., 1963	86 18- to 20-year-old college students	12.0

Note: Adapted from Weiner 1982.

If that is the case, we may go on to speculate that clinicians are assuming a false base rate of pathology in their tacit internal portrait of "the adolescent." Some evidence that this is in fact so is provided through an ingenious study by Offer, Ostrov, and Howard (1981), which asked a group of sixty-two mental health professionals (psychologists, psychiatrists, and so on) to fill out a self-report inventory, designed for adolescents, as they believed a "mentally healthy/well-adjusted adolescent" would. The "scores" given by the professionals were considerably more "pathological" than those achieved by actual adolescents. Indeed, the imagined scores were more pathological than those obtained by seriously delinquent adolescents, and by deeply disturbed (hospitalized) youngsters. The normal adolescent receives a standard score of 50; the hospitalized, a score of 43; the delinquent, a score of 42. The mental health professional imagined the "well-adjusted" as scoring at 40.

It is not hard to see how and why, given that mind-set, the clinician is so often led to error in his work with adolescents. He will tend much of the time to underdiagnose adolescent problems, that is, to minimize their severity; and at times to misdiagnose them completely. Let me illustrate from one of my own misjudgments. Some years ago a colleague and I organized an analytic group for adolescents. A sixteen-year-old boy found his way to our office, complaining of depression. We discovered that it began when he was thrown over by his girlfriend, who complained that he was becoming "too intense." We could see what she meant, for he is a brilliant youngster and very much in command of the language of passion. As we listened to his vivid account of the tempestuous love affair—his initial exhilaration, his slavish devotion, the shock of the loss, his current inconsolability—in one part of our minds we were able to recognize his suffering, yet in another we were busily discounting, our heads filled with familiar literary prototypes—Romeo, Werther, Moravia's adolescents—along with the familiar psychoanalytic observations we spoke of earlier, of the defensive and regressive aspects of adolescent love attachments. In these sources, both literary and psychodynamic, the emphasis is placed upon the *expectable* disruptions of adolescence, these being seen as transient, as characteristic of the period, or as necessary to later growth. In our diagnostic interviews with this boy, we were able to construe the defensive nature of the passionate falling-in-love, as a retreat from a revival of incestuous feeling.

Now that formula, as it happens, was quite correct, for we were able to see quite clearly during the therapy, especially through the intense transference reactions to the female group therapist, that this boy was indeed struggling against the reappearance of archaic oedipal attachments, and trying to handle them by displacements and by various modes of splitting. Yet at the same time that formula was deeply misleading. In the tacit assumption that these are commonplace intrapsychic conflicts, one is led to the belief that the crisis will work itself out in the ordinary course of events, as the drive diminishes in intensity, as the regressive forces ebb, as the ego is strengthened, and the more primitive defenses are discarded. None of that took place, neither in this case nor—as I would argue—in most like instances. The boy was at the beginning of what was to be a tragic emotional career, one not yet completed, that involved several psychotic episodes, several serious suicide attempts, and a life so troubled as to inhibit completely his extraordinary intellectual gifts.

More often than not, the appearance of symptoms in adolescence is the precursor, or the first visible expression, of an established and continuing pattern of psychopathology. The prudent clinician ought not to assume that the youngster or those about him—the family, or the school—are overreacting to what will be a transient phase in development. On these matters the laity seem to have a shrewd sense of what is and is not normative, and the decision to refer or self-refer can be taken as fairly good testimony that the youngster's distress should be addressed and treated.

The Milieu of the Adolescent

As we have seen, the "turmoil" theory of adolescence imputes—I believe mistakenly—a high degree of internal discord to the period. In addition it assumes, as a normal state of affairs, the youngster to be in conflict with his social setting. The child's relation to family members is said to be marked by discord, as he seeks to emancipate himself from their expectations and values, and find new ones more appropriate to his own generation. The peer group in particular is viewed as a central instrument of emancipation, and at the same time the source of new values. Two phrases—now catchphrases—have been employed to capture these putative shifts in orientation: from parental to peer influence; and the generation gap.

Let us begin by looking at the adolescent's relation to the family, noting first the truly astonishing paucity of information on the topic. If you were to sample a series of the leading textbooks on adolescence, you would discover that most of them devote a chapter to the topic, and that these contain discussions, generally thoughtful, of such matters as the dissolution of the traditional family, the invention of alternative forms, the effects of the rising divorce rate, the impact of mothers working or of changes in sex roles, and in general the nature and effect of recent social, structural, and ideological changes as these impinge on the adolescent's family. What you would not find in these chapters is a systematic report of the actual distribution and range of family forms, nor an empirical account of the processes of reward, punishment, indoctrination, and the like, nor any material based on extensive *in situ* observation, of the sort commonplace in anthropological field studies.

In the absence of such direct observation, the best empirical evidence we have is from the reports of adolescents themselves. Here the testimony is quite clear, and entirely at odds with the supposition of intense conflict. We saw earlier that the recent Gallup statistics show U.S. adolescents speaking of their parents with approval, reporting good overall relations, satisfactory discipline, and a sense of moral reliance. These recent findings are not in any way unique, as we said, and confirm what all other studies have shown. Some of this research is based on questionnaires, some on interviews, and some on fairly probing clinical methods; in all cases an essentially positive picture emerges. The most consistent trend is that showing the stability and strength of parental as against peer influence. Curiously enough, that topic was initiated as a means of discovering the tempo at which the adolescent escapes parental influence, it being assumed by the early investigators that their job was to measure carefully what was otherwise palpable. What they discovered instead was the persistence of parental values into late adolescence and the onset of adulthood, the influence of the peer group being limited much of the time to such issues as hairstyle and other modes of consumption. It is of particular interest that on such major issues as whether to attend college, parental opinion is considered to be far more significant than that of best friends (Floyd and South 1972; Kandel and Lesser 1969; Lerner and Knapp 1975).

Of course such studies can be looked at skeptically, in that they rely on self-report and may be suspect of striving to give a good—that is, sanctimonious—impression to the inquirer. But in those instances where we can make a direct comparison between adolescents and parents, much the same impression emerges, of continuity, agreement, and harmony as against the reverse. There is a substantial body of work stemming from political science—work not generally known among psychologists—on the transmission of political attitudes, where comparisons are made among the responses of adolescents and young adults, their parents, and their friends. These data have shown that parents were "more influential in shaping adolescent [political] orientations than were peers" (Jennings and Niemi 1981). To be sure, the degree of parent-child concordance is modest, the child is by no means the parents' clone, yet the findings are consistent over a wide range of studies using a wide range of methods and measures and samples and countries.

To write in this vein is to expose oneself to the suspicion of an advanced Pollyannaism. Surely adolescents as a group are not the Eagle Scouts these studies seem to say. Surely they are not, and I hope it will be understood that the intention here has not been to turn the "turmoil" theory on its head simply for the sake of the argument. Our view is not that adolescents are paragons of mental health, only that they are fundamentally ordinary people, in a somewhat younger version, and show that range of strengths and weaknesses we would find in the general population.

Why do we believe otherwise? No doubt it is partly due to an occupational bias, which leads us to extrapolate our experiences with disturbed young to the age group at large. A second reason may be a subtle class bias, in that we tend to make our judgments about adolescents as a group from those most visible to us, the children of academics and professionals, who are as a cadre "normal" psychologically yet atypically articulate in speech and febrile in temperament.

There is a third reason which deserves particular attention because it may seem to confute the position taken here. There has been a rise in all forms of social and psychological pathology among adolescents in recent years. The increases have been substantial. A survey by Shapiro and Wynne (1982), based on U.S. government statistics, shows increases ranging from two to four times on indices of suicide, homicide, and illegitimate births. Roughly equivalent trends can be found in surveys of teenage arrests, drug use, and the like—though in many of these instances we do not yet have genuinely long-range data. We may add to these such specific syndromes as the anorexia-bulimia pattern, once exotic, now apparently epidemic among upper-middle-class adolescent girls.

What we have had during the post-World War II era is an enormous rise in the size of age cohorts, such that the decade of the 1970s in particular was marked by a "youth bulge," meaning a substantial increase in the number of adolescents. There was in addition an extraordinary increase in the rate of certain pathologies. The rise in numbers compounded by the rise in rate has meant an explosive increase in the number of cases of destructive and self-destructive behavior. In turn, this has tended to sustain the idea of adolescence as a particularly vulnerable period of life. Yet we do well to keep the issues separate. Consider that the "pathological" view of adolescence was at the height of intellectual acceptance in the 1950s, just at the time when the true rate of adolescent pathology was at the lowest point in recorded U.S. history, for many indices. That the rates are high now tells us nothing about the normative vulnerability of the adolescent period; it tells us only that there are processes at work in the culture that are stressful to those populations exposed to them.

The most exciting new hypothesis we have on this matter is that the source of these stresses is demographic. The position has been stated elegantly in a persuasive book by Richard Easterlin (1980) that points out the many ways in which a crowded age cohort works to the extreme disadvantage of its members. In a crowded generation there is more competition for a relatively smaller number of places, producing a variety of effects: on the psychological side, a lowered self-esteem and heightened feelings of alienation; and with respect to the hard facts of social pathology, such phenomena as increases in crime, suicide, divorce, and drug use. Some of the relationships teased out by the demographers are quite unexpected, e.g. that young men's suicide rates have a strong negative correlation with female fertility, and that the same inverse relationship occurs between homicide and fertility. Easterlin argues that the three indices all reflect a common causal factor: "variations in the ability of young persons to achieve their life-style aspirations." In a small generation, one is more likely to marry and have children, and indices of mental stress decline, with the converse taking place in crowded generations.

Once we look at matters in this way, it becomes evident that the rise in social pathology tells us little about the intrinsic nature of adolescence, except insofar as it is a period in which certain important life events do or do not take place. If the demographers are right, we shall soon be seeing a decline in these rates, as generation size declines, and in fact we do seem to be seeing the first signs of that decline. And there is every reason to believe that we will be seeing a continuation of the pathology now affecting the young, though in older age groups, as that generation matures, and as the disadvantaged adolescents of today become the disadvantaged adults of tomorrow.

Some Conclusions

It may be useful to sum up, apodictically, some of the propositions emerging from this analysis.

1. The empirical evidence we have gives us no reason to believe that adolescence is marked by an unusual degree of psychopathology, or by excessive vulnerability to stress.
2. Psychological disturbances appearing in adolescence are unlikely to be transient, and are more likely the debut appearance of chronic or continuing disorders.
3. The more severe the symptom picture in adolescence, the more likely it is that later disturbances will be serious or disabling.
4. Strong feelings of resentment, anger, or alienation felt toward the parents will likely continue later in life, though they may be expressed differently. The same may be said for strong feelings of any kind—dependency, for example.
5. All of the propositions above reflect a conservative reading of the current evidence. It is quite possible to look at that evidence differently. The skeptical reader is advised to consult the brilliant analysis of longitudinal work in adolescence by Livson and Peskin (1980), who conclude that neither the "turmoil" nor the "stability" theories of the adolescent period are yet proven.

References

Blos, P. *On Adolescence*. New York: Free Press, 1962.
———. "The Second Individuation Process of Adolescence." In *Psychoanalytic Study of the Child*, vol. 22, edited by R. S. Eissler et al. New York: International Universities Press, 1967.
———. "The Genealogy of the Ego Ideal." In *Psychoanalytic Study of the Child*, vol. 29, edited by R. S. Eissler et al. New Haven: Yale University Press, 1974.
Douvan, E., and Adelson, J. *The Adolescent Experience*. New York: Wiley, 1966.
Easterlin, A. *Birth and Fortune*. New York: Basic Books, 1980.
Floyd, H. H., Jr., and South, D. R. "Dilemma of Youth: The Choice of Parents or Peers as a Frame of Reference for Behavior." *Journal of Marriage and the Family* 34 (1972): 627–734.
Freud, A. *The Ego and the Mechanisms of Defense*. New York: International Universities Press, 1936.
Freud, A. "Adolescence." In *Psychoanalytic Study of the Child*, vol. 13, edited by R. S. Eissler et al. New York: International Universities Press, 1958.
Gilligan, C. *In a Different Voice: Psychological Theory and Women's Development*. Cambridge: Harvard University Press, 1982.
Greenberger, E., and Steinberg, L. D. "The Workplace as a Context for the Socialization of Youth." *Journal of Youth and Adolescence* 10 (June 1981): 185–210.
Greenberger, E., Steinberg, L., and Vaux, A. "Adolescents Who Work: Health and Behavioral Consequences of Job Stress." *Developmental Psychology* 17(1981): 691–703.

Hall, G. S. *Adolescence*. New York: Appleton, 1904.

Hudgens, R. W. *Psychiatric Disorders in Adolescents*. Baltimore: Williams & Wilkins, 1974.

Jennings, M., and Niemi, R. G. *Generations and Politics*. Princeton: Princeton University Press, 1981.

Kandel, D. B., and Lesser, G. S. "Parental and Peer Influences on Educational Plans of Adolescents." *American Sociological Review* 34 (1969): 213–23.

Kysar, J. E., Zaks, M. S., Schuchman, H. P., Schon, G. L., and Rogers, J. "Range of Psychological Functioning in 'Normal' Late Adolescents." *Archives of General Psychiatry* 21 (1969): 515–28.

Lerner, R. M., and Knapp, J. R. "Actual and Perceived Intrafamilial Attitudes of Late Adolescents and Their Parents." *Journal of Youth and Adolescence* 4 (1975): 17–36.

Leslie, S. A. "Psychiatric Disorder in the Young Adolescents of an Industrial Town." *British Journal of Psychiatry* 125 (1974): 113–24.

Livson, N., and Peskin, H. "Perspectives on Adolescence from Longitudinal Research." In *Handbook of Adolescent Psychology*, edited by J. Adelson. New York: Wiley, 1980.

Masterson, J. F. *The Psychiatric Dilemma of Adolescence*. Boston: Little, Brown, 1967.

Offer, D. *The Psychological World of the Teenager*. New York: Basic Books, 1969.

Offer, D., and Offer, J. B. *From Teenage to Young Manhood*. New York; Basic Books, 1975.

Offer, D., Ostrov, E., and Howard, K. L. "The Mental Health Professional's Concept of the Normal Adolescent." *Archives of General Psychiatry* 38 (February 1981): 149–52.

Petersen, A., and Taylor, B. "The Biological Approach to Adolescence." In *Handbook of Adolescent Psychology*, edited by J. Adelson. New York: Wiley, 1980.

Shapiro, J., and Wynne, E. O. "Adolescent Alienation: Evaluating the Hypothesis." *Social Indicators Research* 10 (1982): 423–35.

Steinberg, L. D. "Jumping off the Work Experience Bandwagon." *Journal of Youth and Adolescence* 11, no. 3 (1982): 183–205.

Steinberg, L., Greenberger, E., Garduque, L., Ruggiero, M., and Vaux, A. "The Effects of Working on Adolescent Development." *Developmental Psychology* 18 (1982): 385–95.

Weiner, I. B. *Child and Adolescent Psychopathology*. New York: Wiley, 1982.

10

Inventing the Young

I was recently told the following story: A nationally known authority on the young was asked to speak to an adult audience in his community. He arrived bearing a tape recorder and announced to his listeners that to understand today's youth one has to listen to its music, and while the audience watched in numb amazement, danced before the lectern. After about twenty minutes of music and dancing he undertook the lecture proper, which berated adults for victimizing the young, who were described as tribunes of a new era of peace and love. In the midst of this harangue he was interrupted by a messenger and left the stage, to return shortly and declare: "I must leave. My students need me." He departed, taking the tape recorder but leaving behind a dazed and enraged audience.

I treasure this anecdote for its grotesque charm and for its demonstration of how much an apostle of love will allow himself, and also because it illustrates so vividly the temptations besetting an expert on the young. It shows how we move to closeness, and beyond that to identity, with those we study; I will return to this later. It also shows the degree to which we invent the young. I choose the word *invent* precisely for its ambiguity. We invent, in the first sense, in that we construct or hypothesize our social categories. We do so because we must, for social theory, even when "empirical" in character, rests ultimately upon some invention or model of society and its categories. But I use the word *invent* in another sense as well, to connote fancy and the making of myths. Here too we invent because we must, for the young are in fact so diverse, complex, and obscure that they force us to imagine not so much what is out there, in reality, as what is inside our minds. Hence we invent what we wish to perceive. We invent the young so that they may, like figures in a morality play, take their places in that larger tableau of social action that our minds have devised.

The incident I have recounted also informs us of the two dominant imaginings of the young: as victims and as visionaries. When our expert makes his sudden departure, crying out that his students are in need of him, we are offered a dramatization in miniature of the theme of the oppressed young; we take it that they are suffering some brutality and require the nurturance and protection of their leader. When he tells his audience that the young herald an era of love and understanding, he is casting them as visionaries, prophets of a new age. Between them, the images of victim and visionary control our current perception of youth. The view of the young as victimized receives its most intense expression in the writings of Edgar Z. Friedenberg, who represents U.S. society roughly along the lines of Kafka's *In the Penal Colony,* with its educational system an equivalent of "The Harrow." The view of the young as seers, as millenarian prophets, has found its most extreme spokesman in Charles Reich, who sees every twitch of the elite young culture—its postures, its argot, the very flare of its trousers—as silently prefiguring a new age of amity and equality.

More often than not the two images coalesce. Either the young are oppressed because of their visionary capacity, because they see so fully what the established powers fear to see at all; or because their victimization, the very posture of humiliation they are forced to endure, allows them a prescience beyond the common understanding. The figure of the prophetic victim, though it draws upon traditional religious imagery, and though it resonates with earlier U.S. archetypes (Billy Budd, for example), becomes the dominant image of the young in the postwar era. It flowers initially in the writing of J. D. Salinger—the Holden Caulfield and the Glass family, the first of these stressing victimization, the second a fatal visionary talent. In the 1960s it sweeps all before it; can we recall a novel or film on youth during this decade that does not in one way or another evoke these images?

And in the 1960s we note an important change. The young victim now transcends his victimization; he overcomes his passivity and in doing so achieves strength and heroism. He is the prophet armed, his rebellion justified by his prior oppression, his vision of a better world setting the goals of his movement. Indeed in this decade the themes of oppression, prophecy, and rebellious heroism become the dominant motifs of collective fantasy, as the metaphor of victimization is politicized, and as other groups—Blacks, women, homosexuals, freaks, prisoners, the psychotic—are defined, by themselves, or more often through self-appointed spokesmen, as victims, visionaries, and revolutionary heroes.

All of which makes for spirited sermons, stirring political rhetoric, best-selling fiction, and popular motion pictures. It also makes for bad art, bad history, and bad social science. To the degree that these images possess us, they constrict and coarsen our experience. When we can see ourselves and others only as victims, villains, and heroes, we reduce brutally the range of our grasp of the human. Thus what we find (or should find) offensive in women's liberation literature is a representation of both men and women so gross as to remind us of sadomasochistic pornography: the men ravening beasts, the women terrorized and fawning slaves. Through this last sorry decade, as the obsessions of militancy have seized us, we witness a painful retrogression in intellectual and artistic life; think of the distance we have traveled, ever backward, from Ralph Ellison to LeRoi Jones, or in feminine psychology from Helene Deutsch to Kate Millett. As Richard Hofstadter said shortly before his death, we have been living in "an age of rubbish."

It may be said that we cannot demand of polemical literature that degree of complexity we look for in more measured and reflective writing, but the point is that these days the polemical spirit will not voluntarily contain itself. It spreads into art and scholarship, concealing itself by simulating the devices and mannerisms of the media it invades.

A case in point is that large and ever-growing body of writing on the young radical. Given the general susceptibility to illusion when we consider the young; given the ease with which the polemical impulse, wittingly or not, can express itself on the topic of radicalism; given the widespread erosion of self-discipline in the social sciences (as the need to be "relevant" escalates); given all these, it is not at all surprising to discover how much of the work on student activism is at the least suspect and at the worst near to worthless, in that the necessary boundaries between illusion and reality, and between polemics and scholarship seem irretrievably blurred. The problem is not so much in those writings, and they are many, which are more or less openly tendentious. When we read someone like Richard Flacks (a founding member of Students for a Democratic Society, SDS), or a Friedenberg, we can, if we so choose, exercise our own forms of skepticism as we judge the work. The more subtle complications are to be found in the scholarship that presents itself to us (and often believes itself to be) dry, objective, unillusioned. One of the best examples is Kenneth Keniston's *Young Radicals,* which is also the most influential and widely known treatise on activist youth.

Keniston's view of the radical young is difficult to present in brief compass: let me stress its emphases. The radical young are drawn from families in the managerial and professional classes. Far from being rebellious toward or alienated from parental values, they in fact share and wish to implement them. They are intelligent, cosmopolitan in outlook, academically successful. Their histories are in fact marked by success, but at some point along the way they begin to question conventional definitions of success and become preoccupied with the discrepancy between the ideals that they have learned and internalized, and the various moral failures of U.S. society. Thus, they find themselves committed, and their commitment brings further commitment and ultimately radicalization. This summary is, let me confess, skeltonized, perhaps to the point of caricature, but I believe that it captures the essence of the argument. I may not, however, capture the susurrus of commendation that lies behind it.

What is wrong with this account is as much or more in what it omits, in what it chooses not to perceive, as in what it says. Let us say that it bears the same relationship to the realities of the radical scene as a picture of a smiling, ruddy Stakhanovite worker bears to Soviet industrial reality. To put it another way, it is a kind of court portraiture: the warts have been removed, the blemishes hidden, the chin strengthened. We are asked to attend only to beauty, grace, and strength. It is, in short, a Panglossian exercise. Not unexpectedly, students on the Left appreciate Keniston's assessment of them and are fond of citing it—an ominous sign, I should think, for an objective study. Nevertheless, there has been, even on the Left, some rising conviction that Keniston's muted panegyrics do not quite tell the whole story. For example, I recently saw an unpublished study of radical activists, carried out by scholars whom I believe to be of Left sympathies, that makes much of the impulsivity, the provocativeness, and the compulsive oppositionalism of the radical young who had been interviewed. Not long ago a radical student of mine confessed, albeit with some chagrin, that he found Keniston's book to be effusive and one-sided. Although he himself remained a radical, he said his own experience in radical politics had been bitterly discouraging. He pointed to the intellectual dogmatism that so often made it difficult to share common action, to an endemic depressiveness among radical students, and their tendency to overcome it in spasms of action; and above all to a hypersensitivity to opposition that made personal relationships rancorous when not in fact explosive. In recent months I have more than once heard radical faculty members lament the frenzy and irrationalism of their radical students.

To such observations, however occasional, from those on the Left, we must add equally mordant assessments from less friendly sources: the pervasive anti-intellectualism of so many members of the movement, and with it, the preference for jargon, slogans, and cant as against hard thought, especially in the realm of politics. It is the quality my colleague Frederick Wyatt has called "target hunger": the restless, relentless search for enemies and conspiracies; the curious mixture of public piety and private cynicism among leaders of the movement; the even more curious mixture of self-pity, self-indulgence, and self-admiration we find in many radical personalities; the shallow, shifting quality of personal ties in the movement. To be sure, these tendencies, singly or together, by no means characterize all of those on the Left, but they are to be found with more than the ordinary frequency, as both sympathetic and disenchanted witnesses of the movement have noted.

Yet in a book—an entire book, after all—that purports to offer a portrait in depth of the radical personality, there is a persistent obtuseness to these and other negative qualities. It is illuminating to interpose, as I have recently done, readings of Young Radicals between readings of the current underground press. The one is all sweetness and light and high moral purpose; the other, slogans and self-righteousness, and above all else, a murderous hatred. The one Woodstock, the other Altamont.

Which brings us, as it must, to the topic of violence, that bone in all our throats. If there is anything that has characterized the movement, that has distinguished it from other expressions of U.S. radicalism in the century, it has been the infatuation with violence. The incidents of actual violence—the bombings, the arson, the vandalism, the personal assaults—are far from being the entire story; they rest upon those incitements to destruction that dominate so much of the radical press, and the quality of indifference and indeed insouciance with which leaders of the movement accept and indulge the more than occasional eruptions into real violence. (On this too, more later.) To say that Keniston has been insensitive to the presence of violence is, if anything, to understate the case. In his view, young radicals are not only free from the disposition to violence, they are in fact entirely opposed to it; they are victims rather than instigators. He tells us:

> Although in behavior most of these young radicals were rather *less* violent than their contemporaries, this was not because they were indifferent to the issue, but because their early experience and family values had taught them how to control, modulate, oppose, and avoid violence. Verbal aggression took the place of physical attack. They learned to argue, compromise, and to make peace when confronted with conflict. Still, too, although their adolescent experience was full of inner conflict, they acted on their violent feelings only during a brief period of indignant rebellion against the inconsistencies of their parents. These young radicals are unusual in their sensitivity to violence, as in their need and ability to oppose it.

Such a grievous misreading of reality can and I suppose will be excused on the grounds that when *Young Radicals* was written, in 1967-68, the turn to violence was not yet evident, that it grew out of the frustrations of Vietnam, that if moves toward peace had been made at that time, the temptation to violence would have subsided. Perhaps so; we will never know. But it needed neither an in-depth study nor the wisdom of Solomon to sense, well before 1968, that the student Left was moving toward an experiment in violence. In my own case, for example, the shock of recognition came as early as 1965, when I began to discern among radical students at Michigan a violence of spirit and language, an eagerness for confrontation, which was new and strange and infinitely worrisome. One of my students, an undergraduate at an Eastern liberal arts college during that same period, can recall a dispute about parietal hours, of all things, and there was much agitated talk among his peers about breaking windows if demands were not met. In 1966 a graduate student at Michigan carried out a study of members of SDS, at that time still officially devoted to nonviolence; one of her respondents even then was willing to write that he looked forward to "a radical movement . . . which would work for a full radical platform violently if not allowed to act nonviolently."

So it is not merely hindsight that allows one to say that by 1967 one could perceive, if one so chose, that turn to violence that has since become normative in the movement. In any case, the question is not whether it was inevitable, and thus predictable, but whether it was visible enough as a potential to warrant some serious attention in a book devoted to young radicals. What we ask of our experts is not that they divine the future but simply that they provide an adequate sense of the contours of the present so that we gain some apprehension of the possible.

It is not difficult to see what has gone wrong. In *Young Radicals,* as in so much current work on the young, there is a fatal failure of distance. There is a good analogy to be found in the studies of a colleague of mine who has been investigating the problems encountered by novice psychotherapists. The most common difficulty, it appears, is in their tendency to substitute identification for empathy. In their wish to get into the patient's skin, to see the world as he sees it, they succeed all too well, in that the impulse to empathy is insidiously transformed into identification, into a being-at-one-with, so that the therapeutic perspective is lost. In striving to see as his patient does, the young therapist takes over and begins to share those very distortions of perception that have contributed to and sustained his client's neurotic problems. Thus the patient acquires a friend and a partisan, and beyond that a double. All may go well in the short run; the patient is buoyed by his therapist's friendliness, and he may shed momentarily his habits of self-doubt and self-blame. The therapist's identification encourages the patient to externalize, to blame others, to see his problems as lying entirely outside himself, to view himself as the victim of an unjust destiny. But in the not-so-long run, therapy begins to falter. The patient has gained a friend but has lost the help of a disinterested presence. The therapist's compassion is not enough, nor is the self-pity or rage induced by externalization. Sooner or later, if this patient is to be helped, the therapist must urge him to look inward to deeper recesses of self and motive.

Keniston's mission was not, of course, therapeutic, but diagnostic; nevertheless the analogy stands. Like the novice therapist he seems unable to distance himself. He is all too eager to believe anything he is told. His respondents tell him they are nonviolent; he believes it. They tell him they act only out of the highest moral principles; he believes it. No doubt if they told him they could walk on water he would believe that too. In an age so bereft of belief, it is touching to find belief reborn. The ingenuousness with which Keniston has approached his topic has produced, as one would expect, a remarkably nondynamic account of radical character. Though the language of *Young Radicals* is, much of the time, psychoanalytic, the fundamental perspective is not. It seems afraid to peer beneath the surface, to explore disinterestedly those complications of motive and experience that might give us a plausible account of the activist personality. What we have instead is a determination both to share and validate the radical world view.

In Keniston's account of radical motivation, the emphasis is constantly external; radical rage is, for example, largely reactive to the moral disarray out there, in the world. We hear much of the fear of technological death, of the sterility of organized life, of the disappointments of affluence—all the touchstones of contemporary intellectual chic. In accepting this grammar of motives, Keniston has accepted the strategy of externalization by which the movement and the counterculture explains, justifies, and forgives its most dubious beliefs and deeds. What we have, then, is not analysis but journalism, and journalism of the worst sort, of the fan-magazine variety, which gushes over its subjects and makes no effort to stand aside, disengaged.

The failure of psychodynamic sensitivity can be seen in Keniston's superficial treatment of the moral dimension in radical politics. He takes the position that the radical young are actuated by universalistic moral principles; offended by the injustices of the world, unable to achieve the moral obtuseness and hypocrisy that shield the rest of us, enraged by the gaps between the ideals we profess and the callousness of our practices, they are led by morality into politics. Theirs, then, is a politics of intense moral concern.

Let me say first that I am more than a little skeptical about the universalism imputed to this political morality; for a universalistic morality it is in practice strangely selective, not to say programmed, in that it burns with outrage about certain injustices and yet is serenely indifferent about others. It rages about the death of Fred Hampton, for example, and is entirely silent about Alex Rackley; it is furious about the indictment of Angela Davis, but finds not a word to say about the innocents killed and endangered by the action for which she was indicted; and so on.

But all this is, in a way, beside the point. Even if we agree that radical politics is more morally concerned than most, should we greet this news with hosannas, or should we not, instead, respond with some fear and trembling? If there is anything this grim century has taught us, it is about what Lionel Trilling has called the "dangers of the moral life itself," that "the moral passions are even more willful and imperious and impatient than the self-serving passions" and that "their tendency is to be not only liberating but restrictive." The dangers of the moral life itself: if anyone should know them, it is the psychoanalytic psychologist. Each day reminds us of the deceits and complexities of conscience. Each day reminds us of the deeply entangled connections between the superego on the one hand and will and aggression on the other. The superego arises, in large part, out of the struggle against aggression and the unbridled will, and it is a struggle never fully won. If the superego, much of the time, constrains cruelty and license, it remains at the same time susceptible to the very corruptions it opposes. If the superego, in certain of its phases, forgives us nothing, then it can, in other moments, forgive us everything.

All of this seems to elude Keniston. Thus, when he confronts, as he now must, the joining of high moral purpose and violence in the radical movement, he resorts to the mechanism of splitting. There are, he argues, good (i.e. ethical, peaceful) radicals and bad (i.e. amoral, violent) ones. The violent ones are attracted to the movement for the worst reasons and their behavior gives it a bad name. There is, I should think, some truth to this, radicals being as various as the rest of us, and yet this argument avoids all manner of hard questions. Are we to believe that peaceful and violent radicals really have so little to do with one another? Are they not sometimes in unconscious collusion, living off each other symbiotically, the peaceful ones providing the high-minded rhetoric that legitimizes the rage of the violent, while the violent act out the disavowed yearnings of the peaceful? It would not be the first time in human history that the respectable elements of a movement used an underclass to do their dirty work for them. The Left would have no trouble recognizing and pointing to such collusion on the Right, as it did, and correctly, in detecting a connection of aim, though not of consciousness, between White Citizens Councils and the Klan, or between good Germans and the SS. The collusion usually consists of the familiar rationalizations, "I don't condone violence, but . . .," and the typical mote-and-beam accusations, "The violence we may do is as nothing compared with the greater violence done by those we oppose." One might even ask whether the collusion is all that unconscious. Is it unconscious when the "respectable" leader of a campus demonstration announces to his audience before it takes to the streets that each person should feel free to express his outrage as he wishes? Is it unconscious when a scholar—most respectable, most distinguished—announces to one and all, following some gratuitous vandalism on campus, that the university "deserved a trashing"?

But the strategy of collusion, of the right hand not quite owning up to what the left hand is doing, is only one of the many possible outcomes of the life of moral purpose. The more interesting, more hazardous, more tragic consequences are to be found within the personality itself, and it is these complications that Keniston's view of the moral life does not capture. Can there by anything more difficult, more ridden with tension than the effort to achieve a secular sainthood? And is it anywhere more difficult than in the United States, where there are neither the traditions nor the institutions to lend support to the effort? In the life of sainthood, that which within the self has been put aside, disavowed—rage, spite, pride, self-indulgence, duplicity—all these threaten to emerge, to overcome the self's constraints. What we know of our recent saints—of a Gandhi, a Schweitzer, a Tolstoy, now apparently a Martin

Luther King—tells us of the costs to be paid, costs paid by friends, followers, family and, above all, costs to the self's wholeness.

It is a psychoanalytic commonplace that the distended superego can be as destructive to the total personality as the unchecked id. The superego swollen in triumph will blunt or choke off the ego, and with it both reason and the full sense of reality. (Thus, the contempt for thought, and the fantastic over-estimation of one's power, both so commonly noted in the radical movement.) It damages the human affection: the other comes to be seen as a mere instrument of one's moral purpose; he is a friend when and only when he is a moral ally, and even one's ally may be sacrificed to the larger good—think of the cynicism with which leaders of the movement deploy their "masses," as at the Chicago convention. And if the other is an enemy, his rights and his very humanity count for nothing. Ultimately the superego may ally itself with the previously disavowed, darker sides of the self; and with that we have the triumph of the totalitarian spirit. We have Bernadine Dohrn, in her latest broadside, speaking, as callously as any Pentagon general, of "anti-personnel bombing." We have her telling us that though many in her collective did not want to take part in random bombing, nevertheless "they struggled day and night, and eventually, everyone agreed to do their part."

I suppose I will be understood to be saying that radicals like Bernadine Dohrn are moral monsters. To the contrary, they are not; that is the problem before us. In this connection I can only think of Diana Oughton and Bill Ayers, both of whom were students at Michigan and were known by some of my students and colleagues. Without exception, they comment on their intelligence, their charm, their personal sweetness, their moral authenticity. Then they were, for reasons unknown, transformed. They became Weathermen—tough, reckless, a little crazy. Ayers took to wearing a leather jacket, provoking fights with high-school toughs, hoping thereby to recruit them into the revolution. Then the "Days of Rage" in Chicago, and finally, the Eleventh Street townhouse explosion, where Diana Oughton was killed and Bill Ayers escaped to go underground. What moved them from a peaceful to a violent radicalism, I do not know. Why they were so moved and not so many others just like them, I do not know. But I do know that Keniston's theory of the moral life will not contain them. His young radicals have all the moral weight and complexity of a troop of Eagle Scouts. When all is said and done, they are no more than sincere and principled and idealistic. A century after *The Possessed,* eighty-five years after *The Princess Casamassima,* a generation after Koestler, Silone, and Orwell, we have every reason to expect a harder, less sentimental, more subtle grasp of the interplay between morality and politics. Kenneth Keniston's failure to perceive the real moral tensions of the radical life, strangely enough, diminishes those he means to idealize.

It is the moralism of the young radicals, and not their morality, that attracts Keniston, and it is that very moralism in his own writing that has made his invention of the young radical so palatable to U.S. establishment thought. We do like to think of our young as possessing exemplary moral vision; it speaks so well of them and equally well of ourselves. What has not been sufficiently understood is that the moralism of the movement draws upon and continues the cursed habit in this nation of pursuing moral uplift in the realm of politics. From Woodrow Wilson to John Foster Dulles to the present day, our hortatory mania has led us to the brink of disaster and beyond. At the same time the moralizing style is quintessentially middle class; Lionel Trilling, the essay cited earlier, reminds us that indignation is a characteristic middle-class sentiment. And is it not indignation that figures as the dominant political sentiment of the day in this most middle-class of nations? Thus we have the scions of the haute bourgeoisie indulging the most delicious emotion at the expense of the petit bourgeoisie, and being repaid in kind. In periods of crisis, all these tendencies exacerbate, and between American piety and middle-class indignation, the stink of holiness has so infected our political discourse as to make that discourse unbearable.

The ultimate problem in Keniston's book is that he is the captive of that very sensibility that we must distance and transcend if we are to try to understand the recent debacles of radicalism. Student activism, at least in its present form, seems to be dying. What will not vanish, however, and may in fact grow, is the moralizing upper-middle-class sensibility, which is the seedbed of the "radical" mentality. It is that class's political and cultural style that I believe to be at the heart of the matter; to my mind, the radical youth ambience is no more than the reflection, though sometimes distorted, of the cognitive, moral, and affective qualities of that class. That class—let us face it, our class—has extraordinary strengths: intelligence, energy, effectiveness, sensitivity, and sometimes hypersensitivity, to the new and emergent. But we must learn to look as coolly as possible at the more problematic qualities of that class: its political style, joining indignation with sentimentality; its middlebrow aesthetics, with all the limitations of vision and depth that that imposes; its oscillations between asceticism and self-indulgence; its love of high-minded cliches; its propensity to guilt balanced against its inclination to moral self-satisfaction; its narcissistic investment in its children, along with its tendency to neglect them emotionally. We have had, here and there, some successful efforts to shed some light on the political and cultural dispositions of this stratum: David Bazelon's brilliant (and shamefully neglected) observations on the New Class; Edward Banfield's perceptive (but cranky and needlessly bitter) comments on the moralizing style; David Riesman's characteristically sharp insights scattered through his writings; penetrating but all too occasional remarks by Robert Nisbet. And we have also had, hidden away in the psychiatric and social science literature, data and observations that, more often than not unknowingly, give us moments of astonishing illumination. But it is all, so far, scattered, incomplete, and embryonic. Unfortunately it will be a task of self-examination, that most difficult of the arts, for the intellectuals and social scientists who must accomplish it are themselves imprisoned by the assumptions of their class. If we judge by the obtuseness and self-satisfaction that has characterized much of the scholarship on the young radical, it may well be a task beyond us.

11

What Generation Gap? (1970)

Can the truth prevail against a false idea whose time has come? The idea that there is a generation gap is not totally false, perhaps. But it is false enough, false in the sense of being overblown, oversimplified, sentimentalized. This may be too strong a way of putting it. Let us say, then, that the idea of a generation gap is at the least unexamined, one of those notions that seems so self-evident that we yield to it without taking thought, and without qualms about not taking thought.

Once we examine the idea, we find it is almost too slippery to hold. What do we mean by a generation gap? Do we mean widespread alienation between adolescents and their parents? Do we mean that the young have a different and distinctive political outlook? Are we speaking of differences in styles of pleasure-seeking; greater sexual freedom, or the marijuana culture? Or do we simply mean that the young and the old share the belief that there is a significant difference between them, whether or not there is?

These questions—and many others one might reasonably ask—are by no means easy to answer. Few of them can in fact be answered decisively. Nevertheless, enough information has been accumulated during the last few years to offer us some new understanding of the young. As we will see, this evidence contains some surprises; and persuades us to cast a very cold eye on the more simpleminded views about this young generation and its place in our society.

Parents and Children

One definition of generational conflict locates it in rebellion against parental authority, or in the failure of parents and their adolescent youngsters to understand and communicate with each other. (In short, *The Graduate*.) On this particular issue there is, as it happens, abundant evidence; all of it suggests strongly that there is no extensive degree of alienation between parents and their children. Vern Bengtson, one of the most careful scholars in this area, has collected data from more than five hundred students enrolled in three Southern California colleges. About 80 percent of them report generally close and friendly relationships with their parents; specifically, 79 percent feel

149

percent feel somewhat close or very close, 81 percent regard communication as good, and 78 percent feel that their parents understand them all or most of the time.

Essentially similar findings have emerged from Samuel Lubell's perceptive studies of college youth. He reports that only about 10 percent of the students he interviewed were in serious discord with their parents, and there was in most of these cases a long history of family tension. Any clinician working with college-age students would agree; among the rebellious or alienated, we find that their troubles with their families go back a long way and surfaced well before the college years.

In some respects the findings of Bengtson and Lubell are not really surprising. What they do is bring us up to date, and tell us that a long-established line of findings on adolescence continues to be true. A few years ago my colleague Elizabeth Douvan and I studied 3,000 youngsters aged twelve to eighteen, from all regions of the country and all socioeconomic levels. We concluded that there were few signs of serious conflict between them and their parents; on the contrary, we found that it was more usual for the relationships to be amiable.

The recently published study by psychiatrist Daniel Offer, of a smaller group, but using more intensive methods of scrutiny, arrives at much the same conclusion. Incidentally, there is no support for the common belief that the adolescent is hostage to the influence of his friends and turns away from parental guidance. A number of studies here and abroad tell us that although peer opinion may carry some weight on trivial issues—taste, clothing, and the like—on more central matters, such as career and college choice, it is parental opinion that counts.

Whatever the supposed generation gap may involve, it does not seem to include deep strains between the young and their parents. The idea of the adolescent's family milieu as a kind of Götterdämmerung, as the scene of a cataclysmic struggle between the forces of authority and rebellion, is exaggerated. As Lubell put it: "We found both much less authority and much less rebellion than popularly imagined."

Politics

Those who are convinced that there is a generation gap also tend to identify youth in general with radical or militantly liberal beliefs. Thus, the young are sometimes seen as a New Breed, impatient with the political pieties of the past, less subject to that fatigue and corruption of spirit characteristic of the older generation of voters.

There is indeed a generational element in politics; there always has been. But to identify the young with liberal or left militancy makes sense only from the perspective of the elite university campus. Once we look at the total population of the young, a decidedly different picture emerges. We have, for example, a brilliant and revealing analysis of the 1968 election by the University of Michigan's Survey Research Center, based upon 1,600 interviews with a representative national sample of voters. Perhaps the most interesting finding was that the under-thirty voter was distinctly overrepresented in the George C. Wallace constituency, and that the Wallace movement outside the South drew proportionately more of its strength from younger than from older voters.

Some of the center's commentary on generational influences is worth quoting at length.

> One of the most important yet hidden lines of cleavage split the younger generation itself. Although privileged young college students angry at Vietnam and shabby treatment of the Negro saw themselves sallying forth to do battle against a corrupted and cynical older generation, a more head-on confrontation at the polls, if a less apparent one, was with their own age mates who had gone from high school off to the factory instead of college, and who were appalled by the collapse of patriotism and respect for the law that they saw about them. Outside of the election period, when verbal articulateness and leisure for political activism count most heavily, it was the college share of the younger generation— or at least its politicized vanguard—that was most prominent as a political force. At the polls, however, the game shifts to "one man, one vote," and this vanguard is numerically swamped even within its own generation.

To overemphasize the role of generational conflict in politics is to ignore or dismiss what we have learned over the years about the transmission of political sentiments in the great majority of cases—it seems to average about 75 percent in most studies—children vote the same party their parents do; it has often been noted that party preference is transmitted to about the same degree as religious affiliation; among studies on this matter there is hardly one that reports a negative relationship between parental attitudes and those of their children.

My own research during the last few years has dealt with the acquisition of political values during adolescence, and it is patently clear that the political outlook of the parents, particularly when it is strongly felt, tends to impress itself firmly on the politics of the child. Thus, the most conservative youngster we interviewed was the daughter of a leader of the John Birch Society; the most radical was the daughter of a man who in 1965 had ceased paying income taxes to the federal government in protest against our involvement in Vietnam.

The strongest recent evidence on this subject seems to come from studies of the student radical. These studies make it evident that the "rebellious" student is, for the most part, not rebelling against the politics he learned at home. Radical activists are for the most part children of radical or liberal-left parents; in many instances their parents are, overtly or tacitly, sympathetic to what their children are doing. (This is shown in the letters written to the press by parents of the students expelled by Columbia and Chicago; the rhetoric of these letters reveals how strong the bond of political sympathy is between the parents and their children. For instance, a letter from a group of Columbia parents states: "We are, of course, concerned about the individual fates of our sons and daughters, but more so with resisting such pressures against a student movement which has done so much to arouse the nation to the gross horrors and injustices prevalent in our country.")

Values

Are the young abandoning traditional convictions and moving toward new moral and ideological frameworks? We hear it said that the old emphasis on personal achievement is giving way to a greater concern with self-realization or with leisure and consumption; that a selfish materialism is being succeeded by a more humanistic outlook; that authority and hierarchy are no longer automatically accepted, and are replaced by more democratic forms of participation; that rationalism is under attack by proponents of sensual or mystical perspectives; and so on.

The most ambitious recent survey on this topic was sponsored by *Fortune* magazine. *Fortune* seems to believe that its findings demonstrate a generation gap and a departure from "traditional moral values" on the part of many of the educated young. A careful look at the survey suggests that it proves neither of these propositions but only how badly statistics can deceive in a murky area.

The *Fortune* pollsters interviewed a representative sample of people eighteen to twenty-four years old, dividing them into a noncollege group; a college group of upwardly largely mobile youngsters interested in education for its vocational advantages; and a so-called forerunner group (largely students interested in education as self-discovery and majoring in the humanities and social sciences). Some substantial, though not surprising, differences are found among these groups: the "forerunners" are more liberal politically, less traditional in values, less enchanted about business careers (naturally) than the two other groups. But the findings tell us nothing about a generation gap because the opinions of older people were not surveyed. Nor do they tell us anything about changes in values because we do not have equivalent findings on earlier generations of the young.

What the findings do tell us (and this is concealed in the way the data are presented, so much so that I have had to recompute the statistics) is, first, that an overwhelming majority of the young—as many as 80 percent—tend to be traditionalist in values; and, second, that there is a sharp division within the younger generation between, on the one hand, that distinct minority that chooses a liberal education and, on the other, both those who do not go to college and the majority of college students who are vocationally oriented. In brief, the prevailing pattern (of intragenerational cleavage) is quite similar to that which we find in politics.

The *Fortune* poll brings out one interesting thing: many of those interviewed—well over 80 percent—report that they do not believe that there are great differences in values between themselves and their parents. This is supported by other investigations. Bengtson's direct comparison of college students demonstrates that they "shared the same general value orientations and personal life goals." He concludes that "both students and parents in this sample are overwhelmingly oriented toward the traditional middle-class values of family and career." From his careful study of normal middle-class high-school boys, Daniel Offer states flatly, "Our evidence indicates that both generations share the same basic values."

Despite the impressive unanimity of these appraisals, the question of value change should remain an open one. It is hard to imagine that some changes are not taking place, in view of the vast social, economic, and technological changes occurring in industrialized countries: the growth of large organizations, shifts in the occupational structure, the rapid diffusion of information, etc., etc. Yet the nature of these changes in values, if any, is by no means evident, and our understanding remains extremely limited. We simply do not know which areas of values are changing, how rapidly the changes are taking place, which segments of the population they involve, how deeply they run, how stable any of the new values will turn out to be. Many apparent changes in "values" seem to be no more than changes in manners, or in rhetoric.

All in all, the most prudent assessment we can make, on the basis of the evidence we now have, is that no "value revolution" or anything remotely like it is taking place or is in prospect; and that if changes are occurring, they are doing so through the gradual erosion, building, and shifting of values.

Pleasure

Let us limit ourselves to the two areas of pleasure where generational differences are often held to be present: sex and drugs. Is there a sexual revolution among the young? And has a drug culture established itself as a significant part of youth culture?

Announced about ten or fifteen years ago, the sexual revolution has yet to take place. Like the generation gap itself, it may be more apparent than real. Support for this statement is provided by the Institute for Sex Research at Indiana University, which has just completed a new study, begun in 1967, in the course of which 1,200 randomly selected college students were interviewed. Comparing the findings with those obtained in its study of twenty years ago, the institute reports increasing liberalism to sexual practices but that these changes have been gradual. One of the study's authors states, "There remains a substantial commitment to what can only be called traditional values." Most close students of the sexual scene seem to agree that the trend toward greater permissiveness in the United States probably began back in the 1920s and has been continuing since. Sexual attitudes and habits are becoming more liberal—slowly. We are becoming Scandinavians—gradually.

The sexual changes one notes on the advanced campuses are of two kinds. First, there is a greater readiness to establish quasi-marital pairings, many of which end in marriage; these are without question far more common than in the past, and are more often taken for granted. Second, there is a trend, among a very small but conspicuous number of students, toward extremely casual sexuality, sometimes undertaken in the name of sexual liberation. To the clinician, these casual relationships seem to be more miserable than not: compulsive, driven, shallow, often entered into in order to ward off depression or emotional isolation. The middle-class inhibitions persist, and the attempt at sexual freedom seems a desperate maneuver to overcome them. We have a long way to go before the sexually free are sexually free.

As to drugs, specifically marijuana: Here we have, without much question, a sharp difference between the generations. It is a rare citizen over thirty who has had any experience with marijuana, and it is not nearly so rare among the young, particularly those in college. Still, the great majority of youngsters—almost 90 percent—have had no experience with marijuana, not even to the degree of having tried it once, and, of course, far fewer use it regularly. Furthermore, a strong majority of the young do not believe marijuana should be legalized. What we have here, then, is both a generation gap and (as we have had before) a gap in attitude and experience within the younger generation.

It would be nice if we could keep our wits about us when we contemplate the implications of marijuana for our society. That is hard to do in the presence of hysteria on one side, among those who hold it to be an instrument of the devil, and transcendent rapture on the other, among those who see it as the vehicle and expression of a revolution in values and consciousness. In any case, the drug scene is too new and too fluid a phenomenon for us to foretell its ultimate place in the lives of the young. Drug use has grown rapidly. Will it continue to grow? Has it reached a plateau? Will it subside?

A more interesting question concerns the sociological and ideological factors involved in marijuana use. As marijuana has become more familiar, it has become less of a symbol of defiance and alienation. Lubell points out that just a few years ago the use of marijuana among college students was associated with a liberal or left political outlook; now it has become acceptable and even popular among the politically conservative. From what I have been able to learn, on some campuses and in some suburban high schools drug use is now most conspicuous among the *jeunesse doree*—fraternity members and the like—where it succeeds or complements booze, and coexists quite easily with political indifference or reaction and philistine values. To put it another way, marijuana has not so much generated a new life style—as Timothy Leary and others had hoped—as it has accommodated itself to existing life styles.

Is there a generation gap? Yes, no, maybe. Quite clearly, the answer depends upon the specific issue we are talking about. But if we are talking about a fundamental lack of articulation between the generations, then the answer is—decisively—no. From one perspective, the notion of a generation gap is a form of pop sociology, one of those appealing and facile ideas that sweep through a self-conscious culture from time to time. The quickness with which the idea has taken hold in the popular culture—in advertising, television game shows, and semiserious potboilers—should be sufficient to warn us that its appeal lies in its superficiality. From another perspective, we might say that the generation gap is an illusion, somewhat like flying saucers. Note: not a delusion, an illusion. There is something there, but we err in our interpretation of what it is. There is something going on among the young, but we have misunderstood it. Let us turn now to the errors of interpretation that bedevil us when we ponder youth.

Parts and Wholes

The most obvious conceptual error, and yet the most common, is to generalize from a narrow segment of the young to the entire younger generation. With some remarkable consistency those who hold that there is a generation gap simply ignore the statements, beliefs, and activities of the noncollege young, and indeed of the ordinary, straight, unturned-on, nonactivist collegian. And the error goes even beyond this: on the university scene, the elite campus is taken to stand for all campuses; within the elite university, the politically engaged are taken to reflect student sentiment in general; and among the politically active, the radical fraction is thought to speak for activists as a whole.

It is not surprising to come across these confusions in the mass media, given their understandable passion for simplification of the complex, and their search for vivid spokesmen of strong positions. Thus, the typical television special on the theme "What Is Happening to Our Youth?" is likely to feature a panel consisting of (1) a ferocious black militant, (2) a feverish member of SDS, (3) a supercilious leader of the Young Americans for Freedom (busily imitating William Buckley), and (4) a hopelessly muddled moderate, presumably to represent the remaining 90 percent. But we have much the same state of affairs in the quality magazines, in which the essays on youth are given to sober yet essentially apocalyptic ruminations of the spirit of the young and the consequent imminent decline (or rebirth) of Western civilization.

Not too surprisingly, perhaps, the most likely writer of these essays is an academic intellectual, teaching humanities or the social sciences at an elite university. Hence he is exposed, in his office, in his classes, to far more than the usual number of radical or hippyesque students. (And he will live in a neighborhood where many of the young adolescents are preparing themselves for such roles.)

On top of this, he is, like the rest of us, subject to the common errors of social perception, one of which is to overestimate the size of crowds; another, to be attracted by and linger upon the colorful and deviant. So he looks out his office window and sees what seems to be a crowd of thousands engaging in a demonstration; or he walks along the campus, noting that every second male face is bearded. If he were to count—and he is not likely to count because his mind is teeming with insights—he might find that the demonstrators number in hundreds rather than thousands, or that the proportion of beards is nearer one in ten than one in two. It is through these and similar processes that some of our most alert and penetrating minds have been led astray on the actualities of the young; that is why we have a leading intellectual writing, in a recent issue of a good magazine, that there are "millions" of activist students.

It is not surprising, then, that both the mass media and the intellectual essayists have been misled (and misleading) on the infinite variety of the young: the first are focused upon the glittering surface of social reality, the second upon the darker meanings behind that surface (an art brought to its highest state, and its highest pitch, by Norman Mailer). What is surprising, and most discouraging, is that a similar incompleteness of perception dominates the professional literature, that is, technical psychological and sociological accounts of adolescence and youth.

Having attended to my sorrow many convocations of experts on the young, I can attest that most of us are experts on atypical fractions of the young: on heavy drug users, or delinquents, or hippies, or the alienated, or dropouts, or the dissident—and, above all, on the more sprightly and articulate youngsters of the upper middle class. By and large our discourse at these meetings, when it is not clinical, is a kind of gossip: the upper middle class talking to itself about itself. The examples run: my son, my colleague's daughter, my psychoanalytic patient, my neighbor's drug-using son, my Ivy League students. Most of us have never had a serious and extended conversation with

a youngster from the working or lower-middle classes. In our knowledge of
the young we are, to use Isaiah Berlin's phrase, hedgehogs, in that we know
one thing, and know it well, know it deeply, when we also need to be foxes,
who know many things less deeply.

What we know deeply are the visibly disturbed, and the more volatile,
more conspicuous segments of the upper middle class. These are the youngsters with problems, or with panache—makers and shakers, shakers of the
present, makers of the future. Their discontents and their creativity, we hear
it said, produce the new forms and the new dynamics of our social system.
Thus, they allow us to imagine the contours of a hopeful new order of things
or, contrariwise, permit us visions of Armageddon.

Perhaps so, but before judging this matter, we would do well to recognize
that our narrowness of vision has led us to a distorted view of adolescence
and youth. We have become habituated to a conflict model of adolescence:
the youngster at odds with the milieu and divided within himself. Now,
adolescence is far from being a serene period of life. It is dominated by
significant transitions, and like all transitional periods—from early childhood
to middle age—it produces more than its share of inner and outer discord.
Yet, we have become so committed to a view of the young based upon conflict,
pathology, and volatility—a view appropriate for some adolescents most of
the time and for most some of the time—that we have no language or framework for handling conceptually the sluggish conformity or the effectiveness
of adaptation or the generational continuity that characterizes most youngsters
most of the time.

Young and Old, New and Old

Another common error is to exaggerate the differences between younger
and older generations. Differences there are, and always have been. But the
current tendency is to assume that anything new, any change in beliefs or
habits, belongs to or derives from the country of the young.

This tendency is particularly evident in the realm of politics, especially on
the left, where "young" and "new" are often taken to be synonymous. Is
this really so? To be sure, the young serve as the shock troops of New Left
action. But consider how much of the leadership is of an older generation;
as one example, most of the leaders of the New Mobilization—Sidney Lens,
David Dellinger, and others—are in their forties and fifties. It is even more
significant that the key ideologues of radical politics—such men as Herbert
Marcuse, Noam Chomsky, Paul Goodman—are of secure middle age and
beyond. The young have, in fact, contributed little to radical thought, except
perhaps to vulgarize it to a degree painful for those of us who can remember

a time when that body of thought was intellectually subtle, rich, and demanding.

For that matter, is New Left thought really new, that is, a product of the 1960s? I was dumbfounded several weeks ago when I stumbled across a book review I had written in the 1950s, a commentary on books by Erich Fromm, Lionel Trilling, and the then-unknown Marcuse. My review suggested that these otherwise disparate authors were united in that they sensed and were responding to a crisis of liberalism. The optimistic, melioristic assumptions of liberalism seemed to be failing, unable to cope with the alienation and the atavistic revivals produced by technological civilization.

Thus, even in the sunny, sleepy 1950s a now-familiar critique of U.S. society was already well established. The seminal ideas, political and cultural, of current radical thought had been set down, in the writings of C. Wright Mills, Marcuse, Goodman, and others, and from another flank, in the work of Norman O. Brown, Mailer, and Allan Ginsberg. That sense of life out of control, of bureaucratic and technological things in the saddle, of malaise and restlessness were, in the 1950s, felt only dimly, as a kind of low-grade infection. In the middle and late 1960s, with the racial explosion in the cities and our involvement in Vietnam, our political and cultural crisis became, or seemed to become, acute.

What I am getting at is that there is no party of the young, no politics indigenous to or specific to the young, even on the radical left. The febrile politics of the day do not align the young against the old, not in any significant way. Rather, they reflect the ideological differences in a polarized nation.

What we have done is to misplace the emphasis, translating ideological conflict into generational conflict. We have done so, I believe, because it suits our various psychological purposes. On the left, one's weakness in numbers and political potency is masked by imagining hordes of radicalized youth, a wave of the future that will transform society. On the right, one can minimize the intense strains in the polity by viewing it, and thus dismissing it, as merely a youth phenomenon—kid stuff. And for the troubled middle, it may be easier to contemplate a rift between the generations than to confront the depth and degree of our current social discord.

Present and Future

A third error we make is to see the mood of the young, as we imagine that to be, as a forecast of long-term national tendencies. In our anxious scrutiny of youth, we attempt to divine the future, much as the ancients did in their perusal of the entrails of birds. Yet consider how radically the image of the U.S. young has changed within as brief a period as a decade.

Ten years ago we were distressed by the apparent apathy and conformism of the young, their seeming willingness, even eagerness, to be absorbed into suburban complacency. We were dismayed by the loss of that idealism, that amplitude of impulse we felt to be the proper mood of the young. By the early 1960s we were ready to believe that that lost idealism had been regained; the prevailing image then was of the Peace Corps volunteer, whose spirit of generous activism seemed so much in the American grain. And for the last few years we have been held by a view of youth fixed in despair and anger.

It should be evident that these rapid shifts in our idea of the young run parallel to changes in the national mood. As we moved from the quietude of the Eisenhower years, to the brief period of quickened hope in the Kennedy years, to our current era of bitter internal conflict dominated by a hateful war and a fateful racial crisis, so have our images of youth moved and changed. Yet, we were in each of these earlier periods as willing as we are today to view the then current mood of youth, as we saw it, as a precursor of the social future.

The young have always haunted our imagination, and never more so than in the past two decades. The young have emerged as the dominant projective figures of our culture. Holden Caulfield, Franny Glass, the delinquents of the *Blackboard Jungle,*the beats, the hippies and the young radicals—these are figures, essentially, of our interior landscape. They reflect and stand for some otherwise silent currents in American fantasy. They are the passive and gentle— Holden, Franny, the flower children—who reacted to the hard circumstances of modern life by withdrawal and quiescence; or else they were the active and angry—the delinquents and the radicals—who responded by an assault upon the system.

In these images, and in our tendency to identify ourselves with them, we can discover the alienation within all of us, old and young. We use the young to represent our despair, our violence, our often forlorn hopes for a better world. Thus, these images of adolescence tell us something, something true and something false, about the young; they may tell us even more about ourselves.

12

The Psychodynamic View of Adolescence

This essay began as a more or less conventional handbook chapter, in both tone and format. In tone it was to be evenhanded; in format, expository; and to some degree these earlier intentions persist. But as we searched the recent literature, we found ourselves increasingly troubled at what seems to us to be a continuing failure to realize the potentials of the psychodynamic approach. In an oft-quoted statement made about two decades ago, Anna Freud (1958) termed the study of adolescence a "stepchild" in psychoanalytic theory. She meant that the period had not received the full attention of psychoanalytic writers, that it was victimized by neglect.

Since that time the degree of neglect is no longer quite so considerable. If one surveys sequentially the volumes of *The Psychoanalytic Study of the Child*, one finds a modest but steady increase in the number of papers devoted to adolescence. There is also now an organization devoted exclusively to adolescent psychiatry, which publishes an annual volume of papers (entitled *Adolescent Psychiatry*) covering the widest range of topics. In addition developmental psychology journals have begun to apply "affirmative action" principles on behalf of manuscripts on adolescence, so that papers dealing with the period are given something of an edge in the editorial process. All of this suggests that the unsatisfactory state of writing in adolescent psychodynamic psychology is no longer due to "neglect," that we ought to look elsewhere for an explanation. Our examination of the literature led us to believe that the problems are due to some unfortunate intellectual habits— specifically, a restricted methodology; a narrowness of range in the populations studied; and an overall parochialism in theory.

It was this dolorous recognition that led, slowly but implacably, to our decision to attempt a critical analysis of the psychodynamic doctrine, with less attention given to explicating who said what when, and rather more to analyzing these tendencies. The loss is rather less than one might imagine because there is a remarkable degree of redundancy in the literature, with B merely repeating what A said many years before or, even more commonly, B repeating himself ad infinitum, and adding very little new to our understanding. Hence this chapter is organized in three major sections: we begin with an exposition of what we take to be the core ideas of the psychodynamic approach, what we take to be the central conceptions by which those of us who are psychodynamically oriented attempt to understand and organize the events of the adolescent period; we then continue on to a discussion—rather briefer because parts of it are considered more fully elsewhere—of some new directions in the canon; and finally, we offer some comments on the intellectual constrictions that to our mind inhibit more rapid conceptual progress in this tradition.

The Core Ideas

Regression

It is by now generally understood that most psychodynamic theories are *historical*, that is, they hold that the person's experience of the present can be grasped fully only by some reference to his past. It is not an inflexible historicism because it is recognized that the burden of the past is at times so light as to be nearly nonexistent, that in many situations the person responds mainly to the exigencies or the clamor of the moment. Nevertheless, in comparison with almost all competing theories, the psychodynamic is distinctive in its emphasis upon personal history. It holds that in truly important moments of one's life one is unwittingly held captive by the past. Whom we marry and how the marriage fares; the work we choose and how well we do it; whether we have children and when and how we raise them and feel about them; when we become ill and how we survive or fail to—all these and other vital events of the life course can be understood in depth only after we have a sufficient understanding of the personal past.

To say this may seem merely to repeat a psychodynamic truism, but what is not fully sensed is the seriousness with which this assumption is held and maintained. Suppose, for example, that having a "natural" bent for the sciences, and hence being free to choose among a variety of vocations—medicine, physics, mathematics, biology, and so on—one chooses physics. In that case the psychodynamic theorist or practitioner would feel constrained to ask, why physics and why not something else?—raising that question in relation to the childhood history. Merely raising the question does not suggest that the answer will be found through a study of the personal history; it may well be that one chooses physics simply because it is at the moment prestigious or lavishly funded, or what have you. Nevertheless the theorist or practitioner would certainly scrutinize earnestly the possibility that the choice is neither "free" nor "objective," that it is in some way conditioned by unknown circumstances in the personal history—for example, that the personal or collective imagery of physics has some particular appeal rooted in one's past;

or that a significant teacher is linked psychologically to a significant family figure. The reverberations from the past are of course felt even more forcefully in such spheres as the erotic, love, and childrearing.

All this may seem sweeping enough, yet in relation to adolescence the psychodynamic approach places an even greater degree of emphasis upon personal history, for it holds that the recrudescence of the past is essential to *normal* development in the adolescent years. Here is Peter Blos (1967) in the course of a highly influential article:

> Adolescent regression, which is not defensive in nature, constitutes an integral part of development at puberty. This regression, nevertheless, induces anxiety more often than not. Should this anxiety become unmanageable, then, secondarily, defensive measures become mobilized. Regression in adolescence is not, in and by itself, a defense, but it constitutes an essential psychic process that, despite the anxiety it engenders, must take its course. Only then can the task be fulfilled that is implicit in adolescent development.

Note that the adolescent regression in normal development is taken not merely as frequent and acceptable but as universal and necessary; as a corollary, it is held that the absence of a sufficient degree of regression is prima facie evidence of a fault in development.

As we will see in a moment, the theory of regression as currently formulated leaves us with many unanswered questions: which systems of personality undergo regression, and to what degree, and under what kinds of circumstances. One sometimes has the feeling in reading the literature that the term is used in an almost incantatory fashion, to explain any and all adolescent phenomena. Yet that should not dissuade us from recognizing the presence and power of regressive phenomena at critical moments in adolescence. Perhaps the most visible—though not necessarily the most profound—expressions of regression are to be seen during the middle years of the period, between fourteen and seventeen (the ages are to be taken as approximate), wherein it is not at all difficult to discern a striking reappearance of the oedipal drama. The boy may suddenly turn surly or sullen or cocky or competitive or scornful vis-à-vis his father; the girl may treat her mother with withering scorn or her most patronizing, brittle "friendliness," or may be overcome with dark, inexplicable rages. With respect to the opposite-sex parent, the oedipal revival is generally more decorous, or more disguised. Yet even so it is not uncommon to see fairly clear signs of it: the boy displaying his muscles to his mother, or the girl reacting to her father with an exaggerated embarrassment or provocativeness, calling attention to the otherwise unspoken sexual dialogue between them.

Still, these are only the most direct, least complex reflections of the oedipal revival (which is, in turn, the most easily perceived aspect of adolescent regressiveness). Much of the time oedipal motifs are expressed indirectly, for example, in erotic or love fantasies, or in response to collective fantasy, to films or novels. In other instances the significant expression of oedipal feeling may involve displacement, via the choice of love objects (or adversaries) who represent the parents and with or toward whom acts of defiance or conquest or rivalry are carried out. Instances of this are seen quite commonly in clinical practice with youngsters, and there is no reason to believe it will not be possible to explore these phenomena in other populations as well. Sherry Hatcher (1973), for example, has provided some revealing examples of the oedipal regression in her study of out-of-wedlock pregnancy among adolescent and young adult women. She found that those who were in the "middle-adolescent" phase of psychosocial growth, as measured by psychological tests, showed patterns that reflected clearly the presence of oedipal motifs both in what led up to the pregnancy and the response to it—e.g. the baby's father was more often a married man; the conception more often took place in the parental home; it was the mother (rather than a friend or the lover) who was first told about the pregnancy; and so on. Hence the pregnancy seemed to represent an unconscious effort to live out the oedipal drama: conceiving and bearing a child by a paternal surrogate.

The most recent psychoanalytic theories of adolescence give an even greater role to regressive processes than earlier ones did; in particular, Peter Blos's phase theory (1962) postulates a sequence from early to midadolescence that involves the sequential recapitulation of preoedipal and oedipal experiences. That drive, ego, and superego regressions are frequent in adolescence seems well supported by the almost universal testimony of clinicians, and to a lesser degree supported by more carefully controlled observation; compare the suggestive evidence from longitudinal studies compiled by Livson and Peskin, particularly their discussion of work in Peskin (1972) and Haan (1974).

Nevertheless, the theory of regression, when examined closely, raises a great many questions still largely unanswered. Like much else in psychoanalytic theory, the idea of regression arises at a specific observation made in specific cases—and then universalized. That sequence, from the particular to the universal, tends in its very nature to omit variations and differentiations. Hence the theory does not yet tell us as much as we need to know about patterns and tendencies in regression: which systems of the personality are vulnerable to regression, and when, and under which circumstances. Until we take some further steps toward achieving that specificity, the theory of regression, and with it psychodynamic theory, will remain radically incomplete. A colleague of ours, a shrewd woman with a long clinical experience with adolescents, told us recently that when she undertakes clinical work with a teenager, she knows that she will uncover a significant regression or recapitulation but that she does not know what it will be—that is, she knows that the neurotic crisis of adolescence will have been brought on by a regressive episode, but it remains unclear initially whether the crisis will relate to an earlier problem in separation, or with the oedipal conflict, negative or positive, or whatever. Clinical testimony of this sort reminds us that adolescence is regression prone, probably more than any other era of the life cycle, but it does not as yet tell us much more than that.

The Drives and Emotions

Here too we have an emphasis in the psychodynamic approach that is understood widely but often not too well. One need not belabor the point that psychoanalysis traditionally has been rooted in instinct theory, and that its conception of adolescence has placed the drives and their destiny at the center. Adolescence seemed to involve a powerful resurgence of the drives, so much so that their control, via the defenses, and their transformation, via displacements and sublimation, have been the essential formula for the psychoanalytic view of the period. To be sure, the drive theory has in recent years been removed from the center of concern, but this is so only because it is deemed so well established that it need no longer be argued. Thus, in current writing more attention is given to such topics as object-attachment (the relationship to others), to the self and its vicissitudes (identity, narcissism, and the like), and to internalized structures of the personality (the superego, the ego ideals).

When we speak of the resurgence of drives in adolescence, we generally intend to connote more than the appearance of conscious sexual urges. Although these can represent acute problems, especially for boys, they are only part of the picture, and in most respects the least important part. The boy coping with *recognized* sexuality—with erections, prurience, "insane" impulses, and the like—is certainly subject to periods of profound distress, because of anxiety, shame, guilt, embarrassment, what have you. Yet as painful as these feelings may sometimes be, they are probably not quite as troublesome for the youngster's adjustment as are drives and derivatives not so easily recognized, in particular, dependency and sadism. Here again it is the regressive aspect of these drives that is the most difficult for the child to deal with, in that the instinctual upsurge threatens to revive atavistic elements of the personality, in particular, primitive oral dependencies and yearnings, anal cruelties and rages, and the like. As we will see in the next section, the task of *defending* against the emergence of these drives has for some years been understood as the central intrapsychic problem of adolescence in the psychoanalytic view of things.

The emphasis on instincts, and latterly on object attachments, has so tended to dominate discourse that the emotions intensely felt at adolescence have been somewhat neglected as an object of study. Of course, most writers do

make note of the emotional volatility of the period, that being far too conspicuous to overlook, yet there has been less attention given to a particularized
understanding of the affects, to their sources, their effects, their vicissitudes,
the defenses against them, the strategies the social order develops for controlling and channeling them. For example, no one who has worked with
adolescents clinically can fail to be impressed by the importance of shame,
and defenses against shame, in the social transactions of adolescence, the
ways in which rumor and gossip and the expectation of shame govern the
way adolescents deal with each other. The vicissitudes of shame—pride,
"shamelessness," display, mortification, morbid shyness—are central in the
phenomenology of adolescence. Indeed, we are fairly certain that shyness is
the most common "symptom" normal adolescents complain about, and one
is also struck by the frequency with which youngsters who seem to be free
of shyness are envied by their peers. Beyond that, the social system—the
family, the peer group, and such institutions as church and school—use these
and other exfoliations of shame in the course of socializing youngsters toward
"larger" social goals, or in the aim of containing and channeling the potentially explosive energies of the young.

The Ego and the Defenses

In our view the definitive account of the psychodynamics of adolescence,
both for better and for worse, is Anna Freud's characteristically lucid, succinct
treatment of the topic, written in 1958. It is worth noting that the paper places
at its forefront of concern the role of the defense mechanisms in adolescent
adjustment. In so doing, Miss Freud was, a generation later, continuing the
emphasis of her earliest contributions to this field, in which she was able to
illustrate both the defensive sides of adolescent psychology, and the pathological variations of ego functioning, by close and revealing examination of
the ego's defensive operations in the adolescent years (Freud 1936).

In the earlier discussion Miss Freud was concerned to demonstrate that the
increased urgency of the instincts produced in turn a heightened vigilance of
defense. Hence many of the peculiar aspects of adolescent behavior ought to
be understood as ways of taming the instinctual beast: the child who becomes
"ascetic," who turns away from the temptations of the flesh, and in the
course of doing so seems to have abandoned or lost the usual animal spirits
of adolescence; or the child who loses himself in the pursuit of interests that
soon take on an obsessive, even magical meaning (these days one is particularly apt to see this among those youngsters who become transfixed by
computers); or the youngster who gives himself over to one or another form
of fanaticism.

In these instances and in like others we might describe, the most efficient formula for some years had seemed to be along id versus ego-superego lines. In time that formula began to seem both thin and a bit mechanical, especially so as we began to grasp the importance of object attachments. It was gradually understood that the child's attachment to his parents, and the revival of archaic feelings toward them were the source of many of the anomalies of adolescent experience. Here is Miss Freud (1958):

> The danger is felt to be located not in the id impulses and fantasies but in the very existence of love objects of the individual's oedipal and preoedipal past. The libidinal cathexis to them has been carried forward from the infantile phases, merely toned down or inhibited during latency. Therefore the reawakened pre-genital urges or—worse still—the newly-acquired genital ones, are in danger of making contact with them, lending a new and threatening reality to fantasies which had seemed extinct but are, in fact, merely under repression.

In a penetrating and brilliant analysis of psychopathology from this stand-point—it cannot be done justice in brief compass—Miss Freud describes central forms of defense against infantile object ties. The youngster may withdraw libido suddenly from the parents and transfer it to others, to parent substitutes, or to leaders who represent "ideals," or to peers. Or he may defend himself not by the displacement of libido but rather through a reversal of affect, from love to hate, or from dependence to revolt. Or the instinctual fears may produce genuinely ominous defensive solutions: a withdrawal of libido to the self, culminating in grandiose ideas of triumph or persecution; or regression, in which there is a grave loss of ego boundaries.

The detailed scrutiny of defensive functions does not have a counterpart in an equally careful study of ego growth during adolescence. It is a period of remarkable maturation in thinking and cognitive grasp in general, and there has been an impressive increase in our understanding of these processes, yet little of this is evident in the psychodynamic literature. One sees some lip service given to the idea that the child's development in this period is pro-gressive, adaptive, and functional, as well as regressive; one will nowadays see the name Piaget mentioned, though a bit uncomfortably, mechanically. Yet the emphasis remains on psychopathology, on the psychic system under stress, and little productive attention has yet been given to the interaction between progressive and regressive ego capacities.

How this is to be done is quite unclear, given the few opportunities clinicians have to examine adaptive functioning among adolescents (or for the matter anyone else). Both the methods and the *situs* (couch, clinic) of the clinician encourage regression and the emergence of the irrational in much the same way as method and *situs* (classroom, lab) among academic developmentalists encourage an overemphasis on the rational. A division of labor has developed that is pernicious in its effect, in that the study of particular functions, such as thinking or moral cognition, tends to generate, tacitly, a model of that adolescent in which that function is dominant. Hence, the picture of the adolescent we construe from a steady reading of *Child Development* is of a youngster engaged in an implacable expansion of intellectual and moral capacity, whereas the one we will develop from a regular diet of *Adolescent Psychiatry* is of a youngster miraculously holding onto his sanity, and doing so only by undertaking prodigies of defense. Yet in truth we may be observing the same youngster through separate perspectives. Any clinician working with adolescents soon becomes aware that some deeply disturbed youngsters show no signs of difficulty in other realms of functioning, that the conflict-free sphere of the ego can maintain itself and indeed expand during periods of intense personal disorder, and not merely in the realm of special skills, such as mathematics, music, or chess, but also in areas where one would expect to observe intrusions of the personal conflict, in such areas as judgment and personal sensitivity. Such discrepancies are to be found in other stages of the life cycle but they are particularly striking when seen in adolescence, simply because at that time one can so easily observe periods of emotional perturbation along with astonishing growth in the acquisition and refinement of complex ego function.

Family and Friends

The psychodynamic theory is also distinctive in both the degree and nature of its emphasis upon the family. Other approaches seem to see the family as one institution among several, and indeed a declining one during this period, when the family finds itself competing with other sources of influence. That tends to a decathected view of the family; in some textbook writing on adolescence, much of the material is organized under the rubric ''parent versus peer influence,'' as though an arithmetic calculation of influence could capture the complex dynamics at work in the child's struggle to disengage.

To its credit, the psychodynamic view avoids such superficiality. It holds that the family by no means moves from the center; to the contrary, all of the regressive forces of the era draw the child closer to the family, dangerously close, so much so that much of the adolescent's psychological life is given over to oscillation between closeness and flight. As we have seen, the youngster finds himself beset by atavistic images of the parents, and archaic feelings toward them, both of these being essentially unconscious. That the inner world is once again so highly charged is troubling enough in itself, yet the child must also reckon with the all-too-palpable presence of those very persons who were the original source and target of those feelings. We have heard it remarked that for some adolescents, life in the family is akin to life lived on the psychoanalytic couch, in the midst of a transference neurosis. One is in the grip of erratic and at times uncanny emotions, subject to storms of affect—rages, depression, enthusiasms, and the like—that seem to possess a life of their own.

We must now mention another important element: the child's coming into maturity will often evoke equally strong regressive feelings in the parents. The child's nubility may awaken conflicted, unconscious emotions of rivalry and desire, along with a sense of time's passing and the waning of one's own power and beauty. One will often discern, even in households characterized by self-control, a certain amount of semiconscious, semierotic "gesturing" between parents and their adolescent children. How common and how significant such displays are is hard to say; we would guess that more or less "unconscious" sexual signaling between parents and children is more the norm than otherwise, and would even argue that the child's sense of himself as sexually valuable is attendant upon a certain degree of such gesturing or signaling from the opposite-sex parents. But in adolescence such display may loom larger, may seem more dangerous, may threaten to get out of hand because of the sexual maturity of the adolescent children. If that is commonly the case in "normal" households, then one can easily imagine the hothouse quality of life in more disorganized or ideologically atypical families. We have ourselves been startled, and more than once, by the degree of sexualization reported by adolescents and young adults in their families; it may be worth remembering that the first adolescent seen in psychoanalysis—the celebrated Dora—found herself entangled in her father's erotic affairs.

Yet sexual nubility and its complications are only part of the problems of the adolescent family, and in many respects a minor part. Many of the more difficult transactions between parents and their adolescent youngsters stem from the repetition, through the regression, of earlier, presumably "settled" areas of conflict. The anal struggles of childhood over autonomy, compliance, cleanliness, and the like, may be revived; or the child may be overcome by a sudden descent into passivity; and so on. It is very nearly impossible to generalize about patterns and outcomes, so various, indeed so protean are the forms of adolescent regression and the familial responses to them. In fact, it has often seemed to us that one of the common errors of clinical writing has been the tendency to generalize too boldly from the clinical observation of particular patterns of regression and response.

Nevertheless, certain general observations may be of value. First, the areas of conflict that appear in adolescence are likely to be precisely those that are, in fact, "unsettled" (appearance to the contrary notwithstanding). A struggle about, say, power and control between the child and the parents (whether or not oedipal in origin and meaning) will suggest to us that the earlier solution was either thin or false—an accommodation, or an uneasy truce. In this sense the intrafamiliar struggles of adolescence can be said to expose (often by amplifying) the unresolved issues of childhood. Second, it is important to bear in mind that although we tend to see these conflicts as belonging to or stemming from the adolescents themselves, they almost always involve the family as well—indeed, the family "system," and as we have learned more about family dynamics through psychotherapies devoted to them, we have become acutely aware how nearly seamless is the web joining children and parents so far as psychopathology is concerned. Third, here as elsewhere appearances can deceive, in that the issues that ostensibly divide child and parents will often serve to conceal latent issues of far greater significance. In particular, adolescent conflicts often tend to center upon the question of autonomy, the youngster's need to establish independence; that motif may in fact disguise entirely different conflicts, particularly the revival of archaic longings for fusion with the mother. Finally, it may be noted that in recent psychodynamic writing on adolescence it has been the recrudescence of those dangerous preoedipal attachments that has been at the forefront of attention, just as in psychodynamic theory in general we have seen a shift in interest from the oedipal to preoedipal sources of action and character.

A few words about the strengths and weaknesses of the psychodynamic approach to peer relationships. Its strength is in its depth, its ability to look beneath the surface and to perceive the murk and complication that may inform the most quotidian of human relationships, the friendship. Its weakness is in its tendency to see friendship as merely the shadow or reflection of something else, something deeper and earlier, and thus presumably more important. The reductionist bias in the psychodynamic approach is nowhere more evident than in its essentially dismissive attitude toward the adaptive function of adolescent friendship. Our survey of the literature has uncovered only a handful of studies rooted in the psychodynamic tradition that give serious attention to the role of friendship in adolescent life, and fewer still (e.g. Douvan and Adelson 1966) that concentrate upon friendship as a means through which the ego's capacities are nourished and enhanced. On the other hand, it is in this respect like all other theories of adolescence. Friendship, which looms so large in the life of the teenager, both in its presence and in its absence, remains essentially unexplored by psychology.

Some New Ideas

The Reorganization of Personality

During the past two decades or so, much of the intellectual energy of psychodynamic theory has had as its target an understanding of character change and consolidation in adolescence. There has been no agreement reached as to the best way to formulate the processes, nor is any visible. The idea of ego-identity represents one effort to come to grips with the question; another, still largely nascent, is in the attempt to develop an extended theory of the self; a third, the mainstream effort, involved the extension or reworking of such structural concepts as the superego or the ego ideal. Because these writings are discussed elsewhere, we will make no effort here to provide a detailed account. Instead we want to call attention, in general terms, to what seemed to us to be the opportunities and problems facing this aspect of psychodynamic theory.

Perhaps we can best begin by discussing a specific phenomenon in adolescent psychology: "adolescent asceticism." It is one of the clinical problems discussed by Anna Freud in her earliest observations on adolescent psychopathology, in *The Ego and Mechanisms of Defense* (1936), and it is a topic she returned to in what seems to have been her last major article on adolescence (1958). It is not hard to see why. Although it is not, in our view, a common adolescent syndrome, it is hard to imagine a better example for illustrating the instinct-defense paradigm that remains at the center of traditional psychoanalytic thinking. "Total war is waged against the pursuit of pleasure as such. Accordingly, most of the normal processes of instinct and need satisfaction are interfered with and become paralyzed" (A. Freud 1958). The ascetic adolescent will abjure not only sex as such but the activities normally propadeutic to it as well—dating, dancing, drinking, and the like. He may in fact turn away from all sources of gratification.

Yet once we begin pondering the matter, it becomes evident that the ego-id formulation, though necessary, is not by itself a sufficient explanation of what is involved. The choice of the *ascetic moment* is itself a reflection of a larger cultural or spiritual ideal. The transformation of that moment into permanence, as in the choice of the ascetic vocation (religious or political, these days) requires more, conceptually speaking, than the theory of instinct and defense can provide. It would not help us to understand St. Francis (or, for that matter, Cromwell or Lenin or Gandhi) or dozens of other personalities whose lives are or were ascetic in intention and practice. Here we find asceticism at or near the center of being; it is either the essential value of being, or directly instrumental to the achievement of some central value. It organizes character. It organizes the perception and interpretation of reality. Beyond that it persists, amplifies, and becomes permanent. Hence a full account of asceticism, or any other important tendency or constellation of character, must venture beyond an id-ego paradigm to consider those forces and structures involved in its becoming an integral and enduring feature of the personality. Furthermore, adolescence has seemed to be a particularly fruitful moment for studying the organization of personality because it is a time when old structures appear to be dissolving and new ones taking their place.

Thus in the last several decades the thrust of psychodynamic theory has to some degree moved from the explication of conflict in adolescence to the study of the origins of adult personality structure. One can discern this simply enough by examining titles in the influential journals and reviews, where we may note, inter alia, such efforts as Peter Blos's papers on the ego ideal (1972; 1974). The task is intrinsically difficult, of course, but has not been made easier by certain inclinations within the psychodynamic theory, above all its uneasy relationship to the concept of the self. The essential genius of Freudian theory at its inception involved a bypassing of the self, that is, the theory set itself against a tendency to give an undue weight to consciousness and its agencies (will, intention) as motivators of action. Until quite recently it has been more comfortable in seeing the self and consciousness as exiguous in its impact upon conduct; the theory is at its heart epiphenomenalistic, that is, holding to "the doctrine of consciousness as merely an epiphenomenon of physiological processes" (*Random House Dictionary*). As the limits of that tendency became evident—in the study of adolescence and elsewhere — psychodynamic theory began to reach out to the self, at first through extensions of the ego concept, later in the development of Erik Erikson's ideas on ego-identity (e.g. 1959), and still later in an increased concern with the sources and pathologies of self-regard, as in the work of Heinz Kohut and his collaborators (Kohut 1971; Goldberg et al.,1978).

Yet the inner conflict between what we may term—crudely—the dynamic and the structural modes of formulation have persisted, albeit unwittingly. It is of some interest to note that despite Erikson's enormous prestige in the intellectual culture at large, very little of his thinking on ego-identity has as yet been absorbed into mainstream psychoanalytic theory. To some degree this is due to the protean and at times diffuse nature of the concept itself; it is also, due, we suspect, to the problems inherent in phrasing identity itself as a source of conduct. An even more troubling and revealing event, along these lines, is that Kohut, who has developed a considerable body of doctrine on the self and its vicissitudes, has recently been rebuffed by his colleagues at the Chicago Institute, the gravamen of the charge being the departure of his theory from the orthodoxy. Leaving the Byzantine, not to say Torque-madan politics of the psychoanalytic movement aside, that action reflects a genuine though largely unrecognized intellectual dilemma: how to revise the philosophical vocabulary of psychodynamic theories so as to include an adequate recognition of the self, or at least of the events that the self theory has been developed to explain.[1]

The absence of the vocabulary and of an adequate theory of the self in action is, we feel, especially limiting when the object of attention is the adolescent. In no other phase of the life cycle do we find a more heightened awareness of self (as in self-consciousness, embarrassment, shyness, shame);

at no other time do we find quite so acute a concern about questions of self-regard. The most promising attempt to address these questions is in the work of Kohut. It has not yet been applied systematically and in detail to adolescence itself, though we can piece together from occasional comments and writings how the application would be made.

It is the Kohutian view that the reorganization of the self is the essential task of adolescence. Specifically, it is not the onset of puberty but rather a change in the self caused by a transformation of the ego ideal that sets the adolescent process in motion. The restructuring of the self is discussed in an important yet little known paper by Wolf, Gedo, and Terman (1972), who describe adolescence as a period wherein the ego ideal established in childhood is discredited and a new ideal constructed. This period of change can and often does constitute a narcissistic peril, especially where there were defects in the original consolidation of the self in early childhood. The structural and psychosocial changes of adolescence may result in some regressive shifts to an earlier narcissistic position, and thus threaten the cohesiveness of the entire personality. The vulnerability of this period is to be seen in the frequent oscillations of self-esteem so often manifest during adolescence. According to Wolf et al., friendships and peer relationships are especially vital in easing the adolescent transition. As the old idealized parental models are deidealized and replaced by newly internalized ideals, the use of ''an intense peer relationship'' helps the youngster maintain a cohesion of the self, as well as sufficient narcissistic balance, until such time as a new ego ideal can be established. Once this new structure is formed, the ''alter-ego'' is no longer needed, and is either discarded or transmuted into ordinary friendship.

In general, the developmental sequence in the Kohutian view runs somewhat as follows: a disillusionment with the parents leads to a dissolution of the child's ego ideal. In pursuit of a new ideal, transformations of the self occur. The adolescent group encourages the process of deidealization of earlier parental images through the espousing of new values. The group also offers cohesion to the self in that period prior to the formation of new guiding ideals. Because such changes in the ideal system can occur anywhere from the age of eleven until sometime after the age of twenty, Wolf et al. state, ''This would suggest adolescence is not the consequence of sexual maturation. The essential requirement for its occurrence seems to be the emergence of an inner necessity for new ideals, accompanied by opportunities encountered for such a transformation of the self.''

The Phases of Adolescence

Without question the most influential contemporary writer in the psychodynamic tradition is Peter Blos. His most important contribution, in our view, has been his account of adolescence as a temporal process extending from the latency period to young adulthood, and his patient, searching exploration of the phases within those years. It has been on the whole an admirable effort, particularly so because there has been so little intellectual support from other writers; almost all we know, or think we know, about the internal history of adolescence derives from Blos. Having said that, let us also confess to some reservations about some aspects of his work. The writing is labored—which might be putting it gently—and hence not easily accessible except to the most devoted reader. As a whole, the Blosian canon is redundant, with far too much attention given to explications of minor variations and nuances of doctrine. Above all, one is troubled by the elaborateness of the theoretical system, in view of the limited observations on which it is based; in particular one is disturbed by the facile extension of clinical observations to other populations, although in this respect Blos is very much like all other writers discussed in this chapter.

Blos begins his account of the adolescent period with a discussion of latency because he believes that the consolidation so marked during this phase is a prerequisite for the more turbulent phases that follow. Latency is characterized by sexual inhibition, and by a considerable increase in control of ego and superego over the instinctual life. Ego functions and skills are enhanced, as are the child's resources. On the whole, affect and mood are stable. This period of relative quiescence is brought to an end by the instinctual upsurge that characterizes puberty. It is here that we see the struggle between a resurgent id and reactive defenses that were discussed earlier in this chapter. In this phase the child is so intent on warding off instinctual dangers that he becomes difficult to reach, to teach, and to control.

In the boy, castration anxiety reappears in relation to the archaic phallic mother so that the male preadolescent's central conflict involves a fear and envy of the female, feelings often defended against by a homosexual defense. (It might be remarked here that this differs from the second homosexual phase in "early adolescence," wherein the same sex is taken as a love object; the homosexual defense in "preadolescence" lacks the erotic component that it takes on in the later period.) Whereas the boy in preadolescence is struggling with his anxieties about the phallic mother, the girl is defending herself against a regressive pull toward the preoedipal mother, by a forceful turning toward heterosexuality. It is she, therefore, who tends to become the aggressor and seducer. The tendency is reinforced by the fact that the girl at this stage, between eleven and thirteen, approximately, is generally taller than the boy.

In the next two phases, "early adolescence" and "adolescence proper," the central concern is the problem of object relations. In the first of these stages we see the first sign of the youngster's turning away from the primary incestuous love object, in the relationship to the friend, who is then idealized. Characteristically, a series of close, idealizing friendships occur with same-sex peers. At the same time a sustained interest in creativity tends to diminish as the child begins to grope for values that are in opposition to those of his parents. The parents' internalized moral injunctions are decathected, so that the superego weakens, and tends to leave the ego weak and self-control inadequate. In extreme cases, we see a delinquent development.

The end of "early adolescence" and the entry into "adolescence proper" are marked by heterosexual object-finding; this signals the final renunciation of the incestuous object and a decisive break from childhood. Now the adolescent abandons the bisexuality of the earlier stage, along with earlier preoedipal and oedipal attachments, turns to genitality, and chooses a non-incestuous heterosexual object. In this phase (also referred to as "middle adolescence"), we see an object-hunger developing as the youngster disengages himself from the primary love objects. The adolescent is now, as it were, in a state of "mourning." That the first heterosexual love choice is really an attempt at displacement from the primary love object is to be seen in the fact that these choices are quite frequently determined by some physical or mental similarity or dissimilarity to the parent of the opposite sex. Yet the actual parent, at one time idealized, is now devalued—a fallen idol.

During "adolescence proper" one also sees an increase in narcissism, reflected in the self-absorption, extreme touchiness, and self-aggrandizement so often observable in youngsters at this time. Though on the whole the child's movement is progressive, toward greater emotional maturity, the subordination of pregenital drives to genital primacy tends to produce instinctual anxiety, thus calling into play the rather stringent defenses characteristic of this phase—asceticism and intellectualization among others. However, at the same time we see some considerable growth of the adaptive ego processes. Cognition becomes increasingly objective and analytical; the reality principle assumes increasing dominance. The adolescent begins to think in terms of the future, though it is not until the late adolescent period that the larger questions of ego identity and futurity come to the fore.

In "late adolescence" the anxious question "Who am I?" is on its way toward resolution, as a positive awareness and acceptance of the self gradually emerges. Self-esteem becomes stabilized, emotions become more even and predictable, and a firm sexual identity is established. Thus, "late adolescence" is primarily a phase of consolidation, as the ego becomes increasingly unified in expressing itself through stable manifestations in work, love and ideology. In terms of sexual identity, by the ages of eighteen to twenty the final overt sexual choice has by and large been made, and the predisposition to a specific type of love relationship is established. The result is a new stability in the personality of the young adult.

The final phase described by Blos is "post-adolescence," which involves the implementation of the goals set forth as life tasks during late adolescence.

Permanent relationships, expressed ultimately in courtship, marriage, and parenthood, are defined and achieved. The young male must come to terms with his father image and the young woman with her mother image before each of them is able finally to move into adulthood and maturity. Strengthened by the diminution of earlier instinctual conflicts, the ego becomes totally absorbed in these life tasks. In short, the ego activity of the young adult in postadolescence is essentially involved in the final task of "settling down."

A Critical Overview

In a chapter already suffused with critique, it may seem gratuitous to end with a section devoted entirely to critique. Yet we believe that anyone reading the psychodynamic literature carefully will conclude that its growth is painfully slow, especially so in view of its potential intellectual power. To be sure, that sluggishness represents a more general state of affairs in adolescent psychology as a whole; nevertheless, other approaches have shown far greater vitality, the cognitive orientation being one example. What we see in the cognitive schools is a continuing interaction between theory and research, each reinforcing the other; and that is precisely what we now seem to lack in the psychodynamic school. There are some noteworthy exceptions—the many studies conducted by Daniel Offer and his associates at Michael Reese Hospital (inter alia, Offer 1969; Offer and Offer 1975); the work on ego identity by James Marcia and others—but by and large it is difficult to find cases wherein sustained programs of research were inspired by psychodynamic thinking and, even more important, instances in which the findings of such studies have had much impact on the theory itself. The realm of theory and the realm of empirical inquiry exist separately, and fail to recognize or support each other.

To some degree this is due to the notorious insularity of the psychoanalytic movement, which has until now provided most of the theory we term "psychodynamic." Yet that insularity, though characteristic, need not be inevitable. We find an instructive contrast in the one area where the psychodynamic approach in developmental psychology has made significant progress in recent years: the study of early childhood. The work of Mahler, Fraiberg, Escalona, Provence, and others has entirely transformed our understanding of the experience of young children in the first two to three years of life. There are several reasons this has happened, in our view. There has been an openness to new and more appropriate methods of observation and inference, involving essentially a shift to ingenious *in situ* methods of direct observation (as against earlier methods, relying heavily on retrospective accounts from older samples, or from tortured inferences derived from studies of acutely disturbed individuals). There has been a willingness to study normal along with troubled populations. There has been an eagerness to absorb findings and theory from other schools, in particular, from Piaget and those influenced by him. There has been a readiness to rely on experimentation and other nonclinical methods, the exemplary instance here being Mary Ainsworth's work on attachment.

In all vital respects, the situation has been entirely different in the psychodynamic study of adolescence, where we find on the whole a striking conservativism of method compounded by a concentration upon fairly narrow segments of the population. The primary method is the one-on-one therapeutic or diagnostic interview, a superb instrument of inquiry in and of itself, but limited and to some degree distorting unless supplemented by other methods. Even more troubling is the reliance on inferences drawn from the study of atypical portions of the total population of the young. It is obvious enough that we find an excessive degree of attention given to clinical populations— youngsters seen in psychotherapy, or youngsters whose disturbances strain the tolerance of the total community—those who are delinquent, or addicted to drugs or alcohol. What may be less obvious is the skewing with respect to social class, most of our observations being made in work with the New Class (professional, managerial, public-sector) strata of the upper middle class (whose children form the largest group of those undertaking extended psychotherapy); and with the more impoverished and disorganized strata, who are drawn substantially from the underclass or from disorganized and downwardly mobile families. What may be least obvious of all is the degree— precisely unknown but we suspect considerable—to which the reliance on clinical population has meant *eo ipso* a reliance on the study of males, leading to a psychology that is tacitly, unwittingly "masculine" in its formulations.

This skewing in the populations observed or studied has resulted in some considerable error in the theory itself. The most striking illustration is to be found in relation to the issue of "adolescent turmoil." The controversy is by now fairly familiar to those having any interest at all in adolescent psychology, but it very much warrants some brief discussion here because it exemplifies the current rigidities of psychodynamic doctrine, and some of their sources. From the beginning the psychoanalytic view of adolescent has seen it as an era marked by extreme inner turbulence. Although this conception has earlier roots in the seminal work of G. Stanley Hall, its preeminence today undoubtedly rests upon the highly influential work of Anna Freud, dating from 1936, and discussed earlier in this chapter. That view has since held and has become dogma, unquestioned in its essentials by any of the influential writers in the psychoanalytic tradition. One characteristic statement of the position holds that the five qualities that distinguish adolescence are emotional volatility, need for immediate gratification, impaired reality testing, failure of self-criticism, and indifference to the world at large (Fountain 1961). That phrasing suggests that youngsters of this age are all impulse and feeling, and very little ego or superego.

Where can such a view derive from, what observations shape it? It is clear from the most cursory perusal of the literature that the formulations are achieved through the study of disturbed youngsters. Once we turn to more ordinary groups we get an entirely different sense of the adolescent process. The "turmoil" theory has been disputed by each and every study that has based itself on a representative sampling of adolescents (e.g. Block 1971; Douvan and Adelson 1966; Elkin and Westley 1955; Offer 1969; Offer and Offer 1975; Vaillant and McArthur 1972). That this is not due to a difference in theory is suggested by the fact that most of those studies are based explicitly on psychoanalytic assumptions. It has made little difference; the steady accumulation of contrary evidence seems to have had almost no effect on the doctrinal orthodoxy.

When the psychodynamic theorist turns away from the study of the disturbed, and looks about for examples of "normality," his eye is likely to fall on those most near and dear—his own children and those of his friends and neighbors, or, if he is connected to a university, his students. In short he will tend to understand the "ordinary" adolescent through the observation of a narrow social enclave, one that tends to emphasize for its youngsters the values of "expressiveness" (as against inner restraint), of "rebelliousness" (as against conformity), and of adversarial indignation (as against the acceptance of social givens). Hence we find a continuing failure to give sufficient weight to those habitual strategies of coping found among many and perhaps most adolescents, those that involve ego restriction, and an identification with the values and standards of the family and dominant social institutions. The emphasis, instead, is given to traits and qualities well represented in the upper middle class: the intellectualizing strategy being one example; and another, the stress placed upon ideals, values, and the taking of moral positions on social issues. The issue here is not the importance of these qualities for understanding the common adolescent experiences of the youngsters of modernity; rather, it is the ready tendency to universalize what is specific to a particular social cadre in a particular historical era. One well-known psychoanalyst has written that "developing a social conscience is a universal need" (Solnit 1972). One may doubt that it is a need; one may be certain that it is not universal. In the sense in which it is employed, "social conscience" is an attitude rare or unknown during most of human history and throughout most of the world today. But it is an attitude frequently seen in the morally uneasy youngsters of a moralizing class in a historically moralistic nation. And it is those youngsters, that class, and that nation that provide the social and historical milieu occupied by most writers in the psychodynamic tradition. In the absence of methods that would expose them to more diverse strata, the result is a social and historical parochialism.

The masculine bias in psychodynamic theory, and elsewhere in the study of adolescence, is rather more subtle, more difficult to document as to its specific effects, but there should be no question about its reality. Adolescent girls have simply not been much studied. One example: a distinguished scholar in women's psychology was asked to write a chapter on feminine adolescent development for a handbook; after a careful survey of the literature she concluded that there was not enough good recent material to warrant a separate chapter. Much the same conclusion on our state of knowledge has been reached by other students of adolescence (e.g. Petersen 1978).

This neglect of female adolescents almost certainly reflects an inattention to women in psychology as a whole, at least until quite recently. But to some degree it may also reflect the fact that adolescent boys are more troublesome to society, hence more visible to the caretakers and theorists of disorder. Many adolescent boys manage internal conflict by acting out, through delinquency, vandalism, and the like. One also suspects that even the more ordinary pathologies are thought to be more troublesome when seen in boys than in girls, perhaps because life chances are felt to be more directly endangered. At any rate one is stuck by the disproportionate representation of boys over girls in the clinical literature, even when we leave aside youngsters seen for acting-out disorders. Our own informal count of psychoanalytic case studies reveals that boys are written about more frequently in a two-to-one ratio.

How this has affected the theory is hard to say with any certainty; all we can know is the state of the doctrine as it now exists, and not what it might otherwise be. But we are willing to venture the opinion that the inattention to girls, and to the processes of feminine development in adolescence, has meant undue attention to such problems as impulse control, rebelliousness, superego struggles, ideology, and achievement, along with a corresponding neglect of such issues as intimacy, nurturance, and affiliation. To read the psychodynamic literature on adolescence has until very recently meant reading about the psychodynamics of the male youngster writ large. What is particularly troubling is that the biases reinforce one another: the separate though interacting emphases on pathology, on the more ideologized, least conformist social strata, and on males has produced a psychodynamic theory of adolescence that is both one-sided and distorted.

It is hard to imagine a satisfying theory of adolescence without the strongest contribution from psychodynamic theory. No other approach can offer, potentially, a comparable depth and range of observation; no other approach is as well-suited, again potentially, to pull together evidence drawn from other sources. Yet it is even harder to imagine that happening today, given the sad state of the art. It is at the moment a fossilized doctrine resisting innovation in method, unshakably parochial in outlook. The illusion of being up-to-date is occasionally provided by the attention—excessive, in our view—given to fashionable topics: the politically active young, or new modes of pathology. That work is rarely illuminating, given an insular theory and tired, overemployed concepts—above all, the concept of regression, which is used as a universal solvent for all conceptual difficulties. We have tried in the course of this essay to suggest that what is needed is a vastly increased pluralism, an openness to new research methods, diverse populations, competing ideas. We have already seen this take place in the study of infancy and early childhood, despite far greater formal difficulties in research methodology. There is no reason to believe a similar evolution is beyond the reach of those of us committed to the study of adolescence.

Note

1. Some of these issues are taken up in an interesting exchange between Marohn (1977), offering a Kohutian discussion of several adolescent delinquents, and Giovacchini (1977), criticizing it from an orthodox standpoint. Roy Schafer's recent work (1976; 1978) represents another attempt to treat these problems.

References

Adelson, J. "The Political Imagination of the Young Adolescent." In *12 to 16: Early Adolescence*, edited by J. Kagan and R. Coles. New York: Norton, 1972.

Block, J. *Lives Through Time*. Berkeley, Calif.: Bancroft Books, 1971.

Blos, P. *On Adolescence*. New York: Free Press of Glencoe, 1962.

——. "The Second Individuation Process of Adolescence." *Psychoanalytic Study of the Child* 22 (1967): 162–86.

——. "The Function of the Ego Ideal in Late Adolescence." *Psychoanalytic Study of the Child* 27 (1972): 93–97.

——. "The Genealogy of the Ego Ideal." *Psychoanalytic Study of the Child* 29 (1974): 43–88.

Douvan, E., and Adelson, J. *The Adolescent Experience*. New York: Wiley, 1966.

Elkin, F., and Westley, W. A. "The Myth of the Adolescent Peer Culture." *American Sociological Review* 20 (1955): 680–84.

Erikson, E. H. "Identity and the Life Cycle." *Psychological Issues* 1 (1959): 1–171.

Fountain, G. "Adolescent into Adult: An Inquiry." *Journal of the American Psychoanalytic Association* 9 (1961): 417–33.

Freud, A. "Instinctual Anxiety during Puberty." In *The Writings of Anna Freud: The Ego and the Mechanisms of Defense*. Rev. ed. New York: International Universities Press, 1966.

Freud, A. "Adolescence." *Psychoanalytic Study of the Child* 13 (1958): 255–78.

Giovacchini, P. Discussion of Richard Marohn's chapter, a critique of Kohut's theory of narcissism. In *Adolescent Psychiatry*, vol. 5, edited by S. Feinstein and P. Giovacchini. New York: Jason Aronson, 1977.

Goldberg, A., et al. *The Psychology of the Self: A Casebook*. New York: International Universities Press, 1978.

Haan, N. "The Adolescent Antecedents of an Ego Model of Coping and Defense and Comparisons with Q-sorted Ideal Personalities." *Genetic Psychology Monographs* 89 (1974): 273–306.

Hatcher, S. "The Adolescent Experience of Pregnancy and Abortion: A Developmental Analysis." *Journal of Youth and Adolescence* 2 (1973): 53–102.

Kohut, H. *The Analysis of the Self*. New York: International Universities Press, 1971.

Marohn, R. "The Juvenile Imposter: Some Thoughts on Narcissism and the Delinquent." In *Adolescent Psychiatry*, vol. 5, edited by S. Feinstein and P. Giovacchini. New York: Jason Aronson, 1977.

Offer, D. *The Psychological World of the Teenager*. New York: Basic Books, 1969.

Offer, D., and Offer, J. *From Teenage to Young Manhood*. New York: Basic Books, 1975.

Peskin, H. "Multiple Prediction of Adult Psychological Health from Preadolescent and Adolescent Behaviors." *Journal of Consulting and Clinical Psychology* 38 (1972): 155–60.

Petersen, A. Personal communication, 1978.

Schafer, R. *A New Language for Psychoanalysis*. New Haven: Yale University Press, 1976.

——. *Language and Insight*. New Haven: Yale University Press, 1978.

Solnit, A. "Youth and the Campus: The Search for Social Conscience." *Psychoanalytic Study of the Child* 27 (1972): 98–105.

Vaillant, G., and McArthur, C. "Natural History of Male Psychologic Health: The Adult Life Cycle from 18–50." *Seminars in Psychiatry*, vol. 4 (1972).

Wolf, E., Gedo, J., and Terman, D. "On the Adolescent Process as a Transformation of the Self." *Journal of Youth and Adolescence* 1 (November 1972): 257–72.

Part IV
Adolescents and their Politics

13

Growth of Political Ideas in Adolescence: The Sense of Community

(with Robert P. O'Neil)

During adolescence the youngster gropes, stumbles, and leaps towards political understanding. Prior to these years the child's sense of the political order is erratic and incomplete—a curious array of sentiments and dogmas, personalized ideas, randomly remembered names and party labels, half-understood platitudes. By the time adolescence has come to an end, the child's mind, much of the time, moves easily within and among the categories of political discourse. The aim of our research was to achieve some grasp of how this transition is made.

We were interested in political ideas or concepts—in political philosophy— rather than political loyalties per se. Only during the last few years has research begun to appear on this topic. Earlier research on political socialization, so ably summarized by Hyman (1959), concentrated on the acquisition of affiliations and attitudes. More recently, political scientists and some psychologists have explored developmental trends in political knowledge and concepts, especially during childhood and the early years of adolescence; the studies of Greenstein (1965) and of Easton and Hess (1961, 1962) are particularly apposite.

Our early, informal conversations with adolescents suggested the importance of keeping our inquiry at some distance from current political issues; otherwise the underlying structure of the political is obscured by the clichés and catchphrases of partisan politics. To this end, we devised an interview schedule springing from the following premise: Imagine that a thousand men and women, dissatisfied with the way things are going in their country, decide to purchase and move to an island in the Pacific; once there, they must devise laws and modes of government.

Having established this premise, the interview schedule continued by offering questions on a number of hypothetical issues. For example, the subject was asked to choose among several forms of government and to argue the merits and difficulties of each. Proposed laws were suggested to him; he was asked to weigh their advantages and liabilities and answer arguments from opposing positions. The interview leaned heavily on dilemma items, wherein traditional issues in political theory are actualized in specific instances of political conflict, with the subject asked to choose and justify a solution. The content of our inquiry ranged widely to include, among others, the following topics: the scope and limits of political authority, the reciprocal obligations of citizens and state, utopian views of man and society, conceptions of law and justice, the nature of the political process.

This paper reports our findings on the development, in adolescence, of *the sense of community*. The term is deliberately comprehensive, for we mean to encompass not only government in its organized forms, but also the social and political collectivity more generally, as in "society" or "the people." This concept is of course central to the structure of political thought; few if any issues in political theory do not advert, however tacitly, to some conception of the community. Hence the quality of that conception, whether dim, incomplete, and primitive, or clear, complex and articulated, cannot fail to dominate or temper the child's formulation of all things political.

The very ubiquity of the concept determined our strategy in exploring it. We felt that the dimensions of community would emerge indirectly, in the course of inquiry focused elsewhere. Our pretesting had taught us that direct questions on such large and solemn issues, though at times very useful, tended to evoke simple incoherence from the cognitively unready, and schoolboy stock responses from the facile. We also learned that (whatever the ostensible topic) most of our questions informed us of the child's review of the social order, not only through what he does not know, knows falsely, cannot state, fumbles in stating, or takes for granted. Consequently we approached this topic through a survey of questions from several different areas of the schedule, chosen to illuminate different sides of the sense of community.

Method

Sample

The sample was comprised of 120 youngsters, equally divided by sex, with 30 subjects at each of 4 age-grade levels—fifth grade (average age, 10.9), seventh (12.6), ninth (14.7), and twelfth (17.7). The sample was further divided by intelligence: At each grade level, two thirds of the subjects were of average intelligence (95–110) and one third of superior intelligence (125 and over), as measured by the California Test of Mental Maturity. Table 1 shows the distribution by grade, intelligence, and sex. For each grade, school records were used to establish a pool of subjects meeting our criteria for age,

TABLE 1
Distribution of Sample by Grade, Sex, and Intelligence

	Boys		Girls	
	Average IQ	Superior IQ	Average IQ	Superior IQ
5th grade: N	10	5	10	5
Mean IQ	106.1	127.8	105.1	128.4
7th grade: N	10	5	10	5
Mean IQ	104.1	140.0	104.5	134.4
9th grade: N	10	5	10	5
Mean IQ	106.6	133.2	105.1	134.0
12th grade: N	10	5	10	5
Mean IQ	106.1	140.8	103.8	134.8

sex, and IQ; within each of the subgroups so selected, names were chosen randomly until the desired sample size was achieved. Children more than 6 months older or younger than the average for their grade were excluded, as were two otherwise eligible subjects reported by their counselor to have a history of severe psychological disturbance.

This paper will report findings by age alone (to the next nearest age) and without regard to sex or intelligence. We were unable to discover sex differences nor—to our continuing surprise—differences associated with intelligence. The brighter children were certainly more fluent, and there is some reason to feel that they use a drier, more impersonal, more intellectualized approach in dealing with certain questions, but up to this time we have not found that they attain political concepts earlier than subjects of average intelligence.

The interviews were taken in Ann Arbor, Michigan. We were able to use schools representative of the community, in the sense that they do not draw students from socioeconomically extreme neighborhoods. The children of average IQ were preponderantly lower-middle and working class in background; those of high intelligence were largely from professional and managerial families. Academic families made up 13% of the sample, concentrated in the high IQ group; 5% of the "average" children and somewhat over one quarter of the "brights" had fathers with a professional connection to the University of Michigan. In these respects—socioeconomic status and parental education—the sample, which combined both IQ groups, was by no means representative of the American adolescent population at large. Yet our inability to find differences between the IQ groups, who derive from sharply different social milieux, makes us hesitate to assume that social status is closely associated with the growth of political ideas as we have measured them, or that the findings deviate markedly from what we would find in other middle-class suburbs.

Interview

The aims, scope, and form of the interview schedule have already been described. In developing the schedule we were most concerned to find a tone and level of discourse sufficiently simple to allow our youngest subjects to understand and respond to the problems posed, yet sufficiently advanced to keep our older interviewees challenged and engaged. Another aim was to strike a balance between the focused interview—to ease scoring—and a looser, more discursive approach—to allow a greater depth of inquiry and spontaneity of response. Our interviewers were permitted, once they had covered the basic questions of a topic, to explore it more thoroughly.

The interviews were conducted at the school. There were six interviewers, all with at least some graduate training in clinical psychology. The interviews were tape-recorded and transcribed verbatim. Those conducted with younger subjects were completed in about one hour, with older subject in about one and a half hours.

Reliability

In order to appraise the lower limits of reliability, only the more difficult items were examined, those in which responses were complex or ambiguous. For five items of this type, intercoder reliabilities ranged from .79 to .84.

Results

When we examine the interviews of 11-year-olds, we are immediately struck by the common, pervasive incapacity to speak from a coherent view of the political order. Looking more closely, we find that this failure has two clear sources: First, these children are, in Piaget's sense, egocentric, in that they cannot transcend a purely personal approach to matters which require a sociocentric perspective. Second, they treat political issues in a concrete fashion and cannot manage the requisite abstractness of attitude. These tendencies, singly and together, dominate the discourse of the interview, so much so that a few sample sentences can often distinguish 11-year-old protocols from those given by only slightly older children.

The following are some interview excerpts to illustrate the differences: These are chosen randomly from the interviews of 11- and 13-year-old boys of average intelligence. They have been asked: "What is the purpose of government?"

11A. To handle the state or whatever it is so it won't get out of hand, because if it gets out of hand you might have to . . . people might get mad or something.

11B. Well . . . buildings, they have to look over buildings that would be . . . um, that wouldn't be any use of the land if they had crops on it or something like that. And when they have highways the government would have to inspect it, certain details. I guess that's about all.

11C. So everything won't go wrong in the country. They want to have a government because they respect him and they think he's a good man.

Now the 13-year-olds:

13A. So the people have rights and freedom of speech. Also so the civilization will balance.

13B. To keep law and order and talk to the people to make new ideas.

13C. Well, I think it is to keep the country happy or keep it going properly. If you didn't have it, then it would just be chaos with stealing and things like this. It runs the country better and more efficiently.

These extracts are sufficiently representative to direct us to some of the major developmental patterns in adolescent thinking on politics.

Personalism

Under *personalism* we include two related tendencies; first, the child's disposition to treat institutions and social processes upon the model of persons and personal relationships; second, his inability to achieve a sociocentric orientation, that is, his failure to understand that political decisions have social as well as personal consequences, and that the political realm encompasses not merely the individual citizen, but the community as a whole.

First, "government," "community," "society," are abstract ideas; they connote those invisible networks of obligation and purpose which link people to each other in organized social interaction. These concepts are beyond the effective reach of 11-year-olds; in failing to grasp them they fall back to persons and actions of persons, which are the nearest equivalent of the intangible agencies and ephemeral processes they are trying to imagine. Hence, subject 11A seems to glimpse that an abstract answer is needed, tries to find it, then despairs and retreats to the personalized "people might get mad or something." A more extreme example is found in 11C's statement, which refers to government as a "he," apparently confusing it with "governor." Gross personalizations of "government" and similar terms are not uncommon at eleven and diminish markedly after that. We counted the number of times the personal pronouns "he" and "she" were used in three questions dealing with government. There were instances involving six subjects among the 11-year-olds (or 20 percent of the sample) and none among 13-year-olds. (The most striking example is the following sentence by an eleven: "Well, I don't think she should forbid it, but if they, if he did, well most people would want to put up an argument about it.")

Although personalizations as bald as these diminish sharply after eleven, more subtle or tacit ones continue well into adolescence (and in all likelihood, into adulthood)—the use of *they*, for example, when *it* is appropriate. It is our impression that we see a revival of personalization among older subjects under two conditions: when the topic being discussed is too advanced or difficult for the youngster to follow or when it exposes an area of ignorance or uncertainty, and when the subject's beliefs and resentments are engaged to the point of passion or bitterness. In both these cases the emergence of affects (anxiety, anger) seems to produce a monetary cognitive regression, expressing itself in a loss of abstractness and a reversion to personalized modes of discourse.

Second, the second side of personalism is the failure to attain a sociocentric perspective. The preadolescent subject does not usually appraise political events in the light of their collective consequences. Since he finds it hard to conceive the social order as a whole, he is frequently unable to understand those actions which aim to serve communal ends and so tends to interpret them parochially, as serving only the needs of individuals. We have an illustration of this in the data given in Table 2. Table 2 reports the answers to the following item: "Another law was suggested which required all children to be vaccinated against smallpox and polio. What would be the purpose of that law?"

TABLE 2
Purpose of Vaccination

	Age			
	11	13	15	18
Social consequences (prevention of epidemics, etc.)	.23	.67	1.00	.90
Individual consequences (prevention of individual illness)	.70	.33	.00	.10

Note.—$\chi^2(3) = 46.53$, $p < .001$. In this table and all that follow $N = 30$ for each age group. When proportions in a column do not total 1.00, certain responses are not included in the response categories shown. When proportions total more than 1.00, responses have been included in more than one category of the table. The p level refers to the total table except when asterisks indicate significance levels for a designated row.

A substantial majority—about three quarters—of the 11-year-olds see the law serving an individual end—personal protection from disease. By thirteen there has been a decisive shift in emphasis, these children stressing the protection of the community. At fifteen and after, an understanding of the wider purposes of vaccination has become nearly universal.

Parts and Wholes

Another reflection of the concreteness of younger adolescents can be found in their tendency to treat the total functioning of institutions in terms of specific, discrete activities. If we return to the interview excerpts, we find a good example in the answer given by subject 11B on the purpose of government. He can do no more than mention some specific governmental functions, in this case, the inspecting of buildings and highways. This answer exemplifies a pattern we find frequently among our younger subjects, one which appears in many content areas. Adolescents only gradually perceive institutions (and their processes) as wholes; until they can imagine the institution abstractly, as a total idea, they are limited to the concrete and the visible.

Table 3 is one of several which demonstrates this. The subjects were asked the purpose of the income tax. The responses were coded to distinguish those who answered in terms of general governmental support from those who mentioned only specific government services. (In most cases the services referred to are both local and visible—police, firefighting, etc.) We observe that the percentage of those referring to the government in a general sense rises slowly and steadily; all of the high school seniors do so.

Negatives and Positives

Before we leave this set of interview excerpts, we want to note one more important difference between the 11- and 13-year-olds. Two of the former

TABLE 3
Purpose of Income Tax

	Age			
	11	13	15	18
General support of government	.23	.33	.47	1.00*
Specific services only	.23	.17	.23	.00
Do not know	.53	.50	.30	.00

Note.—*p* level refers to row designated by asterisk.
*$\chi^2(3) = 9.54$, $p < .05$.

emphasize the negative or coercive functions of government. ("To handle the state . . . so it won't get out of hand"; "So everything won't go wrong.") The 13-year-olds, on the other hand, stress the positive functions of the government—keeping the country happy or working properly. This difference is so important and extensive that we will treat it in depth in a later publication, but it should be discussed at least briefly here. Younger subjects adhere to a Hobbesian view of political man: The citizenry is seen as willful and potentially dangerous, and society, therefore, as rightfully, needfully coercive and authoritarian. Although this view of the political never quite loses its appeal for a certain proportion of individuals at all ages, it nevertheless diminishes both in frequency and centrality, to be replaced, in time, by more complex views of political arrangements, views which stress the administrative sides of government (keeping the machinery oiled and in repair) or which emphasize melioristic ends (enhancing the human condition).

The Future

The adolescent years see a considerable extension of time perspective. On the one hand, a sense of history emerges, as the youngster is able to link past and present and to understand the present as having been influenced or determined by the past. On the other, the child begins to imagine the future and, what may be more important, to ponder alternative futures. Thus the present is connected to the future not merely because the future unfolds from the present, but also because the future is *tractable*; its shape depends upon choices made in the present.

This idea of the future asserts itself with increasing effect as the child advances through adolescence. In making political judgments, the youngster can anticipate the consequences of a choice taken here and now for the long-range future of the community and can weigh the probable effects of alternative choices on the future. The community is now seen to be temporal, that is, as an organism which persists beyond the life of its current members; thus judgments in the present must take into account the needs of the young and of the unborn. Further, the adolescent becomes able to envision not only the communal future, but himself (and others) in possible statuses in that future as well.

The items which most clearly expose the changing meaning of the future are those dealing with education. When we reflect on it, this is not surprising: Education is the public enterprise which most directly links the generations to each other; it is the communal activity through which one generation orients another toward the future. Several questions of public policy toward education were asked; in the answers to each of the needs of the communal future weigh more heavily with increasing age. One item runs: "Some people suggested a law which would require children to go to school until they were sixteen

years old. What would be the purpose of such a law?'' One type of answer
to this question was coded ''Continuity of community''; these responses stress
the community's need to sustain and perpetuate itself by educating a new
generation of citizens and leaders. Typical answers were: ''So children will
grow up to be leaders,'' and ''To educate people so they can carry on the
government.'' Looking at this answer alone (analysis of the entire table would
carry us beyond this topic), we find the following distribution by age (see
Table 4).

Another item later in the interview poses this problem: ''The people who
did not have children thought it was unfair that they would have to pay taxes
to support the school system. What do you think of that argument?'' Again
the same category, which stresses the community's continuity and its future
needs, rises sharply with age as shown in Table 5.

Finally, we want to examine another education item in some detail, since
it offers a more complex view of the sense of the future in adolescent political
thought, allowing us to observe changes in the child's view of the personal
future. The question was the last of a series on the minimum education law.
After the subject was asked to discuss its purpose (see above), he was asked
whether he supports it. Almost all of our subjects did. He was then asked:
''Suppose you have a parent who says 'My son is going to go into my business

TABLE 4
Purpose of Minimum Education Law

	Age			
	11	13	15	18
Continuity of community	.00	.27	.33	.43

Note.—$\chi^2(3) = 11.95$, $p < .01$.

TABLE 5
Should People without Children Pay School Taxes?

	Age			
	11	13	15	18
Continuity of community	.10	.10	.47	.60

Note.—$\chi^2(3) = 18.61$, $p < .001$.

anyway and he doesn't need much schooling for that.' Do you think his son should be required to go to school anyway? Why?''

Table 6 shows that as children advance into adolescence, they stress increasingly the communal function of education. Younger subjects respond more to the father's arbitrariness or to the economic consequences of the father's position. They are less likely to grasp the more remote, more general effects of a curtailed education—that it hinders the attainment of citizenship. Representative answers by 11-year-olds were: "Well, maybe he wants some other desire and if he does maybe his father is forcing him''; and ". . . let's say he doesn't like the business and maybe he'd want to start something new." These children stress the practical and familial aspects of the issue.

Older subjects, those fifteen and eighteen, all but ignored both the struggle with the father and the purely pragmatic advantages of remaining in school. They discoursed, sometimes eloquently, on the child's need to know about society as a whole, to function as a citizen, and to understand the perspectives of others. Here is how one 18-year-old put it:

> A person should have a perspective and know a little bit about as much as he can rather than just one thing throughout his whole life and anything of others, because he'd have to know different things about different aspects of life and education and just how things are in order to get along with them, because if not then they'd be prejudiced toward their own feelings and what *they* wanted and they wouldn't be able to understand any people's needs.

Older subjects see education as the opportunity to become *cosmopolitan*, to transcend the insularities of job and kinship. For the older adolescent,

TABLE 6
Should Son Be Required to Attend School
though Father Wants Him to Enter Business?

	Age			
	11	13	15	18
Yes, education needed to function in community	.00	.23	.43	.77***
Yes, education good in itself	.03	.23	.20	.27
Yes, education needed in business	.40	.47	.23	.13
Yes, prevents parental coercion	.57	.47	.43	.23

Note.—*p* level refers to row designated by asterisk.
***$\chi^2(3) = 25.54$, $p < .001$.

leaving school early endangers the future in two ways. On the personal side, it threatens one's capacity to assume the perspective of the other and to attain an adequate breadth of outlook; thus, it imperils one's future place in the community. On the societal side, it endangers the integrity of the social order itself, by depriving the community of a cosmopolitan citizenry.

Claims of the Community

We have already seen that as adolescence advances the youngster is increasingly sensitive to the fact of community and its claims upon the citizen. What are the limits of these claims, the limits of political authority? To what point, and under what conditions can the state, acting in the common good, trespass upon the autonomy of the citizen? When do the community's demands violate the privacy and liberty of the individual? The clash of these principles—individual freedom versus the public welfare and safety—is one of the enduring themes of Western political theory. Many, perhaps most, discussions in political life in one way or another turn on this issue; indeed, the fact that these principles are so often used purely rhetorically (as when the cant of liberty or of the public good is employed to mask pecuniary and other motives) testifies to their salience in our political thinking.

A number of questions in the interview touched upon this topic tangentially, and some were designed to approach it directly. In these latter we asked the subject to adjudicate and comment upon a conflict between public and private interests, each of these supported by a general political principle—usually the individual's right to be free of compulsion, on the one hand, and the common good, on the other. We tried to find issues which would be tangled enough to engage the most complex modes of political reasoning. A major effort in this direction was made through a series of three connected questions on eminent domain. The series began with this question:

> Here is another problem the Council faced. They decided to build a road to connect one side of the island to the other. For the most part they had no trouble buying the land to which to build the road, but one man refused to sell his land to the government. He was offered a fair price for his land but he refused, saying that he didn't want to move, that he was attached to his land, and that the Council could buy another piece of land and change the direction of the road. Many people thought he was selfish, but others thought he was in the right. What do you think?

Somewhat to our surprise, there are no strong developmental patterns visible, though we do see a moderate tendency (not significant statistically, however) for the younger subjects to side with the landowner (see Table 7). The next question in the series sharpened the issue somewhat between the Council and the reluctant landowner:

TABLE 7
Which Party Is Right in Eminent-Domain Conflict?

	Age			
	11	13	15	18
Individual should sell; community needs come first	.30	.20	.30	.40
Detour should be made; individual rights come first	.60	.47	.27	.37
Emphasis on social responsibility; individual should be appealed to, but not forced	.10	.17	.17	.07
Ambivalence; individual is right in some ways, wrong in others	.00	.13	.27	.17

TABLE 8
Should Landowner Be Forced to Sell His Land?

	Age			
	11	13	15	18
Yes, rights of others come first	.40	.37	.63	.70
No, individual rights come first	.57	.50	.33	.07**
No, social responsibility should suffice	.03	.10	.00	.23

Note.—p level refers to row designated by asterisk.
**$\chi^2(3) = 12.17$, $p < .01$.

The Council met and after long discussion voted that if the landowner would not agree to give up his land for the road, he should be forced to, because the rights of all the people on the island were more important than his. Do you think this was a fair decision?

The phrasing of the second question does not alter the objective facts of the conflict; yet Table 8 shows decisive shifts in position. It is hard to be sure why: perhaps because the second question states that the Council has considered the matter at length, perhaps because the Council's decision is justified by advancing the idea of "the people's rights." Whatever the reason, we now see a marked polarization of attitude. The younger subjects—those 11 and 13—continue to side with the landowner; those 15 and 18 almost completely abandon him, although about one quarter of the latter want to avoid coercion and suggest an appeal to his sense of social responsibility.

The final question in the series tightened the screws: "The landowner was very sure that he was right. He said that the law was unjust and he would not obey it. He had a shotgun and would shoot anyone who tried to make him get off his land. He seemed to mean business. What should the government do?"

The landowner's threat startled some of the subjects, though in very different ways depending on age, as Table 9 shows: The younger subjects in these cases did not quite know what to do about it and suggested that he be mollified at all costs; the older subjects, if they were taken aback, were amused or disdainful, saw him as a lunatic or a hothead, and rather matter-of-factly suggested force or guile to deal with him. Nevertheless, this question did not produce any essential change in position for the sample as a whole. Those older subjects who had hoped to appeal to the landowner's social conscience despaired of this and sided with the Council. Otherwise, the earlier pattern persisted, the two younger groups continuing to support the citizen, the older ones favoring the government, and overwhelmingly so among the oldest subjects.

These findings seem to confirm the idea that older adolescents are more responsive to communal than to individual needs. Yet it would be incorrect to infer that these subjects favor the community willy-nilly. A close look at the interview protocols suggests that older adolescents choose differently because they reason differently.

Most younger children—those thirteen and below—can offer no justification for their choices. Either they are content with a simple statement of preference, for example: "I think he was in the right"; or they do no more than paraphrase the question: "Well, there is really two sides to it. One is that he is attached and he shouldn't give it up, but again he should give it up for the country." These youngsters do not or cannot rationalize their

TABLE 9
What Should Government Do if Landowner Threatens Violence?

	Age			
	11	13	15	18
Detour	.60	.63	.37	.10
Government coercion justified	.23	.27	.57	.83

Note.—$\chi^2(3) = 29.21$, $p < .001$.

decisions, neither through appeal to a determining principle, nor through a comparative analysis of each side's position. If there is an internal argument going on within the mind of the 11- or 13-year-old, he is unable to make it public; instead, he seems to choose by an intuitive ethical leap, averring that one or the other position is "fair," "in the right," or "selfish." He usually favors the landowner, because his side of the matter is concrete, personal, psychologically immediate, while the Council's position hinges on an idea of the public welfare which is too remote and abstract for these youngsters to absorb. Even those few children who try to reason from knowledge or experience more often than not flounder and end in confusion. A 13-year-old:

> Like this girl in my class. Her uncle had a huge house in _____, and they tore it down and they put the new city hall there. I think they should have moved it to another place. I think they should have torn it down like they did, because they had a law that if there was something paid for, then they should give that man a different price. But then I would force him out, but I don't know how I'd do it.

What we miss in these interviews are two styles of reasoning which begin to make their appearance in 15-year-olds: first, the capacity to reason consequentially, to trace out the long-range implications of various courses of action; second, a readiness to deduce specific choices from general principles. The following excerpt from a 15-year-old's interview illustrates both of these approaches:

> Well, maybe he owned only a little land if he was a farmer and even if they did give him a fair price maybe all the land was already bought on the island that was good for farming or something and he couldn't get another start in life if he did buy it. Then maybe in a sense he was selfish because if they had to buy other land and change the direction of the road why of course then maybe they'd raise the taxes on things so they could get more money cause it would cost more to change directions from what they already have planned. [Fair to force him off?] Yes, really, just because one person doesn't want to sell his land that don't mean that, well the other 999 or the rest of the people on the island should go without this road because of one.

In the first part of the statement, the subject utilizes a cost-effectiveness approach; he estimates the costs (economic, social, moral) of one decision against another. He begins by examining the effects on the landowner. Can he obtain equivalent land elsewhere? He then considers the long-range economic consequences for the community. Will the purchase of other land be more expensive and thus entail a tax increase? Though he does not go on to solve these implicit equations—he could hardly do so, since he does not have sufficient information—he does state the variables he deems necessary to solve them.

The second common strategy at this age, seen in the last part of the statement, is to imply or formulate a general principle, usually ethico-political in nature, which subsumes the instance. Most adolescents using this approach will for this item advert to the community's total welfare, but some of our older adolescents suggest some other governing principle—the sanctity of property rights or the individual's right to privacy and autonomy. In either instance, the style of reasoning is the same; a general principle is sought which contains the specific issue.

Once a principle is accepted, the youngster attempts to apply it consistently. If the principle is valid, it should fall with equal weight on all; consequently, exceptions are resisted: "I think that the man should be forced to move with a good sum of money because I imagine it would be the people, it said the right of the whole, the whole government and the whole community, why should one man change the whole idea?" And to the question of the landowner's threatening violence: "They shouldn't let him have his own way, because he would be an example. Other people would think that if they used his way, they could do what they wanted to." Even a child who bitterly opposes the Council's position on this issue agrees that once a policy has been established, exceptions should be resisted. "Well, if the government is going to back down when he offers armed resistance, it will offer ideas to people who don't like, say, the medical idea [see below]. They'll just haul out a shotgun if you come to study them. The government should go through with the action."

The Force of Principle

Once principles and ideals are firmly established, the child's approach to political discourse is decisively altered. When he ponders a political choice, he takes into account not only *personal* consequences (What will this mean, practically speaking, for the individuals involved?) and pragmatic *social* consequences (What effect will this have on the community at large?), but also its consequences in the realm of *value* (Does this law or decision enhance or endanger such ideals as liberty, justice, and so on?). There is of course no sharp distinction among these types of consequences; values are contained, however tacitly, in the most "practical" of decisions. Nevertheless, these ideals, once they develop, have a life, an autonomy of their own. We reasoned that as the adolescent grew older, political principles and ideals would be increasingly significant, and indeed would loom large enough to overcome the appeal of personal and social utility in the narrow sense.

To test this belief we wanted an item which would pit a "good" against a "value." We devised a question proposing a law which, while achieving a personal and communal good, would at the same time violate a political ideal—in this case, the value of personal autonomy. The item ran: "One [proposed law] was a suggestion that men over 45 be required to have a yearly medical checkup. What do you think of that suggestion?" The answer was to be probed if necessary: "Would you be in favor of that? Why (or why not)?" Table 10 shows the distribution of responses.

The findings are interesting on several counts, aside from offering testimony on the degree to which good health is viewed as a *summum bonum*. The 11-year-olds, here as elsewhere, interpret the issue along familial and authoritarian lines. The government is seen *in loco parentis*; its function is to make its citizens do the sensible things they would otherwise neglect to do. But our primary interest is in the steady growth of opposition to the proposal. The basis for opposition, though it is phrased variously, is that the government has no business exercising compulsion in this domain. These youngsters look past the utilitarian appeal of the law and sense its conflict with a value that the question itself does not state. These data, then, offer some support to our suggestion that older adolescents can more easily bring abstract principles to bear in the appraisal of political issues. Strictly speaking, the findings are not definitive, for we cannot infer that all of those supporting the law do so without respect to principle. Some of the older adolescents do, in fact, recognize the conflict implicit in the question, but argue that the public and personal benefits are so clear as to override the issue of personal liberties. But there are very few signs of this among the younger subjects. Even when pressed, as they were in a following question, they cannot grasp the meaning and significance of the conflict; they see only the tangible good.

TABLE 10
Should Men over 45 Be Required to Have a Yearly Medical Checkup?

	Age			
	11	13	15	18
Yes, otherwise they would not do it	.50	.07	.00	.03***
Yes, good for person and/or community	.50	.80	.70	.60
No, infringement on liberties	.00	.13	.27	.37**

Note.—p level refers to rows designated by asterisk.
**$\chi^2(3) = 11.95$, $p < .01$.
***$\chi^2(3) = 33.10$, $p < .001$.

Discussion

These findings suggest that the adolescent's sense of community is determined not by a single factor, but by the interaction of several related developmental parameters. We should now be in a position to consider what some of these are.

The decline of authoritarianism. Younger subjects are more likely to approve of coercion in public affairs. Themselves subject to the authority of adults, they more readily accept the fact of hierarchy. They find it hard to imagine that authority may be irrational, presumptuous, or whimsical; thus they bend easily to the collective will.

With advancing age there is an increasing grasp of the *nature and needs of the community*. As the youngster begins to understand the structure and functioning of the social order as a whole, he begins to understand too the specific social institutions within it and their relations to the whole. He comes to comprehend the autonomy of institutions, their need to remain viable, to sustain and enhance themselves. Thus the demands of the social order and its constituent institutions, as well as the needs of the public, become matters to be appraised in formulating political choices.

The absorption of knowledge and consensus. This paper has taken for granted, and hence neglected, the adolescent's increasing knowingness. The adolescent years see a vast growth in the acquisition of political information, in which we include not only knowledge in the ordinary substantive sense, but also the apprehension of consensus, a feeling for the common and prevailing ways of looking at political issues. The child acquires these from formal teaching, as well as through a heightened cathexis of the political, which in turn reflects the generally amplified interest in the adult world. Thus, quite apart from the growth of cognitive capacity, the older adolescent's views are more "mature" in that they reflect internalization of adult perspectives.

We must remember that it is not enough to be exposed to mature knowledge and opinion; their absorption in turn depends on the growth of *cognitive capacities*. Some of the younger subjects knew the fact of eminent domain, knew it to be an accepted practice, yet, unable to grasp the principles involved, could not apply their knowledge effectively to the question. This paper has stressed the growth of those cognitive capacities which underlie the particular intellectual achievements of the period: the adolescent's increasing ability to weigh the relative consequences of actions, the attainment of deductive reasoning. The achievement of these capacities—the leap to "formal operations," in Piaget's term—allows him to escape that compulsion toward the immediate, the tangible, the narrowly pragmatic which so limits the political discourse of younger adolescents.

In turn, the growth of cognitive capacity allows *the birth of ideology*. Ideology may not be quite the word here, for its suggests a degree of coherence and articulation that few of our subjects, even the oldest and brightest, come close to achieving. Nevertheless there is an impressive difference between the younger and older adolescents in the orderliness and internal consistency of their political perspectives. What passes for ideology in the younger respondents is a raggle-taggle array of sentiments: "People ought to be nice to each other"; "There are a lot of wise guys around, so you have to have strict laws." In time these sentiments may mature (or harden) into ideologies or ideological dispositions, but they are still too erratic, too inconsistent. They are not yet principled or generalized and so tend to be self-contradictory, or loosely held and hence easily abandoned. When younger subjects are cross-questioned, however gently, they are ready to reverse themselves even on issues they seem to feel strongly about. When older subjects are challenged, however sharply, they refute, debate, and counterchallenge. In some part their resistance to easy change reflects a greater degree of poise and their greater experience in colloquy and argument, but it also bespeaks the fact that their views are more firmly founded. The older adolescents, most conspicuously those at 18, aim for an inner concordance of political belief.

These then are the variables our study has suggested as directing the growth of political concepts. We must not lean too heavily on any one of them: The development of political thought is not simply or even largely a function of cognitive maturation or of increased knowledge or of the growth of ideology when these are taken alone. This paper has stressed the cognitive parameters because they seem to be so influential at the younger ages. The early adolescent's political thought is constrained by personalized, concrete, present-oriented modes of approach. Once these limits are transcended, the adolescent is open to influence by knowledge, by the absorption of consensus, and by the principles he adopts from others or develops on his own.

A Developmental Synopsis

We are now in a position to summarize the developmental patterns which have emerged in this study. It is our impression that the most substantial advance is to be found in the period between eleven and thirteen years, where we discern a marked shift in the cognitive basis of political discourse. Our observations support the Inhelder and Piaget (1958) findings on a change from concrete to formal operations at this stage. To overstate the case somewhat, we might say that the 11-year-old has not achieved the capacity for formal operations. His thinking is concrete, egocentric, tied to the present; he is unable to envision long-range social consequences; he cannot comfortably reason from premises; he has not attained hypothetico-deductive modes of analysis. The 13-year-old has achieved these capacities some (much?) of the time, but is unable to display them with any consistent effectiveness. The 13-year-olds seem to be the most labile of our subjects. Depending on the item, they may respond like those older or younger than themselves. In a sense they are on the threshold of mature modes of reasoning, just holding on and capable of slipping back easily. Their answers are the most difficult to code, since they often involve an uneasy mixture of the concrete and the formal.

The 15-year-old has an assured grasp of formal thought. He neither hesitates nor falters in dealing with the abstract; when he seems to falter, it is more likely due to a lack of information or from a weakness in knowing and using general principles. His failures are likely to be in content and in fluency, rather than in abstract quality per se. Taking our data as a whole we usually find only moderate differences between 15 and 18. We do find concepts that appear suddenly between eleven and thirteen, and between thirteen and fifteen, but only rarely do we find an idea substantially represented at eighteen which is not also available to a fair number of 15-year-olds.

The 18-year-old is, in other words, the 15-year-old, only more so. He knows more; he speaks from a more extended apperceptive mass; he is more facile; he can elaborate his ideas more fluently. Above all, he is more philosophical, more ideological in his perspective on the political order. At times he is consciously, deliberately an ideologue. He holds forth.

Note

1. The research was supported by grants to the first author from the H. H. Rackham Faculty Research Fund of the University of Michigan and from the Social Science Research Council. It constituted a portion of the second author's doctoral dissertation submitted to the University of Michigan.

References

Easton, D., and Hess, R. D. "Youth and the Political System" in S. M. Lipset and L. Lowenthal (eds.), *Culture and Social Character*. New York: Free Press, 1961, pp. 226–51.

Easton, D., and Hess, R. D., "The Child's Political World." *Midwest Journal of Political Science* 6 (1962): 229–46.

Greenstein, F. *Children and Politics*. New Haven: Yale University Press, 1965.

Hyman, H. H. *Political Socialization*. Glencoe, Ill.: Free Press, 1959.

Inhelder, B., and Piaget, J. *The Growth of Logical Thinking from Childhood to Adolescence*. New York: Basic Books, 1958.

14

The Political Imagination of the
Young Adolescent

The years of early adolescence, twelve to sixteen, are a watershed era in the emergence of political thought. Ordinarily the youngster begins adolescence incapable of complex political discourse, that is, mute on many issues, and when not mute, then simplistic, primitive, subject to fancies, unable to enter fully the realm of political ideas. By the time this period is at an end, a dramatic change is evident; the youngster's grasp of the political world is now recognizably adult. His mind moves with some agility within the terrain of political concepts; he has achieved abstractness, complexity, and even some delicacy in his sense of political textures; he is on the threshold of ideology, struggling to formulate a morally coherent view of how society is and might and should be arranged.

This essay will explore how this transition takes place. It will lean heavily, though not entirely, on the work my colleagues and I have done during the past several years.[1] We have conducted interviews with about 450 adolescents, a varied group, ranging in age from eleven to eighteen, of both sexes, of normal to extremely high intelligence, through the full spectrum of the social classes, and in three nations, the United States, West Germany, and Great Britain. About 50 of these youngsters form a longitudinal sample, having been interviewed first at thirteen and then at fifteen, or first at fifteen and then at eighteen.

Our aim was to discover how adolescents of different ages and circumstances construe the world of political action, and how they organize a political philosophy. Our early, informal interviewing had suggested that it would be best to avoid talking to our youngsters about current political realities. To do so would obviously make it difficult to compare children in different cultures, but beyond that we found that to do so risked being misled about the child's grasp of the political. The younger adolescent may be intimidated by his lack of ''knowledge,'' while the older adolescent may glory in the possession of it. In either case both child and interviewer become so mesmerized by the pursuit of facts and opinions that the quality of the child's thought may be obscured. At any rate we settled upon an interview format that offered the following premise: imagine that a thousand people venture to an island in the Pacific to form a new society; once there they must compose a political order, devise a legal system, and in general confront the myriad problems of government.

Having established this framework the interview schedule continued by offering questions on a large number of hypothetical issues. Our youngsters were, for example, asked to choose among several forms of government and to argue the merits and liabilities of each. They were asked didactic questions: What is the purpose of government, of law, of political parties? Proposed laws were suggested, and they were asked to offer opinions about them; for example, should the government require citizens over forty-five to have annual medical examinations? Problems of public policy were explored: Should a dissenting religious sect be required to undergo vaccination, or what should be done when a law is commonly violated and hard to enforce? In general we tried to touch upon the traditional issues of political philosophy: the scope and limits of political authority, the reciprocal obligations of citizen and state, the relations between majorities and minorities, the nature of crime and justice, the collision between personal freedom and the common good, the feasibility of utopia, and so on.

Let me offer here a brief synopsis of the findings. Surprisingly, it appears that neither sex nor intelligence nor social class counts for much in the growth of political concepts. There are simply no sex differences; and while there are some expectable differences associated with intelligence and social class (the bright are capable of abstract thought a bit earlier; the upper middle class are somewhat less authoritarian), these differences are on the whole minor. What does count, and count heavily, is age. There is a profound shift in the character of political thought, one that seems to begin at the onset of adolescence—twelve to thirteen—and that is essentially completed by the time the child is fifteen or sixteen. The shift is evident in three ways: first, in a change in cognitive mode; second, in a sharp decline of authoritarian views of the political system; and finally, in the achievement of a capacity for ideology. National differences in political thought, though present, are by no means as strong as age effects. A twelve-year-old German youngster's ideas of politics are closer to those of a twelve-year-old American than to those of his fifteen-year-old brother.

The Quality of Thought

The most important change that we find in the transition from early to middle adolescence is the achievement of abstractness. On the threshold of adolescence the child adheres to the tangible; he is most comfortable (and capable) with the concrete event, the actual person. As he matures, he fights free of the concrete and its constraints and begins to reach for the abstract. As an example, consider these responses given by twelve- and thirteen-year-olds who have been asked, "What is the purpose of laws?"

- They do it, like in schools, so that people don't get hurt.
- If we had no laws, people could go around killing people.
- So people don't steal or kill.

Now compare these with the answers given by youngsters just two to three years older:

- To ensure safety and enforce the government.
- To limit what people can do.
- They are basically guidelines for people. I mean, like this is wrong and this is right and to help them understand.

An essential difference between these two sets of responses—there are others, as we will see later—is that the younger adolescents are limited to concrete examples: stealing, killing, and the like. In some cases a more general principle seems to govern the concrete response, but ordinarily that principle cannot be articulated. The older adolescent, on the other hand, can move from the concrete to the abstract and then back again. Having stated a principle, he illuminates it by a concrete instance, or having mentioned specific examples, he seeks and finds the abstract category that binds them.

Several important consequences follow from the young adolescent's difficulty in managing the abstract. The processes and institutions of society are personalized. When we ask him about the law, he speaks of the policeman, the judge, the criminal. When we talk of education, he speaks of the teacher, the principal, the student. When we mention government, he speaks of the mayor, or the president, or the congressman, and much of the time none of these but rather a shadowy though ubiquitous set of personages known as "they" or "them." ("They do it, like in schools, so that people don't get hurt.") As one thirteen-year-old put it, when asked the purpose of government: "It's more or less a great leader and it makes our decisions and things of that sort."

The child's adherence to the personal and the tangible makes it difficult for him to adopt a sociocentric perspective. Because he cannot easily conceive of "society," or of other abstract collectivities, he does not take into account, when pondering a political action, its function for society as a whole. He thinks instead of its impact upon specific individuals. For example, when we asked adolescents the purpose of a law requiring the vaccination of children, the younger interviewers said that it is to prevent children from getting sick, while older adolescents replied that it is to protect the community at large.

To put it another way, at the threshold of adolescence the youngster gives few signs of a sense of community. Unable to imagine social reality in the abstract, he enters adolescence with only the weakest sense of social institutions, of their structure and functions, or of that invisible network of norms and principles that link these institutions to each other. Furthermore, the failure to achieve abstractness does not permit him to understand, except in a most rough and ready way, those concepts essential to political thought, such ideas as authority, rights, liberty, equity, interests, representation, and so on.

Once abstractness is achieved, the adolescent enters into a distinctly new realm of thought and discourse. Let me illustrate this by describing the changing pattern of responses, through adolescence, to a question dealing with the problem of minority rights. The youngster was told that 20 percent of the people on the island were farmers and that they were concerned that laws might be passed that would damage their interests. What might be done about this?

At the beginning of adolescence our subjects could do very little with the question. Much of the time they offered no response at all. Sometimes they denied, rather blithely, that there was a problem—people wouldn't hurt the farmers. Sometimes they expressed alarm, along with the wistful hope that something would be done for the poor farmers. And sometimes they resorted to *machtpolitik*: the farmers should fight, or should move to another part of the island, or should refuse to grow or sell food in order to get even. In the next phase, still in early adolescence, the idea of negotiation or communication takes hold: the farmers should talk to the rest of the people and make their problems understood. But there is as yet little grasp of institutionalized or collective means of carrying this out: an amorphous mass of farmers will somehow communicate with an equally amorphous mass of citizens. Toward the middle of adolescence youngsters acquire an understanding of the nature of collective institutions and of representation. Now they propose that the farmers form themselves into a union or some other organization, that they appoint representatives and have them petition or negotiate with the legislature. The final step takes place during the middle and later years of adolescence, when our subjects try to view the farmers' interests in the context of the entire community. They now observe that the farmers, having 20 percent of the votes, can expect to have an equal proportion of legislators, and thus are automatically represented in the government and can exercise their will through the normal democratic processes. The more optimistic assume this is done by persuasion, the more cynical suggest bloc voting, logrolling, and the filibuster.

Time Perspective

Another important change in thought involves an extension of time perspective. In the early years of adolescence the child's mind is locked into the present. In pondering political and social issues he shows little sense of history or a precise and differentiated sense of the future. The past is not seen to weigh upon the present, via precedent and tradition, nor can the child perceive the manifold and varying potentialities within the present. The young adolescent will rarely look back to the antecedent sources of the present, and when he thinks of the future, or is forced to by the question we ask him, he can imagine only the immediate and direct outcome of a current event.

During the middle years of adolescence, we begin to see a distinct, though modest, extension of temporal range. A sense of the past begins to appear. In trying to decipher the causes of a human action—as in examining the roots of crime—the youngster may speculate about the miscreant's personal history: Has he done this before? Is he known to be delinquent from his previous behavior? What was his upbringing like? When the midadolescent offers his judgments on laws and institutions proposed for our hypothetical island, he will sometimes look to the past: Where do the islanders come from? What was their earlier history? Are there successful precedents for this law?

Yet for most of our subjects, even the older ones, the sense of history is undeveloped. What is far more visible as the child passes through the early years of adolescence is a more powerful imagining of the future. Many of our questions asked youngsters to give their opinions on social and political proposals. At the entry into adolescence there seems to be little sense of the consequential; answers are brisk and brusque: that's a good idea or, that's a bad idea. Gradually he begins to look beyond the short-run impact of, say, a proposed law to wonder and worry about its long-term effect. As this capacity is consolidated, he can not only perceive the consequences of a single decision but also weigh and choose between alternative futures, that is, he can trace out the remote consequences of present possibilities: if A is chosen, then X and later Y may follow, but if B is chosen, X' and later Y' will result. Thus, when offered possibility A, the adolescent may spontaneously add an alternative B, and choose between them on the relative merits of outcomes Y and Y'. What we have here, of course, is that leap from concrete to formal operations that Piaget and his associates have posited to be the key cognitive advances in the transition from childhood to adolescence.

Motivation

The youngster enters adolescence with a remarkably thin repertoire of motivational and psychological categories available to him. He is like a naive behaviorist; he does not look beneath action to its internal springs. There is little sense of inner complication. Men act as they do because they are what they are. A man acts selfishly because he is selfish; the crime is committed because the man is a criminal. The vocabulary of motives is both impoverished and redundant. Character—character seen simplemindedly—is destiny.

All this changes very slowly. At the end of early adolescence few youngsters show much astuteness about motivation. Certainly we do not see those rapid and dramatic changes when more purely cognitive tasks are set. But changes there are: in a gradually thickening texture of psychological constructs, in the dropping out of black-white, good-evil judgments of personality, in a generally heightened sense of human complexity.

Consider the following: after a series of questions on crime and punishment, we introduced the problem of recidivism. Most people who go to jail seem to end up there again. Why? A hard question, certainly, and penetrating answers are hard to come by at any age. Yet there are clear differences in the quality of psychological inference between adolescents in the early and middle periods. The twelve- and thirteen-year-olds say such things as "Well, they don't know anything, and you have to teach them a lesson," or "Well, it is in his mind that he has to do it and keep doing it over again," or "Well, their conscience might tell to do this or something." At fifteen a deeper sense of motive is apparent. One youngster says that "going to jail produces a grudge against others," another suggests that they "become bitter or feel mocked," a third speculates that they brood and thus "establish themself as being a criminal."

The increased grasp of human complexity has an impact upon the child's apprehension of the political realm. On the topics of crime and punishment, for example, it produces the appreciation that men are subject to motivation, that if some motives may induce men to delinquency, other motives may persuade them to good behavior. Hence the child becomes responsive to education and rehabilitation, and sometimes even to psychotherapy, as methods of personal reform. Yet if he is more optimistic about human change in this domain, he is less so elsewhere, for his heightened understanding of human will leads him to a greater cautiousness, a greater skepticism about law and politics as ways of altering the human condition. He no longer, as the child does, sees men as infinitely tractable to the will of law. He now reckons with human resistance, with the human tendency to resist authority. The very young adolescent, limited to an empty-organism model of the person, sees men as malleable, as yielding easily, even willingly, to authority; the older adolescent sees law as only one resort among many, and comes to recognize that indirection and inducement also serve as vehicles of social change.

Modes of Reasoning

One hesitates to say boldly that the young adolescent cannot reason about political problems, and yet one hesitates equally to say that he does. At the beginning of adolescence discourse is often so stark, so naked of embellishment, qualification, or nuance, that the listener cannot tune in, not confidently, to the modes of reasoning that may underlie and govern discourse. Given a problem to reason through, our younger interviewees, if they answered at all—and much of the time they could not—seemed to jump at the answer. Even when the answer was plausible—and much of the time it was not—it allowed little sense of the reasoning processes involved. A good deal of the time, then, the logical processes influencing response seemed entirely tacit, or solutions were, apparently, arrived at by an essentially intuitive logic, through some spoken, unstatable framework of conviction.

Furthermore, one must reckon in this age group with an occasional descent into sheer confusion. What is one to make of the following statement? The young man, thirteen years old, has been asked why a certain law, forbidding the smoking of cigarettes on the island, has proved difficult to enforce: "Because people who are used to it now . . . well that would be awful. Then people would go ahead and drive around, but you could see it. Well maybe you could have no newspapers, but then all the people in the newspaper business would go bapoof.'' What has happened here? Apparently, he begins by wanting to say that those who are habituated to smoking are unable to stop, but for some reason he does not complete the thought. He then introduces automobiles, and in all likelihood he means to say that cigarette smoking can be carried out surreptitiously and automobile driving cannot. But the next statement, on newspapers, simply eludes understanding; newspapers have never been mentioned in the interview. Is he referring to newspaper advertising of cigarettes? Or to the prohibition of newspapers? Who can tell? Statements such as these, marked by a certain looseness of association, probably reflect the effects of anxiety upon the unready cognitive capacity of the young adolescent. This is an occasional, though not a common phenomenon in this age group; most young adolescents, unable to answer a question, remain mute, or answer monosyllabically or evasively. It is, however, quite uncommon among adolescents past the age of fifteen.

The significant transition in reasoning during the early years of adolescence involves the acquisition of a hypothetico-deductive capacity. We have already alluded to one example of this capacity in discussing the extension of temporal range: the ability to anticipate the remote consequence of a decision. A closely related variant is in the appearance of cost-benefit modes of reasoning, wherein the youngster, pondering the pros and cons of a political choice, can examine and compare explicitly the utilities involved. What are the costs to each party and what are the gains? The calculus of costs and gains will control the decision. Here, for example, are two bright fifteen-year-olds answering a question on eminent domain. The government on the island, they have been told, needs some land to construct a highway; the landowner is unwilling to sell. Who is right, and what is to be done?

> Well, maybe he owned only a little land if he was a farmer, and even if they did give him a fair price, maybe all the land was already bought on the island that was good for farming or something, and he couldn't get another start in life if they did buy it. Then maybe in a sense he was selfish because if they had to buy other land and change the direction of the road, why of course then maybe they'd raise the taxes on things cause it would cost more to change directions from what they already have planned.

> If it's a strategic point like the only way through a mountain maybe without tunneling, then I'm not too sure what I'd do. If it's a nice level stretch of plain that if you didn't have it you'd have to build a curve in the road, I think the government might go ahead and put a curve in the road.

Prior to the emergence of hypothetico-deductive reasoning, problems such as these are handled, when they are handled at all, by a brusque, simplistic decisiveness—affirmations and negations. Later on we see, as in these extracts, the appearance of the *conditional mode*; such locutions as "if" and "it depends upon" begin to dominate discourse on decisions. The youngster avoids either-or positions and thinks in terms of contingencies; the hard-and-fast absolutism of childhood and the first years of adolescence gives way to moral and conceptual relativism. Furthermore, the youngster begins to resist the either-or alternatives proposed by our questions. He *breaks set*, that is, he challenges the assumptions, tacit and otherwise, contained in the inquiry. Should the government do A or do B, we ask. Now he may say "neither," and suggest amendment, or compromise, or some entirely new solution that bypasses or transcends the terms of the question.

Let me conclude this section by a close analysis—an *explication du texte*, as it were—of a single response given by a fourteen-year-old boy, a child who has, cognitively speaking, put childish things away. The response is by no means representative, far from it, but it illustrates and highlights the conceptual achievements that separate early and later adolescent political thought. The question asked was "What would happen if there were no laws?" I will treat each sentence of the answer separately.

1. *At first people would do as they pleased.* This is the conventional response to this question—a vision of self-indulgence and perhaps worse. But note

the "at first," which suggests that he has already begun to look beyond the immediate.

2. *But after a while someone or some party would come to power and impose laws, probably stricter ones than before.* He does indeed look past the immediate to remote, second-order consequences. What makes this statement unusual—in fact, unique in our experience of this age—is that it shows a grasp of social dynamics, in the suggestion that a period of anarchy would be followed by a period of stricter social control. He seems to be positing a kind of Newtonian social principle, that an action may generate an equal and opposing reaction, that reformation breeds a counter equal and opposing reaction, that reformation breeds counterreformation.

3. *But a lot would depend upon the kind of society it was.* The conditional mode is brought into play. Also note the close connection he sees between law and society. Unlike younger adolescents he views law not as a given, unrelated to the social matrix, but as an integral expression of the social system.

4. *Some societies have a strict etiquette, like in ancient China, I think it was, where people were afraid to lose their place in society, because if they did something wrong everyone would look down on them.* An extraordinary statement, for several reasons. It breaks the set provided by the question, that is, it challenges the tacit assumption that laws are necessary for social control. It does so via an attempt at comparative sociology—*autre temps, autre moeurs.* The allusion to a distant and alien culture (and note the use of history) is employed to illuminate the relativism of social forms. The statement brings together the idea of informal social constraint with the idea of a legal code, and sees them as equivalent methods of control. It bespeaks the presence of a concept of social hierarchy, and beyond that the understanding that caste or class relations can compel conduct.

The Decline of Authoritarianism

Unless and until one has spoken at some length to young adolescents, one is not likely to appreciate just how bloodthirsty they can be. Herewith, some excerpts from interviews with three thirteen-year-old boys on crime, punishment, and rehabilitation.

- On the best reason for sending people to jail: "Well, these people who are in jail for about five years and are still on the same grudge, then I would put them in for triple or double the time. I think they would learn their lesson then."
- On how to teach people not to commit crimes in the future: "Jail is usually the best thing, but there are others. . . . In the nineteenth century they used to torture people for doing things. Now I think the best place to teach people is in solitary confinement."

• On methods of eliminating or reducing crime: "I think that I would . . . well like if you murder somebody you would punish them with death or something like this. But I don't think that would help because they wouldn't learn their lesson. I think I would give them some kind of scare or something."

Let me confess that I have chosen some unusually colorful examples; our youngsters were not typically quite so Grand Guignol, so Queen of Hearts in language. But the outlook expressed in these excerpts is entirely characteristic of younger adolescents when talking about law and order. Though they have a rough sense that the punishment should fit the crime, their view of that arithmetic leads them to propose draconian measures even for innocuous misdeeds. If crime is to be stamped out, anything goes, and so they are ready to support elaborate and indeed Orwellian measures of control. To the question on what to do when a law prohibiting cigarette smoking is commonly violated, some of our younger subjects suggested, *inter alia*, such methods as hiring police informers, secreting spies in the closets of peoples' homes, and, yes, providing an elaborate network of closed-circuit television monitors in both public and private places. To achieve communal decorum, young adolescents are disposed simply to raise the ante: more police, stiffer fines, longer jail sentences, and, if need be, executions. To a large and various set of questions on crime and punishment, they consistently propose one form of solution: punish, and if that does not suffice, punish harder. At this age the child does not ordinarily conceive that wrongdoing may be a symptom of something deeper, or that it may be inhibited by indirect means. The idea of reform and rehabilitation through humane methods is mentioned by only a small minority at the outset of adolescence.

The young adolescent's views on crime and punishment reflect a more general, indeed a pervasive authoritarian bias. There is in fact no topic we explored that is free of that bias; wherever the child's mind turns—government, law, politics, social policy—we find it. Furthermore, at the onset of adolescence we find it in both sexes, in all social classes, and in the three nations we studied. It is, in short, a ubiquitous feature of early adolescent political thought.

Consider once again that set of interview excerpts on the purpose of law that initiated the discussion of cognition. In the sample of thirteen-year-olds we observe an exclusive emphasis upon constraint. The purpose of law is to keep people from bad behavior. At fifteen years the stress on restriction, though still present, is distinctly diminished. Now the youngster will far more often advert to the beneficial functions of law; it provides guidelines, he may say, or it ensures safety. An essentially similar pattern appears when we ask youngsters to describe the purpose of government. At the earlier ages they are more likely to answer in terms of constraint: government, they say, "prevents chaos," or it provides "better order in the city," or it keeps "the country from doing anything it pleases." In midadolescence there is a clear shift to the positive: government is now seen as "ensuring freedom," or fostering equality, or organizing efficient services.

What accounts for the authoritarian animus among the young? They are, to begin with, preoccupied by human wickedness. They see men as tending naturally toward the impulsive and the anarchic. They are Hobbesian: it is the war of all against all. They do not seem to have much faith in—or perhaps they do not cognize adequately—the human capacity for self-control, or the demands of conscience.

A second source, related to the first, is an ingenuous belief in the goodness and justice of authority. The young adolescent does not spontaneously imagine that authority might be capricious, arbitrary, or mistaken. He takes much the same position toward law. His first inclination—and his second and third— is to support any law, even when he is not altogether clear about its purposes. The underlying attitude seems to be that if a law is passed, or even proposed, there must be some good reason for it. And if the state makes a demand upon its citizens, it is their duty to obey because solely benign (though perhaps inscrutable) motives actuate the state. In the early years of adolescence the child's orientation to government and law is trusting, uncritical, acquiescent. He transfers to these realms the habits of trust and obedience he has acquired in school and at home. (Interestingly enough, partisan politics does not share this exemption from critique. More often than not our youngsters tended to be cloudy about parties and the party system, but vaguely suspicious and uneasy. "Politics" in this sense is often associated with dispute—the prevailing images are of contention and acrimony. It is as though government and law partake of the sacred, while partisan politics are worldly, secular, and thus potentially corrupt.)

Another source of authoritarian attitude is the child's inability to grasp the idea of rights. It is too abstract, too evanescent a notion for the young adolescent fully to understand. It is only in the middle and, often, the later years of adolescence that the concepts of individual (and minority) rights are firmly entrenched. One example among several: we asked whether the government should require men over forty-five to undergo annual medical examination. Most younger subjects deem this a splendid idea; it is not until late in adolescence that youngsters (and even then only a minority) understand that a principle might be involved, that the citizen's rights of privacy and self-determination might outweigh the tangible benefits of the medical checkup. The young adolescent responds affirmatively to evident good. If what the state proposes, or demands, is visibly, concretely beneficent, he cannot look beyond or beneath to more remote and abstract violations of principle. Should the government require all houses to be painted every five years? Only older adolescents suggest that this law might represent an excessive degree of interference by the state. Should the government insist upon the vaccination of members of religious groups opposed to it? Only the older adolescents are troubled by the idea of state intrusion upon religious principles.

Finally, the child's authoritarianism can be seen to stem from a certain conservatism of mind, which leads him to view values and institutions as fixed and immutable. He does not readily imagine those processes of change, planned and unplanned, that characterize social and political phenomena. What is, has been; what is, will be. Perhaps the clearest expression of this disposition is to be seen in the moral absolutism we mentioned earlier. Moral judgments at this age are marked by a blessed simplicity. Good and evil do not vary over time or between situations, and we see little of the moral relativism that will later complicate clear conviction.

So much may be obvious, but what may be less apparent is that a similar habit of mind dominates the child's perception of social and political institutions. One of our most interesting findings is that the young adolescent does not spontaneously entertain the concept of amendment. If you suggest to him that a law is not working out as expected, he will likely propose that it be enforced more rigorously. He may also suggest, though far less often, that it be abolished. But he will almost never conceive that it can be altered to make it more effective. What it amounts to is that at the onset of adolescence the child cannot think of human actions as provisional, tentative, empirical. He has little sense that social and political decisions are responsive to trial and error. He does not see the realm of government as subject to invention, and thus to experiment, to tinkering, to trying out. It is as though law (and other human artifacts), like the Decalogue, descended from the mountaintop. Once given, once announced, the citizen's duty is to submit and obey.

At fourteen, fifteen, and beyond, the youngster's mood begins to be critical and pragmatic. Confronting a proposal for law or for a change in social policy, he scrutinizes it to determine whether there is more to it than meets the eye. Whose interests are served, whose are damaged? He asks these questions not out of a reflexive suspiciousness but because he weighs heavily, as the younger adolescent does not, the obstacles between the will and the act. He senses that law and social policy must take account of the dead hand of the past, entrenched privilege, human stubbornness, the force of habit. He now understands that law and policy must accommodate competing interests and values, that ends must be balanced against means, that the short-term good must be appraised against latent or long-term or indirect outcomes.

To sum up, the young adolescent's authoritarianism is omnipresent. He has only a dim appreciation of democratic forms (for example, he is more likely to favor one-man rule as against representative or direct democracy);

he shows little sensitivity to individual or minority rights; he is indifferent to the claims of personal freedom; he is harsh and punitive toward miscreants; his morality is externalized and absolutistic. The decline and fall of the authoritarian spirit is, along with the rapid growth in abstractness (to which it is related), the most dramatic developmental event in adolescent political thought. Lynnette Beall developed an index of authoritarianism based on our interview items. At the threshold of adolescence a remarkable 85 percent of our subjects are high on the index; by the senior year in high school only 17 percent score in the high range.

Ideology and Utopia

It is commonly assumed that adolescence is a period marked by political idealism, a preoccupation with utopian reconstructions of society, and a disposition toward the formulation of ideologies. We hear it said that the youngster, once he discovers politics as a vehicle for the free exercise of mind, leaps exuberantly into its possibilities, into ideation, speculation, fantasy, into the building of brave new doctrines and worlds. A utopian impulse, fed by idealism and by newly won cognitive capacities, captures the adolescent imagination. The youngster then gives himself over, both in the privacy of thought and in excited exchange with like-minded friends, to the criticism of current institutions and the search for a more just society.

In plain fact, and for better or worse, nothing very much like this takes place among the great majority of adolescents. Why we think it does is a puzzle: perhaps we remember (and perhaps falsely) our own exceptional lives in adolescence; or perhaps we are attracted by those rare and spectacular instances of precocity in the fraction of articulate, politically engaged adolescents, and then generalize to the total body of the young. Be that as it may, the evidence we have speaks to the contrary. Utopian ideals are not only uncommon in adolescence, the mood of most youngsters is in truth firmly antiutopian. As to idealism, though it is present, it is by no means modal, let alone universal, and is less common than skepticism, sobriety, and caution as a characteristic political affect. As to ideology, with which I will begin, that is a most complicated matter.

The root of the complication is that we may adopt either a weak or a strong definition of *ideology*. By the latter we mean a highly structured, hierarchically ordered, internally consistent body of general principles from which specific attitudes follow. Used in this strong sense, the ideological capacity in adolescence is extremely rare, almost never found before the later years of high school, and even then only among the most intelligent, intellectually committed, and politically intense. In a weak definition, we construe *ideology* to involve the presence of attitudes roughly consistent with one another, and more or less organized in reference to a more encompassing, though perhaps tacit, set of political principles. Used in this sense, ideology is dim or absent at the beginning of adolescence, and the criteria for achieving ideology are apparent only during the middle period. It is in the latter sense that I will use the term.

It should be clear that the child cannot achieve a personal ideology, even in the most modest sense, until he has acquired and to some degree mastered the cognitive skills of the stage of formal operations. He must be able to manage abstractness; he must be able to synthesize and generalize his observations beyond the specific instance; he must be able to transcend the present and imagine the future. So much we have already seen, and now we must add another vital quality: the mastery of principles.

At the onset of adolescence, the youngster's grasp of principle is dim, erratic, shifting. Much of the time, of course, he is simply unaware of the principles that might govern a political decision, but even when he is aware, his command is too uncertain, too unsteady to allow him to bring it to bear on the specific instance. We see examples of this in the early adolescent's penchant for political catchphrases and slogans, which generally serve as a substitute for and approximation of the general principles he senses are relevant but does not truly grasp. To a question on voting the child will say, brightly and confidently, "The majority rules," and a moment later we learn that by majority he means unanimity. Or he may allude solemnly to "freedom of speech," and shortly thereafter call for the total abridgment of dissent. In these and like instances the child senses that a given class of political decisions is controlled by or subsumed under some governing principle, but his mind cannot fully contain the principle or cannot articulate the connection between the specific case and the controlling generality. The cognitive failure or slippage leads him to flail about until he finds an apparently relevant phrase that relates to and stands in place of the more vaguely sensed principle.

The steady advance of the sense of principle is one of the most impressive phenomena of adolescent political thought. Once acquired, it spells an end to the sentimentality that so often governs the young adolescent's approach to political issues; it allows the child to resist the appeal of the obvious and the attractive, particularly where individual or communal *rights* are concerned. Our youngest subjects are so often capricious about individual rights not merely because they idealize authority but also because they have so little sense of those principles that should limit the sway of government. Confronted with an appealing proposition, the younger adolescent proclaims brightly that it "sounds like a real good idea"—a recurring phrase, by the way—and cannot look beyond immediate advantages to discern violations of principle. The same tendency can be found in the opposite direction, in that the child will favor the individual against the government when the former's case is immediate and attractive and the latter's is based on principle. To our question on eminent domain, for example, younger subjects favored the landowner because his case was concrete and attractive, and showed little recognition of the parallel rights of the community.

Knowledge

The growth of ideology in adolescence also feeds upon the child's rapid acquisition of political knowledge. By *knowledge* I mean more than the dreary "facts"—for example, on the composition of county government—that the child learns, or better, is exposed to in the conventional civics course taught to most U.S. ninth graders. Nor by *knowledge* do I mean only information on current political realities. Aside from these facets of knowledge the adolescent also absorbs, often unwittingly, a feeling for those many unspoken assumptions about the political system that make up the common ground of understanding—such matters as what is "appropriate" for the state to demand of its citizens, and vice versa, or the "proper" relationship of government to subsidiary social institutions, such as the schools and churches. Much of the naivete that characterizes the younger adolescent's grasp of politics stems not from an ignorance of "facts" but from an incomplete apprehension of the common conventions of the system, of what is and is not customarily done, and of how and why it is or is not done.

And yet, while I would not want to scant the significance of increased knowledge in the forming of adolescent ideology, let me also say that over the years I have become progressively disenchanted about its centrality, and have come to believe that much current work in political socialization, by relying too heavily on the apparent acquisition of knowledge, has been misled about the tempo of political understanding in adolescence. Just as the young child can count many numbers in series and yet not grasp the principle of ordination, so may the young adolescent have in his head many random bits of political information without a secure understanding of those concepts that would give order and meaning to the information.

Like a magpie, the child's mind picks up bits and pieces of data. If you encourage him, he will drop these at your feet: Republicans and Democrats and the tripartite division of the federal system and Nixon and Agnew and Kennedy and, if he is prodigal enough, the current secretary of labor and the capital of North Dakota. But without the integumental function that concepts and principles provide, the data remain fragmented, random, disordered.

Cathexis

To this point I have emphasized—to put it mildly—the cognitive component of the adolescent's political imagination. That side of things is, after all, the most visible, the most easily discerned and measured, and no one conversant with adolescent thought can escape the compelling force of the child's rapid growth in sheer understanding. But clearly there is another aspect to the growth of ideology: the youngster's increasing investment in matters political. For the typical young adolescent, politics is personally remote. Though he answers your questions politely, even earnestly, it is quite clearly, one senses, alien territory. He wants to please you, he wants to get the answers "right," but aside from that he is essentially indifferent to the political world. By the middle period of adolescence this indifference—perhaps neutrality is a better word—has given way, at least in some cases, to a more keenly felt sense of connection to the political. There is less distance between the cognizing, valuing self and the realm of politics. What accounts for this change?

Clearly, no single thing. The various events of the adolescent experience accumulate and interact to move the child toward a cathexis of the political. His growing intellectual facility stimulates interest, and the political, now cognitively accessible, becomes comfortable and, beyond that, engaging. In turn, interest can be the engine of intellectual growth; the cathecting of the political stimulates and challenges the child's mind, activating heretofore latent capacities for formal thought in the political vein. Add to this an obvious but most important fact: the youngster's increased sense of autonomy, his anticipation of adulthood, his rehearsal of mature modes of self-definition, among which is the readiness for citizenship, and with it the need to have opinions, make judgments, discourse on the world of affairs.

These are the normative pressures and opportunities that move all adolescents toward a greater investment in political ideas; all children experience and respond to them. Yet there are profound individual differences in political cathexis. Some youngsters, even of fifteen, seem deeply involved in political talk and thinking; most do not. To some degree this difference reflects general intellectual capacity and interest, but there are many exceptions. Some of our most astute interviewees at this age seem largely disengaged affectively. One of the most advanced interviews I have ever done was with a fourteen-year-old who showed a remarkable grasp of political concepts and information. He told me, for example, that he had been reading Trotsky's *History of the Russian Revolution* and could discuss it intelligently. Yet he did not read any newspaper, nor did he watch television news, nor did he discuss politics with family or friends. He said he found politics "boring." On the other hand, a fifteen-year-old much given to long-winded and dogmatic assertions of political opinion, many of them eccentric (among other things, he has given serious thought to being dictator of the world), showed only modest attainments in political cognition. Such anomalies abound in the middle period. Youngsters show surprising gaps in knowledge, and between levels of understanding from one topic to another, and one also can find astonishing discrepancies between cathexis and cognition.

And yet we can venture some generalizations about those youngsters intense about politics and striving toward ideology. The most apparent common denominator is their origin in families that are politically active and for whom politics is morally passionate. The youngster takes not only the direction of political thought from his parents but also their moral intensity. It is an unusual phenomenon in the adolescent population, but a memorable one when it appears, and we find it on both Left and Right. On the Right the religious component in politics is often not far from the surface; politics is only moderately displaced from piety. One of our adolescents, the daughter of a John Birch Society leader, in fact made little distinction between political goals and the fundamentalist values she held; both were oriented toward the assurance of order and the reduction of wickedness. On the Left, political earnestness seems more a substitution for than a mere extension of the religious impulse. We find here a politics dominated by guilt, where the themes of restitution and atonement command the political perceptions. In a sense, however, both Right and Left politics are dominated by guilt. In the former case, the moral impulse is largely externalized and others must be coerced into goodness; in the latter, an internalized sense of guilt, an aching sense of one's own unmerited privilege, is dominant, at least initially, although in many cases (as these last years remind us) the moral passion is ultimately directed toward external enemies. We note in these cases a decided absence of playfulness, irony, or detachment, at least when politics is discussed. Politics has come under the sway of the superego. Whatever losses and gains may follow from this state of affairs, there can be no question that among the consequences are a heightened attention to the political, some considerable precocity of attitude, an early crystallization of belief, and a strong sense of family unity.

We now approached the important but difficult topic of ideology's connection with psychodynamics. It is difficult first because we made no systematic effort to explore personality, and beyond that because both ideology and personality at this age seem too fluid, too shifting to allow us more than the most hesitant of impressions. But let me venture one impression: a certain consistency of motif, based in part upon psychodynamics, dominates the political thought of certain adolescents in the middle period. There is, for example, a politics of dependency (found with unusual frequency in the German sample, as we will see later), in which the imagined and described political world is organized around the idea of government as a succoring parent and the citizen as a receptive child. There is a politics of envy, of resentment, dominated by the conviction that the high and mighty unjustly retain the world's resources for themselves. And there is a politics of power, in which we can discern a preoccupation with domination and control. These themes—guilt, dependency, envy, power, and no doubt others— seem to emerge from an interaction between salient values in the child's milieu and certain dispositions in personality. When felt strongly enough they order the political perceptions and provide a framework for the organization of ideology.

Let me offer a brief example. The young man in question was one of the longitudinal sample, interviewed first in the ninth grade, then three years later as a high school senior. He is one of the two or three most intelligent adolescents in the entire sample; at fifteen his views are unusually well developed. Unlike most of our highly intelligent youngsters, there is nothing in the least liberal about his opinions. He expects to become a scientist, like his father, who is a manager of scientists working in the defense industry and a Goldwater-style Republican; he has, he tells us, taken over his father's political ideas. Government is too powerful, too intrusive; it has stifled autonomy and initiative. So he believes, or believes he believes. Once the interview is under way, however, it becomes evident, in the way he talks about the specific problems that the interview proposes, that he cherishes not the government's weakness but the government's strength. He wants the government to be efficient, tough, powerful. He is the consummate technocrat: hard-headed, "rational," scornful of human muddle, disdainful of the incompetent. Though he will not say so, not at this time, one senses that he yearns for an engineered society.

At eighteen he tells us that he has thought out a scheme for governing society. He has, in fact, developed a fully elaborated utopia. (He is the only adolescent we have ever interviewed to do so.) It is based upon a science-fiction novel he once read, and he has since made his own improvements on the germinal idea. In his ideal society, political power would be completely in the hands of an elite whose nature seems partly militaristic, partly technocratic. The governing class would be self-selected. Young men would volunteer for a five-to-ten-year period of service and training, during which they would undergo tests of courage, submission, and discipline. They would also be trained for political and technical leadership, and would enter the ruling class upon successful completion of the regime. The common people, being well served by their leaders, would devote themselves only to leisure and self-realization, and would not need to bother with politics, policy, or planning.

We have here an example—an unusually choice one, as it happens—of the growth of ideology, of some of its determinants, and of its consistency over time. We note a well-developed identification with the father, one that draws our young man toward a technocratic political ideal; social problems will vanish when in the hands of a tough-minded, scientifically trained, quasi-monastic elite, a kind of Knights Templar of the twenty-first century. We see an emphasis on submission and sacrifice, upon the testing of the self by trials of devotion, upon the ritual initiation into maturity—all the archetypical concerns of some forms of adolescent idealism. Above all, we observe the persistence of the theme of power. At the age of fifteen it is relatively muted, a tendency, a bias, not yet clearly an ideology; at eighteen the ideal of power has flowered into a carefully elaborated fantasy of totalitarian control, one in fact not far removed in some of its details (as in the two-tiered caste system) from *Brave New World*.

I want to stress again how nearly singular the case is. It was, as I have mentioned, the only fully articulated utopia we came across. The belief in naked power is extremely unusual. But it is unusual too in less obvious ways. Rarely do we find so consistent a view, realistic or utopian, of the political world. If we think of ideology not merely as the presence of attitudes and principles but also as involving the successful attempt to bind them, to give them internal coherence, in that sense ideology is an unusual event in adolescence, even at eighteen. Most of our subjects' ideologies seemed very much ad hoc. They answered each question as it came, seeming to make little effort to construct a model that would relate principles to one another. In the great majority of instances, the child merely soaks up the tacit assumptions of the milieu. Those few youngsters who cathect politics are those who will try to delineate, clarify, and justify the tacit, or those who resist it. It is in this sense that, for the most part, political grasp and political energy fuel each other; without a high cathexis of the political world there is, at least in adolescence, little effort given to the construction of a consistent political ethic.

Idealism, Utopianism, and Other Political Affects

The revival of political activism on college campuses has given new life to an older vision of the young as intensely political creatures, motivated by messianic or, at least, idealistic sentiments. From the first, a central goal of this research was the exploration of this putative state of affairs. In earlier work with adolescents I had seen few signs of deep political involvement, much less so political idealism. Nor had other data I had consulted suggested it; to the contrary. But the political beliefs of adolescents had not, at that time, been much studied; nor had the problem of political idealism been studied head on. Hence, several of the items on the interview schedule directly (and many more, indirectly) were addressed to searching out ideals and idealism. Specifically, would it be possible in an ideal society to eliminate crime; would it be possible to diminish or do away with disputes and disagreements among people; what kind of ideal society would you set up? Let me quickly grant the limitations of the questions for providing a full answer to the assessment of adolescent idealism. In particular, I now believe that we should also have included items dealing with more feasible social goals, such as the elimination of poverty or racial strife (as we are now in fact doing in research currently in progress). But we were more interested in determining whether the child could imagine social possibilities beyond those offered by conventional liberalism.

We had expected to discover more idealism among the young than we did, but we were not overly surprised to find it generally absent. What we were totally unprepared for was the prevalence of antiutopian views and the fierce strength with which they were held. Otherwise sleepy interviewees could bestir themselves to lecture us on the limits of human nature and social change. One became accustomed, when the "utopianism" questions were asked, to a shake of the head, a gentle smile, and a polite but determined dismissal of such naive notions. Antiutopian sentiment is found to about the same degree at all ages and in all three nations.

I think we get some insight into its sources when we examine some characteristic interview responses:

• Because you can go back into history and human nature has always been the same—people want things and if they see no other way to get it they'll steal it or kill. Because basically everybody is selfish. So I don't think— no matter what kind of government or system has been devised—there will always be crime. Because you can go back as far as you want and people have always been the same basically.
• People are always out to gain things for their own ends, and if they can gain great wealth quite easily without working for it, and the temptation is there, then it is human nature and they are going to take the chance and the crime is committed.

"You can't change human nature . . . people are basically selfish . . . people will always disagree"—these are the constant refrains heard in the interview when it touches upon the possibilities for substantial changes in human conduct. Our youngsters believe, as many of the Founding Fathers did, in "the assertive selfishness of human nature." They would most likely agree with Madison on "the propensity of mankind to fall into mutual animosities." They might even believe, with Hamilton, "that men are ambitious, vindictive, and rapacious." They are saying that the human being is a creature of interest, that interest will overcome goodness, if not all of the time, then some of the time, and if not in all human beings, yet certainly in some. Hence, the political order, though it may strive to attain perfection in human beings, should not expect to achieve it. To the contrary, society must be arranged to take account of and counter the human tendencies toward self-interest and faction.

There are, I suppose, varying attitudes we can take about the anti-idealism of the young. A colleague of mine, a devotee of Herbert Marcuse and the counterculture, sees in this finding a reflection of how the competitive conditions of capitalism stifle the natural openness and generosity of the young. Another colleague is delighted to learn of it; he believes that utopianism is essentially romantic and that political romanticism is sooner or later antidemocratic. Another feels that this mood among the young suggests no more than the triumph of the Lockean over the Rousseauist tradition in Western political thought. However we understand the counteridealism of our adolescents, we should be clear about what it is not. It is not the thoughtless authoritarianism of the very young, for older subjects are rather more skeptical of human goodness than younger ones. Furthermore, it is our most reflective and sensitive youngsters who offer some of the most telling arguments against what they take to be naive idealism. Nor is it gutter cynicism, or anything like it; it appears in those who are otherwise fairly sanguine about the prospects for human beings and society.

The anti-idealistic attitude is, I suspect, among other things, a reflection of that striving toward realism that is as important as, and far more prevalent than, the reach toward idealism. The child moves during this period toward what he conceives to be an "adult" understanding of the world, which sometimes seems to mean relinquishing what he deems to be "childish"—naivete, or simple-mindedness, or sentimentality. The strain toward "maturity"—that is, toward coolness, prudence, sober judgment, and the like—is as strongly felt as the more idealistic impulses. The striving toward realism, and the consequent tension between "idealistic" and "realistic" modes within the person have been much neglected by students of adolescence, so enthralled have they been by the myth of adolescent idealism.

In view of this it should come as no surprise that few adolescents show signs of having given serious thought to the radical revision of society. That there is little interest in the construction of utopia among the youngest adolescents is hardly unexpected. As we have seen, they have such a rudimentary sense of the concept of society that it would be implausible to find them indulging in social critique, let alone proposing schemes of social betterment whether modest or exalted. But in the middle period, with the capacity for political reasoning established—though not altogether consolidated—we would expect to see, and we do in fact see, the emergence of both critical and melioristic outlooks. These largely span a rather narrow range of attitude. To the question on devising an ideal society, most responses range from fatuous complacency to sharp and succinct wishes for change, the latter very much within the system.

A great many youngsters say, "I like it just the way it is," or some variant thereof, and will not be budged even when pressed by further questioning. Some of the U.S. youngsters in particular think their country ideal, or close to it. Many responses are rather diffuse, for example, "Well probably one where the people could do what they wanted . . . not what they want. What I mean is not go out and have riots and things like that, but do things that they would enjoy and have fun in that and not get into trouble or anything.'' Others offer only modest goals: "A society that would have laws and that would be run by the people, and a country that everyone under eighteen should go to school and everyone over eighteen should go to college, and make something out of themselves." Some propose a utopia by exclusion: "Let's see, I would try to make it better. All the people causing trouble should be sent away by themselves. They could make all the trouble out there. So they wouldn't bother anybody.''

Among the more focused responses, three themes seem dominant. There is a *law-and-order* and/or serenity motif, in which the stress is upon the absence of crime, riots, narcotics, and the like, and the consequent achievement of a tranquil, peaceful, kindly community. There is an *abundance* motif, which emphasizes the elimination of want. One child proposes that everything be free; another, a credit-card utopia, with cards to be in bountiful supply. There is an *equality* motif, which aims at the leveling of differences, both economic and racial. These themes—serenity, bounty, equality—are the elements of most millenarian visions, but it should be emphasized that they seem not to be felt strongly, that these are attenuated millennial dreams, both in their scope and in their affective intensity. On the whole, the mood of our youngsters is conservative. Grievances against the system, when present, do not seem deeply held; the apocalyptic or chiliastic mentality so often imputed to adolescents is scarcely to be found.

We should not look upon any of this in the least surprising. Our samples in all three nations were drawn largely from youngsters of the more or less contented classes of the community, from that vast range of the population extending from the stable working class to the nonintellectual upper middle class. In regard to politics they will ultimately become either passive spectators or intelligent consumers; signs of this are already evident. They are consumed neither by grievances nor by moral passion, and in this respect it is no surprise either that the impulse to utopian thought, in the few instances we find it, appears among inner-city adolescents, largely black but some white, who feel themselves despised and rejected, and by young suburban intellectuals, morally troubled, and feeling in themselves the destiny to innovate and lead. These, too, are no doubt much like their families. The inclination to utopia, in short, is a matter of class and social position, not fundamentally a youth phenomenon.

National Variations

What follows should be read with the utmost caution. They are sketches of national styles in adolescent political thought, attempts to capture the distinctive qualities—the dominant tonalities, as it were—of the three political cultures. To do so, I have stressed what is unique to each, at the cost of ignoring the many more ways in which U.S., German, and British adolescents are alike. Thus the typical German adolescent is not as preoccupied with order and obedience as the sketch given below would suggest; yet taken as a whole, the set of German interviews do show such a preoccupation when we compare them with the other two national samples.

The Germans

I begin with the German interviews because they are the easiest to grasp. The distinguishing themes can be stated boldly and simply. They are also familiar, eerily so. Reading some of these interviews—not all, but a substantial minority, perhaps 30 percent of them—we feel ourselves drawn or thrown back thirty or forty years, to those sentiments about citizen, state, and society that we then took to be "uniquely" German. Despite at least two decades of successful democratic practice, despite the earnest attempt of most educated Germans to wash their hands of the past, much of that political spirit persists—as many observers have noted, and as our interviews made painfully plain. Consider the following statement by an eighteen-year-old German girl, responding to a question on the purpose of government. Nothing like it, nothing remotely like it, appears in the U.S. or British interviews. "We have to have someone who takes responsibility for us, so that they don't become confused, the whole community, so that there's one person who governs us, and shares an interest in what we do and everything."

In this brief extract we catch a glimpse of several of the motifs that distinguish the German interviews: the fear of confusion; the identification of government with a single person; and, above all, the view of authority as parental and of the citizen as a child. The governing power is seen as wise and benevolent, the citizen as weak and dependent, the two joining symbiotically. Given this nuclear view of the political enterprise, most of the singular features of German political thought fall into place.

The ordinary citizen is seen as weak or stupid or incompetent. He does not know enough to come in out of the rain. A disdain for "the people" runs through the interviews: "people must all be guided somehow . . . they can't otherwise make sense out of what happens to them," "the laws are created because otherwise when one lives without laws . . . then one cannot tell if what one is doing is right."

Indeed, it is sometimes implied that stupidity, or a sheeplike docility, *should* be the proper state of mind for the citizen:

• [Laws are needed] so that all the people can live in such a way that they don't have to think about what's going to happen to them very much.

• There should be [a law forbidding smoking] because . . . otherwise people would have to decide for themselves if it's good or bad for their health or not.

They wanted to have a guiding principle that one could defer to without further ado, without reflecting on his deeds and considering whether something is correct or false.

These last quotations point to a recurrent theme in many of the German interviews: the anguish of ambiguity, the pain of deciding among alternatives. Ambiguity begets confusion, and confusion is an internal state most deeply feared. Out of the fear of ambiguity and the deeper fear of confusion, of being adrift in a sea of possibilities, comes the need to reduce diversity, to seek order, clarity, and direction. Hence the German youngster turns to the strong leader. Without firm leadership, there will be chaos, anarchy. By anarchy he has in mind not that state of nature where it is the war of all against all (an Anglo-Saxon notion, to judge by our interviews) but a state of anomie, of being lost, rootless, perplexed, without beacons or guideposts, besieged by a Babel of separate voices. The clear, loud, coherent voice of authority can overcome Babel. It is this consideration that seems to attract a disproportionate number of German adolescents to one-man rule. (Overall, the German sample preferred one-man rule twice as often as the U.S. and British subjects. At the age of thirteen an astonishing 50 percent prefer it over representative or direct democracy.)

• Well, when one man rules it is always better than when many rule. There are no others who have a different opinion and such, and there should be only one ruling. With [a representative system] the people could not determine anything at all, because there are always different voices.
• [One-man rule] I like—that only one person decides; otherwise they might argue. And with [representative democracy] they won't get to agree, and with [direct democracy] there is probably more confusion, when they all at once say this and that.

Even when the choice is made for a representative system, the reasoning is the same:

> If each person decided individually, there would almost certainly be a tremendous chaos, and when only a certain number of people rule, then they guide the people much better. They realize what's important for individual people.

The leadership—whether a single man or a ruling group—is assumed to be, as one youngster put it, ''smarter and wiser'' than the people they rule, and thus entitled to rule. There is little of the cynicism and distrust of authority we find so commonly in the U.S. and British interviews. The omnicompetence of the leader allows the citizen to turn over responsibility to him without qualms, secure in the sense that a strong and wise leadership will provide order, ensure unity, and thus protect the country from chaos and weakness. What haunts the imagination of a few youngsters is the idea of a disunited country weak in the face of its enemies.

- If a state didn't provide any order, in my opinion, if there weren't any internal order, in Germany, then other states would begin to overrun the country because no one would provide unity then.
- [The purpose of government] is first to keep order in the country and then— most of all to unite, perhaps, during a war. The state must not only be strong, it must *appear* to be strong.

If the government gives even the appearance of weakness, then all may be lost. When asked what the government should do about a law being violated by the citizenry, one seemingly unworkable, we have these responses:

- Keep [the law] but alter it. To abolish it they would more or less admit that they had been wrong . . . and, of course, if the government is wrong, the people would have no confidence in it.
- Repealing the law completely would be admitting defeat and so I would disagree.
- Well, they should stiffen the law maybe now, because if they let the people get away with [smuggling], then it would be a very weak government.

The fear of disorder, and of the confusion and weakness that would follow, influences political judgments in many areas. Some German youngsters view the party system, for example, not as a means of expressing political conflict but almost as a way of inhibiting it. They stress the orderliness that the party system provides:

- [Purpose of political parties] So that there is order. Well, because otherwise everyone could almost do as he pleases.
- [Why did parties emerge?] So that there are no disturbances in the country and that everything is in order in the country.

Thus, the Germans: they are not "authoritarian" in the sense that they wish to bully the weak, or even to wield authority over others. To the contrary, they seem to see themselves as weak, childlike, and inept, and they yearn for the strong, comforting hand of a benign and vigilant leader. Offered it, they will follow.

The British

The British were the most difficult of our samples to understand. They are rugged individualists, laissez-faireists of the H. L. Hunt stamp, and yet they are the most welfare-oriented of the national groups, determined that the government provide goods and services. They resent any attempt to do away with their pleasures, and yet they take a low view of their fellow humans on the grounds that they are too obsessed by pleasure. They are edgy and irritated about authorities, whom they suspect to be bossy and hypocritical, and yet they want and expect the authorities to govern, and no nonsense about it. Their politics is a marvelous, bewildering mixture, derived partly from Hobbes, from whom they draw a mordant view of man and his doings; from John Stuart Mill, with whom they share a fierce devotion to liberty; and from the Fabians and their successors, who have taught them to look to the state for welfare and security.

To find our way into the British political temper, let me begin, once again, with a representative quotation from an interview with a thirteen-year-old responding to a question on laws: "There must be certain laws, otherwise people would just go round and eat other people's apples off the next door neighbor's trees or something." This rather innocuous excerpt contains within it two elements that reflect British preoccupations: the oral emphasis, on food and stealing, and the implicit concern with boundaries—the sense of territory, and fear of trespass.

Reading through the British interviews, one is struck most forcefully by their ubiquitous orality. There is a more than usual frequency of oral metaphors and phrasings, as in the example given, but even more evident is what amounts to an obsessive emphasis on greed, envy, theft, and self-indulgence, all of these oral motifs. The concern with stealing is especially prominent. When Americans think about a world without law, they mention murder and other forms of personal violence; the British mention theft and its variants, and only later, as a second thought, think to mention killing. To an open-ended, general question on crime, 49 percent of the British subjects spontaneously cited stealing as an example; to the same question, only 18 percent of Americans did so.

When we look more closely into what they imagine to motivate theft, we find once again a stress upon oral motifs. People steal because they are greedy, that is, they are voracious, insatiable, unsatisfied by what they have. Or they are consumed by envy, that is, they cannot abide the prosperity of the other in the light of their own deprivation. Or they are truly deprived, that is, poor and in want. Or they are merely self-indulgent, unwilling to work as the rest of us must, they take the easier path of theft.

I mention this pervasive orality, this obsessive stress on getting and taking, not as a psychoanalytic curiosity but because it has a vital connection to the political thought of our British adolescents. What matters to the British—far more than to the U.S. or German youngsters—are such issues as the equitable distribution of supplies, the government's stance toward the pursuit of pleasure and self-interest, the enhancement of economic well-being and other matters bearing upon the materialistic interests of the citizen.

As Judith Gallatin has pointed out, the British, in contrast to both the Germans and Americans, are disposed to think in terms of distributive rather than aggregative utility when considering a political proposal. That is to say, they measure the value of a law or political decision by its benefit to the individual citizen rather than its advantages to the community as a whole. Germans, as we have seen, tend to think first in terms of strengthening the state; Americans, as we will see, think in terms of enhancing the common good. For the British, what comes first is the well-being of the individual citizen. Whereas the German or American might say that what's good for the community is good for the citizen, the British clearly believe that what's good for the citizen is good for the country.

The maintenance of material well-being is seen as being very much a governmental responsibility. While both the U.S. and German adolescents more or less ignore the government's economic role, the British put it at the forefront of concern. It is only in the British interviews that we find such statements on the purpose of government as the following: it should "control the economy," "sustain existence," "look after the economic side," "help old people," "look after the welfare of the country," and "increase export and trade."

The government's role in regard to supplies is expected to go beyond the enhancement of the nation's well-being. It must also make sure that what there is (and it is taken for granted that what there is is in short supply) must be distributed equitably, fair shares for all. As one British youngster put it, one of the functions of government is "to see that everybody gets their own share of everything."

What makes this a difficult task is the tendency toward greed and self-interest commonly imputed to at least some of one's neighbors. It is not, I hope, overly cynical to point out that while the British child sees himself as wanting no more than his due (and no less), he is ready to imagine that others are not nearly so modest in their wants; the mechanism, projection, is familiar enough. This preoccupation with the avarice of others is a steady drumbeat in the British interviews, and it does not diminish much with age.

- Everyone would take advantage of everyone else. Nobody would mind taking something from the person next door.
- The majority of people steal because they want to live above what they have been used to.
- I think people would turn greedy, dishonest, and selfish.

So the British youngster is fretful lest he be deprived of his share of the pie, yet vigilant that others may cheat and steal to get more than they merit. It is this mixed mood that seems to generate a peculiarly ambivalent view of authority. If authority is too weak, then people will plunder. One's territory, one's goods, one's privacy, one's autonomy—and the British hold all of these dear—will be despoiled. Hence authority must be firm enough, alert enough, and, above all, disinterested enough to keep human predation in check and to ensure equality of supply. Yet his need of authority does not lead the British adolescent to exalt it. His leaders too are made of human clay; they too may be actuated by self-interest or the vanity of office. At their best his leaders may indeed be disinterested, but in this vale of tears who will count on that? It would be going too far to say that the British are suspicious of authority. It does not quite amount to that. Let us say that they are unillusioned, skeptical. Authority is a necessary evil, necessary because of man's self-love. The British are anarchists *manqués*; were it not for the beastly nature of man, they would as soon do without authority.

Though the British youngster's skepticism about authority is usually polite, or *sotto voce*, it emerges nevertheless, almost despite itself. He half suspects that his leaders are hypocrites, that they will deprive him of things that they permit themselves. (On the question of controlling cigarette smoking it was the British alone who felt that dissuasion of the young by authority would not work because teachers and other elders would continue to smoke, even while inveighing against it for the young.) And if they are not hypocritical, then they are bossy, intrusive, officious—eager to interfere with simple pleasures, ready to invade one's privacy. (As one youngster put it, commenting scornfully on an intrusive law, "Some bureaucrat in an office thought of that.") It should be clear that the British do not see in authority a potential tyrant, a man on horseback. The thought does not even cross their minds. They see authority as potentially a Scrooge or a Mrs. Grundy, or—above all—a Pecksniff.

And so we return to that "fierce devotion to liberty" we talked about at the outset of this argument. The British are not much given to airy sentiments about freedom, much less so than our Germans and Americans, both of whom, each in their way, tend toward philosophy, by which I mean the high-flown and the full-blown. The British love of liberty is earthy, concrete, material, and in many ways selfish; it is, at bottom, based on such self-regarding sentiments as "keep your hands off my sweets" and "get off my turf." It is the British, not the Americans, who emerge in our interviews as "rugged individualists." They have a tough, gritty independence, a stubborn determination to be left alone—to have each man be a tight little island of his own—and at their best, a live-and-let-live attitude toward others.

But I have no wish to sentimentalize. Their independence, their refreshing individualism, is but one side of the coin. The other side is a potential callousness to others, a tendency toward selfishness that the British themselves have named and lamented: "I'm all right, Jack." In that balance between the individual and the collective good that all political cultures must somehow compose, the British clearly emphasize the citizen's self-interest, and at some cost, actual or potential, to the total community. Nor are the British always quite so indulgent of others, so live-and-let-live in outlook as they are at their best. Their tolerance for eccentricity and their acceptance of diversity are often under some strain, and they readily lapse into peevishness, malice, and even vindictiveness as they reflect on the greed and self-indulgence they impute—projectively, I believe—to others. The Pecksniffism and Grundyism they so quickly suspect in their leaders is in fact to be found in themselves. More so than the Germans and Americans, the British seem to struggle with their impulses. The struggle takes its toll in an ambivalent shuttling back and forth between their wish to be generous and fair toward others and their tendencies toward envy and resentment. Let me conclude by showing that struggle directly, in an excerpt from a fifteen-year-old girl's interview. She is composing her ideal society, and what she tells us speaks more vividly than paraphrase of British ambivalence:

I'd like darkies to be accepted because they're not as bad—I don't think they're as bad as they're made out to be. Some are very nice and then again there are some who are horrible. I think they're more nice than horrible. Try to get on with them, you know. They're nice to talk to sometimes. I think they should be accepted because after all they're no different really, except for the color of their skins. The only thing I don't like about them is the way they come over here and in a few days—well, before they've been over here very long, they seem to have got a good job, and they've got a great big car and they've got loads of clothes and it just seems a wonder how they get them—those jobs—just like that as they come over.

The Americans

I begin with four statements, two taken from the press, two others drawn from the interviews:

• What people have to do is build that collective spirit. To overcome that notion of bourgeois individuality which separates one person from the next and which defines the individual as someone who can assert himself at the expense of his neighbor, at the expense of his brother by destroying his brother.

- What we are really into is living together . . . Living in community, learning to love one another . . . Learning to live together! This and not landing a space ship on the moon is the great adventure of our time.
- [The purpose of law] Just to set a certain basis for society so that people can get along together.
- [The purpose of government] to enable . . . a great many people to live together in harmony.

The first quotation is by Angela Davis; the second is from an effusion celebrating life in hippie communes; the third is from a young lady mentioned earlier, the daughter of a John Birch Society leader and a Bircher herself; the fourth is also from a youngster discussed earlier, the boy who wants to be dictator of the world. If we ignore the rhetorical flourishes in the first two excerpts, we can observe that all four speakers are saying much the same thing. They are emphasizing community, togetherness, social amity. And in doing so, and despite their no doubt bitter differences each from the other, and all from the center of American thought, the four do share a togetherness, a community of a sort—they are all Americans, and they share the deep American belief in community, and the American ambivalence about unbridled individualism.

To simplify: if what mattered to the German adolescent was the leader's wisdom and strength, and to the English youngster the needs of the individual, what mattered to the American was the citizen's connection to the community. In the interviews with Americans the preoccupying themes are those of the group and community: how to produce harmony among factions within the community; how to reduce differences in status among members of the community; how to find a balance between the citizen's rights and the group's needs. With remarkable consistency the U.S. sample was the most likely of the three to adduce community welfare and community needs as the essential goals of political action.

What we have, in a sense, is an other-directed politics, a politics of togetherness. But in saying this I do not mean to offer the common and to my mind vulgar idea that Americans are slavishly conformist to the opinions of others. Our data in fact showed that the Americans were the most likely of the three national samples to fear the tyranny of the majority, to uphold minority rights, and to emphasize the right of dissent. (For that matter, the Americans were—by a considerable margin—the least authoritarian of the three samples, a good thing to keep in mind in these hysterically self-flagellating times.) What I do mean to say is that the Americans seemed to be ever mindful of the total community—of its needs, its just demands, its potential for tyranny. The ideal of government is social harmony, the reduction of frictions so that people can live together amicably.

In the pursuit of social amity, a number of specific political goals are stressed. First, there must be harmony among factions, or potential factions within the community. In the good polity, no single group profits at the expense of others. Conflicts should be mediated, differences compromised; a balance among competing interests must be achieved. The concept of *balance* seemed to be of particular importance to the U.S. youngsters:

• To keep people free—worship, free speech, way of thinking. . .so people have rights. . .and the civilization will balance.
• The purpose of government is to balance individual and group interests so that no one group had advantage over others.

The idea of equity among competing factions is extended to minority groups. As I remarked earlier, there is a distinct emphasis upon the protection of minority rights. All voices should be heard, all interests accommodated whenever possible. The wish to reduce differences within the community is seen in its strongest form in the emphasis upon equality. Richard Hofstadter, among others, has pointed out that Americans tend to equate democracy with egalitarianism. Our interviews do much to confirm this. We find a vigorous egalitarian bias, so much so that for some of our subjects a prime function of government is the fostering of equality.

The U.S. interviews, then, emphasized social harmony, democratic practices, the maintenance of individual rights, and equality among citizens. An optimistic view of government: the state not as the antagonist of the citizen but as his collective extension. Does all this seem too good to be true? To some minor degree. In some part the "democratic" quality of these interviews stemmed from a penchant for democratic rhetoric. In some degree it reflected a complacency about "the American way of life"; the Americans were, as I may have mentioned, the most self-consciously patriotic of the national samples. Yet neither of these tendencies—neither the occasional reciting of democratic set-pieces nor the occasional indulgence in national self-congratulation—is the essential source of the American ambience. The optimistic, expansive liberalism of the U.S. interviews could be seen in the most unconscious, most unselfconscious moments of discourse, in the tacit assumptions made while groping toward solutions of the problems posed by the interview.

But there is a fly in the ointment. Beneath the generally optimistic view of government we find some real tensions, involving the potential collision between equally prized values: individualism and the public good. Some of the time the American handles this conflict by a kind of denial. He imagines a social contract between the individual and society wherein the social order protects personal freedom and initiative in the understanding that the individual will voluntarily limit his pursuit of self-interest when this conflicts with the greater good sought by the community. When the spirit of Pollyanna is upon him, the American adolescent wills himself to the belief that the terms of the contract are easily met, that this concert of aims is achieved automatically. In the best of all possible political worlds, individual freedom enhances the common good, the lion of self-interest lies down with the lamb of public good.

In his darker moments we find a fear of unchecked individualism, an apprehension that the citizen will exploit and abuse the opportunities for freedom offered by the community. Let me offer a hypothesis here: that the American handles this political anxiety—at least in part—by displacing it from the realm of politics to the world of crime. There is a striking discrepancy in the U.S. findings between the liberal, humanistic emphasis in the areas of government and political philosophy and the hard, harsh, cold line taken toward crime. (I should mention here that much of our interviewing was done before the consciousness of crime was as acute as it has since become; our U.S. youngsters were as obsessed about the control of crime in 1963 as they are in our latest studies.)

The Americans tend to see crime as a social act. It is a betrayal of the community, a violation of the contract that binds men together in amity. When the American youngster speaks of crime, he speaks not so much of impulses (as the British do) as of its effect upon other people. The criminal is one who, willfully or otherwise, has broken his connection with the community, with other people.

- Well we send people to jail to protect other people in the community. And well if he's a thief or murderer I think that it's his place to be somewhere else where he won't hurt someone else.
- Crime is another way of expressing discontent for existing institutions.
- [Lawbreakers] might not have very good relationships with their families or the community and I think that would have an awful lot to do with it.

The outlaw haunts the American imagination—unfettered, free, free of community and thus of constraint, free and thus alone. Crime, in the deepest American consciousness, is individualism writ large, individualism corrupted, individualism out of control.

Note

1. I cannot emphasize too strongly how much this report owes to the gifted group of students I have worked with during the past several years: Drs. Marjorie Bush, Bernard Banet, and Maury Lachor, and Mrs. Ruthellen Josselson. Detailed findings from our research are available in the following publications and dissertations: J.

Adelson and R. O'Neil, "The Development of Political Thought in Adolescence: The Sense of Community," *Journal of Personality and Social Psychology* 4 (1966): 295–306; J. Adelson, B. Green, and R. O'Neil, "The Growth of the Idea of Law in Adolescence," *Developmental Psychology* 1 (1969): 327–32; J. Adelson and L. Beall, "Adolescent Perspectives on Law and Government," *Law and Society Review* (May 1970): 495–504; J. Gallatin and J. Adelson, "Individual Rights and the Public Good," *Comparative Political Studies* (July 1970): 226–42; unpublished doctoral dissertations (all University of Michigan) by Robert O'Neil (1964), Lynnette Beall (1966), Judith Gallatin (1967), and Marjorie Bush (1970).

15

Rites of Passage

How do youngsters in the vital transitional period of pre- and early adolescence deal with the ideas of the social sciences and the humanities? How do they cope with the concepts they must absorb in learning about history or civics or political science or literary studies? Does psychology have anything useful to tell us about how to teach those subjects during that difficult age? Do we know something that would help us accelerate learning or deepen it or strengthen the child's grasp on what he has been taught?

The work I will report here is based on two major investigations, one crossnational, comparing over three hundred youngsters in our country, England and Germany, ranging in age from ten or eleven to eighteen, from the fifth grade to the twelfth. The second study, in which we interviewed about 450 adolescents, covered the ages from eleven and twelve to eighteen. This study was directed and analyzed by my colleague Judith Gallatin. The second study concentrated upon youngsters in an urban area, largely blue collar in origin, with an equal number of Blacks and Whites.

Our research instrument was the open-ended interview. After a great deal of trial and error, we hit upon an interview format that began with the following premise: a thousand people leave their country and move to a Pacific island to start a new society. We hoped that the use of an imaginary society would help free some of the children, the young ones particularly, from their preoccupation with getting "the right answer." Given this framework, we then offered our youngsters a great many questions on a wide variety of political, social, and moral issues: the scope and proper limits of political authority; the reciprocal obligations of the individual and the community; the nature of crime and justice; the collision between personal freedom and the common good; the prospects for utopia; and so on. Put this way, it all sounds rather formidable, but the questions themselves were straightforward and generally quite concrete. In the second of the studies, we also introduced a number of questions having to do with urban tensions: the sources and outcomes of poverty, the relations between citizens and the police, and the proper channels for citizen protest. The interviews took, on the average, an hour to complete—the older the child, the longer the interview. We tape-recorded and then transcribed faithfully, including silences, uhs, "you knows," and grammatical incoherence, since we felt that the process of achieving a response might in some cases be as interesting as the response itself.

Since there are far too many findings to report even in summary form, I have identified five topics that I think are of central importance, since they influence so many other areas of social thought: the conceptions of community and of law, the growth of principles, and the grasp of human psychology and of social reality. In each of these topics we see some significant and at times startling changes in children's understanding during the adolescent years. I will concentrate here particularly upon those taking place in the earlier part of that period.

The Community

The first piece of advice to give any teacher preparing to work with ten-, eleven-, and twelve-year-olds is that one ought not to assume the child is talking about the same things you are. With respect to such concepts as "government" or "society" or "the state," the youngster may talk in a seemingly appropriate fashion; yet, when you extend the conversation or query him a bit, you may likely find something close to a conceptual void. At the threshold of adolescence, children find it difficult to imagine impalpable social collectivities; they do not yet enjoy the sense of community.

We can illustrate this graphically by looking at the answers eleven- and twelve-year-olds give to the question "What is the purpose of government?" To begin with, many of them cannot answer the question at all. Either they fall mute entirely or provide obviously confused or irrelevant responses. In our cross-national study, we found that 15 percent of eleven-year-olds could give no answer at all to that question. More revealing yet is the number who are unable to give adequate answers—that is, answers of sufficient coherence and complexity to allow their being coded. The category "Simplistic, Missing the Point, Confused, Vague" accounts for 43 percent of responses among twelve-year-olds. A certain confusion about politics, government, law, and society is endemic among preadolescent youngsters. But the failure to understand the idea of government—and similar concepts of the collectivity— is especially significant because these are the regnant ideas in thinking about social, moral, and historical issues, and confusion, murkiness, error, and failure to grasp these concepts makes itself felt throughout a much larger domain of cognition.

But to say that these youngsters are mistaken or confused does not take us very far, since it does not tell us about the specific nature of the cognitive flaw. To understand that, it may be best to turn to some specific responses, chosen at random, from eleven-year-olds of average intelligence, to the question on the purpose of government:

To handle the state or whatever it is so it won't get out of hand, because if it gets out of hand you might have to . . . people might get mad or something.

Well . . . buildings, they have to look over buildings that would be . . . um, that wouldn't be any use of the land if they had crops on it or something like that. And when they have highways the government would have to inspect them, certain details. I guess that's about all.

So everything won't go wrong in the country. They want to have a government because they respect him and they think he's a good man.

What strikes us first about these statements is that, in each case, the speaker seems unable to rise securely above the particular. The child feels most comfortable in remaining concrete, by turning to specific and tangible persons, events, and objects—hence "government" becomes a "him," or the child talks about crops and buildings and highways. Of course an effort is made to transcend particularity, to discover a general principle or idea, but the reach exceeds the grasp, as we can see vividly in the first of these excerpts in which the speaker, seeking a general principle ("to handle the state"), gives up and subsides into concreteness ("people might get mad or something").

The shift from concrete to abstract modes of expression during the course of adolescence is a dramatic one. In our cross-national study, no eleven-year-old child was able to attain high-level abstractness in discussing the purpose of government; and no eighteen-year-old gave an answer as entirely concrete. Most eleven-year-olds (57 percent) can give only concrete responses. At thirteen and fifteen, a low level of abstractness is the dominant mode of conceptualizing government. And at eighteen, a strong majority of youngsters achieve a high level of abstractness.

The findings immediately above are based on our cross-national survey. In other studies we have tried different ways of categorizing responses, but the pattern remains essentially the same.

Unable to imagine "the community"—that is, the invisible network of rules and obligations binding citizens together—the child at the threshold of adolescence does not quite understand the mutuality joining the individual and the larger society. He does understand power, authority, coercion; indeed, he understands those all too well, in that his spontaneous discourse on "government" and the like relies heavily—at times exclusively—on the idea of force, authority being seen as the entitlement to coerce. Yet even that is imagined only concretely: it is the *policeman* who pursues and arrests the criminal, the *judge* who sentences him, and the *jailer* who keeps him. The less punitive purposes of the state are less readily discussed in large part, we believe, because the child, lacking a differentiated, textured view of collectivities, cannot quite grasp how they function or what their larger goals might be. The child at this stage may know that the government does things—fixes the streets, let us say—and that it does so in order to benefit the citizenry as a whole. But beyond such tangible activities leading to such tangible benefits, the need and purposes of the community remain a mystery, impenetrable.

Perhaps the most consistent finding we have is that the adolescent years witness a shift from a personalized, egocentric to a sociocentric mode of understanding social, political, historical, and moral issues. The sociocentric outlook is essentially absent at the beginning of adolescence—that is, when the child is ten, eleven, or twelve; yet, it is more or less universal by the time the child is seventeen or eighteen, with most of the movement taking place in the period we are talking about, somewhere between thirteen and fifteen years of age. The shift is dramatic in that it involves a fairly complete reorganization of how these issues are perceived and interpreted. We have here an expanding *capacity* to think in terms of the community. It does not mean that the youngster, having achieved that capacity, is held captive by it. It does not mean that discourse about society, from that point on, ignores individual needs and perspectives. It does mean, however, that the youngster, having achieved sociocentrism, is able to weigh the competing claims for ego and other, of the individual and the state, or the larger community. Until that point is achieved, social perceptions tend to be truncated, and social judgments and ratiocination are vulnerable to the distortion of a narrow individualism.

The Law

Perhaps the most unnerving discovery we made upon first reading the interview transcripts was that a substantial minority of our youngest respondents were capable, on occasion, of the moral purview of Attila the Hun. On questions of crime and punishment, they were able—without seeming to bat an eyelash—to propose the most sanguinary means of achieving peace and harmony across the land. Here are three examples, all from the discourse of nice, clean-cut middle-American thirteen-year-old boys, telling us their views on the control of crime:

> [On the best reason for sending people to jail]: Well, these people who are in jail for about five years must still own the same grudge, then I would put them in for triple or double the time. I think they would learn their lesson then.

> [On how to teach people not to commit crimes in the future]: Jail is usually the best thing, but there are others . . . in the nineteenth century they used to torture people for doing things. Now I think the best place to teach people is in solitary confinement.

> [On methods of eliminating or reducing crime]: I think that I would . . . well, like if you murder somebody you would punish them with death or something like this. But I don't think that would help because they wouldn't learn their

lesson. I think I would give them some kind of scare or something.

These excerpts are *not* randomly chosen, since we have selected cases marked by colorful language and thought. Yet neither are they altogether atypical, in this sense—they represent only the more extreme expressions of a far more general social and moral outlook; the tendency to see law, government, indeed most other social institutions, as committed *primarily* to the suppression of wayward behavior. In this view, human behavior tends toward pillage and carnage, and the social order is characteristically on the brink of anarchy. That may overstate it a bit, but not by much. Gradually but steadily, however, an entirely different view of the purpose of law emerges in later adolescence. Toward the end of the period we are dealing with and certainly by the time children are fifteen and sixteen, the dominant stress upon violence and injury has begun to diminish markedly, and it will more or less vanish by the time the child reaches the age of eighteen.

Two other motifs similarly signal the end of the pre- and early adolescent period. One of these is the tendency to see laws as *benevolent* as against restrictive, as designed to help people. A characteristic statement: "The purpose of laws is to protect people and help them out." Another motif, somewhat related, we suspect, is one that links law to the larger notion of community, that sees law as providing a means for interpersonal harmony, either among competing social groups or in the nation or the state as a whole ("so that the country will be a better place to live"). These changes from a purely restrictive to a benevolent or normative view of law, are as fundamental and quantitatively decisive as a shift from the concrete thinking to the abstract.

Principles

We have so far observed two major developments in political thought from the onset of adolescence to its end: the achievement of a sociocentric perspective, the ability to think about social and moral and philosophical issues while keeping the total community in mind; and the gradual abandonment of an authoritarian, punitive view of morality and the law. We now add a third theme: the youngster's capacity to make use of moral and political principles—ideas and ideals—in organizing his thinking about social issues. Once available, that capacity alters—decisively and irrevocably—the youngster's definition of social issues, and at the same time it alters the child's sense of himself as a social and political actor. Most current theories of political attitudes and thinking stress the central significance of more or less stable, more or less complex systems of belief, the presence of which allows the person to organize his understanding of social and political reality. It is in the period we now have under consideration that we first see the emergence of those systems, as the child begins to use principles in coming to legal, moral, political and social judgments. To judge by our interviews, however, it is a rather late development in adolescence. We seem to see the first signs of it when the child is between fourteen and sixteen, and the use of principles does not make itself felt fully until the end of the adolescent period.

Perhaps we best begin by showing just how the older adolescent makes use of principles in making judgments on social issues. Here is an eighteen-year-old who has just been asked what the government ought to do about a religious group opposed to compulsory vaccination:

> Well, anyone's religious beliefs have to be tolerated if not respected, unless it comes down to where they have the basic freedoms. Well, anyone is free until he starts interfering with someone else's freedom. Now, they don't have to get their children vaccinated, but they shouldn't have anything to say what the other islanders do, if they want their children vaccinated. If they're not vaccinated, they have the chance they may infect some of the other children. But then that's isolated, that's them, so if they don't get vaccinated, they don't have anyone else to blame. (Do you think that the government should insist these people go along with what the majority has to say, since they're such a small minority?) No, I don't think that the government should insist, but I think that the government should do its best to make sure that these people are well informed. A well-informed person will generally act in his own interest. I never heard of religion that was against vaccination. (There are religions that are against blood transfusions.) If they want to keep their bodies pure . . . well, like I said, I think that a well-informed citizen will act in his own best interests. If he doesn't, at least he should know what the possibilities are, you know, the consequences. So I think the government's job is to inform the people. In that case, at least, to inform them and not force them.

Younger children, when faced by a question of this type, find it difficult to reason on the issue. They come down hard on one side or the other or cannot make up their minds and therefore hedge; in support of their position, they may put forward a principle-like phrase, such as "freedom of religion," but they cannot do much with the idea except to assert it. What we see in the excerpt we have given—which we choose not because it is "brilliant" but because it is characteristic in late adolescence—is the capacity to advance a general and generalizing principle, which then allows the youngster to talk about specific issues with some flexibility. These formulae need not be absolute in nature, nor rigidly applied; indeed, in many cases the youngster brings forward circumstances that call for a suspension or modification of the principle.

How does the youngster come into possession of these principles? As far as we can tell, they are not constructed *de novo* but are acquired by the most mundane processes of learning, in the classroom or through the media, in the church or at home. At moments one can almost see the civics or history textbook before the child's inner eye as he struggles with the question. Here is a youngster trying to answer a question as to which law should be made permanent and unchangeable:

> Well, freedom of speech is one, as you said. And then one law, well, I don't think you should be in prison for a longer time than twenty-four hours without them telling the charge against you. Or freedom of the press or freedom of the religion, that should never be changed, because anybody can pick any religion they want. There's no certain religion that everybody has to go by. (Can you think of any other kind of law that should not be changed or is that about it?) There are some more laws, but I know what they are, but I can't really put it into words because . . . you know, I really know what they are, like the laws, the Bill of Rights, you know, the first ten amendments of the Constitution, uh, them laws, you know, that I haven't mentioned. They should be put in there, in the United States Constitution. I can't remember what they were exactly, but if I had a history book, I'd look them up, you know.

Obviously, he has absorbed some of the principles of constitutional democracy, albeit a bit imperfectly. Nevertheless, it is almost certain that the mode of discourse we see here is not exclusively a function of learning; it depends also upon the growth of cognitive capacity. If we take a look at the interviews of average children in the early and middle-adolescent period, we get some sense of the limits of learning before the child is intellectually ready. Ninth and tenth graders have also been exposed to the fundamental ideas of constitutional government, at least in the students we worked with; yet, it seemed to us that the learning does not quite "take," not completely, not sufficiently to allow the child to make use of it in ordinary conversation. The principles do not "come to mind," even when the child is primed by how the question is phrased. In writing the interview item on permanent laws, we were aware that younger children would not spontaneously think of laws or constitutional provisions guaranteeing fundamental freedoms, and so we decided to prime the pump, so to speak, by mentioning "freedom of speech" as an example. Nevertheless, very few of our younger subjects took the hint. Instead, they concentrated on those issues—crime and punishment, violence and injury—that most concerned them and generally in the straightforwardly authoritarian manner we mentioned earlier:

> They should have a law, like people should stop stealing, and if they do steal, they would have to stay in jail for about a year until they settled down and stopped doing that. And they should stop killing each other because that's not right.

And even when the child is not entirely obsessed with fantasies of danger, the response to this question usually betrays an inability to make general statements:

> Don't litter. Don't steal. Keep off the grass. Don't break windows. Don't run up the stairs. Don't play with matches. Keep matches out of reach of little children.

We do not want to make either too much or too little of the child's acquisition of principle. It does not usher in a golden era of humanistic wisdom. The ordinary youngster acquires the conventional ideas and ideals of the world about him, and unless he is intensely interested in social or philosophical or literary topics, he is unlikely to have ideas that are discernibly unique or penetrating. Yet on the other hand, it is a development of some importance. One obvious reason is that until the child acquires a capacity for general ideas, he does not understand most of the language of social and moral discourse that envelops him. He is in that sense like the tourist in a foreign land, unable to speak or read the indigenous language, and not quite sure what the customs signify. If he is facile enough, he may be able to mimic some of the argot and conduct of the natives around him, yet studied inquiry would soon reveal the lacunae and confusions. Time and again in our interviews with pre- and early adolescents—those, let us say, between eleven and fourteen—we come upon such instances wherein the child's mimetic talent allowed him to talk as though he knew the language when, in fact, he did not. The majority rules, the child says. Ah, we say in turn, so tell us about the majority. Then the child replies, oh, that's when everybody agrees.

Achieving a grasp of principle also means that the child can resist the appeal of the immediate, hence is less vulnerable to mere sentiment. The government wants to build a highway and needs some farm land. The farmer resists; the authorities insist. Who is right? Without some general idea to aid him—either the virtues of property or the common good or eminent domain or some such—the youngster is not far from helpless in telling us what ought to be done, and why. Either he sides with the farmer, sentimentalized as the underdog, or with the government, sentimentalized as the guardian of the public weal. Without the guidance of principle, he is, we feel, so subject to the tug of emotion, and thus of demagoguery, that he cannot make reasoned—and hence reliable—decisions. He is much to responsive to the *evident* good.

One more comment before we leave this topic. It may be worth repeating that the term "principles" refers to both ideas and ideals. The increasing conceptual grasp of the adolescent allows him to come to an understanding of the conventions of social and moral reality as understood by the community at large. At the same time he becomes capable of cognizing the "irreal" as well, and hence of being in touch with the values, hopes, and utopian beliefs of the culture as a whole. Hence the grasp of principles means that the child can become both more "realistic" and "idealistic." It has been our unfortunate habit to concentrate upon "adolescent idealism" as though that were a dominant moral outlook of the adolescent period. In fact, the child's realism, the child's becoming socialized to the conventions of the culture, is a far more conspicuous feature of this era. But what is perhaps most important is that we see a dialectic between these attitudes, between being realistic and being idealistic.

Understanding Human Behavior

Near the beginning of the interview schedule we introduced a series of questions about law and laws, some of which we have already mentioned. What is the function of law? What would happen in a world without law? How and why do people get into trouble with the law? In developing the topic, we want to get some sense of how youngsters understand the psychology of malfeasance. One of our questions put forth the following proposition: some percentage of people need laws to keep them from getting into trouble, while others "follow their consciences naturally and do not need laws." We then asked what accounted for the difference between these two types of people.

What interests us here are not the particular theories proposed—these are fairly commonplace—but rather the somewhat abrupt shift in the child's capacity to talk about human psychology, a shift that in its rudiments seems to take place fairly early in adolescence—most of the time it is visible between the ages of eleven and thirteen. Here are some typical eleven-year-olds trying to distinguish between those who are naturally law abiding and those who need laws to guide them:

> Well . . . most people, some people they don't like, like speeding, they don't like to do this, but some people like . . . maybe . . . grownup people some people like to speed a lot.

> Well about the person I think he had been pushed around and people don't like him and stuff. The people that do not like the laws—well they probably had friends and he didn't get into much trouble so they just got used to it.

> Well . . . (pause, question repeated) well, it could be that the person who thinks that they were law abiding, I mean the criminals, they see things wrong. (How do you mean?) Well I mean they see . . . I can't explain it.

One is struck immediately by the sheer confusion of these comments: ideas—even phrases—do not quite connect to each other. There are gaps in discourse. Our experience has been that this sort of confusion suggests not so much ignorance, or fool's knowledge, as it does the child's earnest attempts to reach something just out of his grasp. He does not quite have the conceptual means to achieve a dimly sensed end. We sense that our third respondent is trying to say something about the social outlook of the delinquent ("they see things wrong"), while the second is speaking psycho-historically, that is, trying to link miscreancy to past experience ("he had been pushed around . . . and stuff"). In these instances we feel that the child's essential problem is a difficulty linking part to whole, particular to general, and vice versa. We may imagine that given the category "law abiding," the child's mind hits upon "speeding" as an instance of that larger category but cannot go beyond that, that is, cannot yet link speeding to other forms of social malfeasance, nor can he develop a differentiated view of the category "law abiding" that will allow him to classify different instances within it.

Even when the eleven-year-old's response is not quite so confused, it generally reveals some distinct limitations in the appraisal of human behavior. Here is a more typical response from a child at this age—it is neither the least nor the most advanced:

> Oh, well, someone—their mom and dad might separate or something and neither one wanted them or something like that, didn't like them very much and oh, if they happened to turn bad, I mean just, and they had trouble—pretty soon if they keep doing that and pretty bad conditions they'll probably get in a lot of trouble.

Once we get into this long, meandering sentence, we discover that it contains not one but two theories of miscreancy and its sources—the first of these having to do with parental rejection, the second suggesting that trivial sins that go uncorrected lead implacably to larger ones. But here we see even more clearly the problem in being unable to find a suitable language. Our youngster speaks only about specific acts or feelings—as though he were the most naive type of behaviorist, one who had vowed to avoid all speculation about internal states of mind. In a year or two this very youngster, proposing the same theory, will almost certainly be able to tell us that kids who come from broken families feel bad about themselves and become trouble makers; but at this moment, although the child seems to have that general idea in mind, even the concept "broken family" may be a bit too abstract (or too unfamiliar) to state. Similarly, even such familiar denominatives as "trouble maker" or "delinquent" may be difficult either to understand or to express comfortably. At any rate, we note at this age level—although not universal even here—a common reliance on action language, the child being unable to talk about "traits" or "character" or other structures or tendencies of the personality. Instead he talks about specific acts of malfeasance.

Children at this age have no stable idea of the personality nor an understanding of motives beyond the most simple (getting mad, getting even, teaching a lesson). The youngster cannot think in terms of *gradations* of motives nor of *variations* in personality. Nor can he formulate the impact of the situation upon the personality. Nor can he propose a theory of incentives beyond simple coercion, nor can he recognize the symbolic or indirect effects of rewards and punishment.

What we have, in short, is a markedly impoverished conception of the personality. Motives are few and starkly simple—fear, anger, revenge, envy, the wish to be liked. Motives tend to be either/or in character—the child cannot easily think in terms of conflict of motives, of compromises among them, or of other dialectical processes that would ultimately determine behavior.

We also see a sharp limitation in time perspective. The child at this age seems unable to grasp fully the effect of the past upon the present, in that he does not seem to consider the effect of personal history upon current conduct. That statement needs some qualification. The child may mention the immediate precipitants of a course of current conduct but finds it difficult to link the present to more remote events in the person's past. Equally striking is the difficulty the youngster shows in tracing out spontaneously the potential effect of current conduct upon later events. Again, we do not want to overstate this: if the question clearly asked for future consequences (what would happen if there were no laws?), the child will imagine those consequences. But in ordinary discourse, the "time window" seems quite narrow. Beyond that, the youngster is rarely able to imagine dialectical processes taking place in the future as the result of decisions taken today—that, for example, an unpopular law may ultimately generate law breaking or other forms of underground opposition.

It may seem to be loading the dice somewhat to take our examples so exclusively from the realm of crime and punishment, given the child's obsessive involvement with these issues. Yet we see these difficulties elsewhere, even when the child is discussing virtue or merit, and for some of the same reasons—an uncertain sense of major and minor, relevant and irrelevant.

Appraising Social Reality

There are some surprising similarities between the preadolescent patterns in learning to understand human psychology and the gradual, at times faltering, steps he takes in developing a sense of social reality. In both instances we come across problems in classification: what belongs to what; how to construct a hierarchy of types and functions; how to specify boundaries and limits. In both instances we perceive a shortness of time perspective, the youngster being unable initially to imagine the effect of the past upon the present, or more than the immediate effect of current social events upon the more or less remote future. And in both instances we note what can only be called a thinness of texture; the child does not seem to grasp ambiguity, complexity, or interaction.

We want to begin by looking at a specific social institution in order to describe the changes that take place in the youngster's grasp of a structure and function and of its relation to larger social processes. We chose the idea of "political party" for several reasons; to begin with, almost all children raised in democratic countries are exposed to information about political parties, and in the fullness of time, achieve an adequate understanding of them; secondly, as an institution, it is neither so diffuse nor so various that different youngsters may have had entirely different experiences of it.

It comes as a surprise to most people how little children at the onset of adolescence actually understand about the nature and purpose of the political party. Since the knowledge of parties seems to be so ubiquitous and since the child is exposed to that knowledge regularly in the mass media, at home, or in school, we are likely to assume that that exposure has resulted in some learning, especially so if the child is the kind who is alert to current events. Nevertheless, a distinct majority of children at the age of eleven, twelve, and thirteen cannot give satisfactory answers to straightforward questions on the purpose and functioning of political parties—and by "satisfactory" we mean no exalted standards of comprehension. Either they cannot answer the questions at all (about 15 percent at age eleven) or they give answers that are either too diffuse to be coded or plainly in error. What is of particular interest is the kind of mistake the child is liable to make when he does venture an opinion. The most common of these is the tendency to confuse the functions of the political party with those of government as a whole. The party is seen as making laws or carrying out either the general or specific tasks of the state. But here are some characteristic expressions of that misunderstanding from some twelve-year-old boys chosen randomly:

> Ah, what, like the United States? I think they have these parties because they want to help the United States be a better state, I mean a better country and things like that. And then that's why they have one every one or two years.

> I guess because if they wanted a law a certain way then they could have it that way. (probe) I guess if they had a law that people couldn't kill, I guess they didn't like it that way. (Didn't like what?) Some people don't like laws and some people do.

> To keep people in order. (What else?) That's all I have to say. (Further probe) To keep people in order like I just said.

In these examples we sense that the child cannot yet classify, that is, cannot yet establish boundaries between the separate functions and structures of the political process. Since he has heard that parties are involved in elections, he may see them as carrying out elections; since he grasps vaguely that they are connected to government, he imputes to them some of the functions of government.

We might mention here, somewhat parenthetically, that these confusions and errors are by no means limited to the topic of the political party. We find much the same pattern in the early years of adolescence, when the child is addressing more general questions about governing. They can find it difficult to distinguish among the legislative, executive, and judicial apparatuses of the state; for that matter, they can find it difficult to distinguish between the government, the state, and the nation, all of which seem to blend into each other. That confusion of element, part standing for wholes and vice versa, characterizes the child's early apprehension of social and governmental institutions.

The next stage is marked by an accurate, although rudimentary, grasp of institutional function. It is a distinct advance over the confusion and error we have seen in the examples just given, and yet compared with what the child will later be capable of, it is marked by what we will call *thin* texture. The child will fasten upon a single, at most two, aspect of structure or function. With respect to political parties, we will be told that the party puts forward candidates or stands for certain ideas or supports candidates. From the interview:

> To help the candidates running to have a better chance of getting the office.
>
> Well, so that the people can express their views.
>
> It's to help the people find their candidates and to back the people when they are candidates.

The change from thin to thick texture is difficult to describe succinctly, since it may involve somewhat different processes. In the most simple form, we find a capacity to describe multiple aspects or functions of the institution being discussed. Thus, in relation to political parties, the youngster may tell us that parties both represent positions *and* support candidates, or that they both finance *and* organize for issues *and* their nominees. A step beyond that level is the ability to synthesize several ideas in a single statement. Here is an eighteen-year-old speaking on the advantages of political parties:

> A well, if you have a whole bunch of people with different ideas but have a government that's to be run, you are not going to get much accomplished, but

if you put them together in a group, and then they pool their assets and ideas, then they have enough power to do something about what they want, than everybody just talking about what they want.

Now this is by no means an extraordinary statement; the ordinary citizen would make it. And yet its very ordinariness may conceal from us that an important conceptual advance has taken place. She is telling us that parties are both efficient and potent in that they are able to unify otherwise disparate political voices: ideas in unison can be powerful, as they are not when voiced separately.

For reasons that are still obscure, at least to me, the degree of achievement of hypothetico-deductive reasoning that Piaget and other cognitive theorists have demonstrated to be involved in advance modes of reasoning in relation to scientific problems seems to be far less widespread in the social and philosophical reasoning of adolescents. When this degree of achievement occurs, it seems to take place much later in the child's development. The kind of cognitive operations that many children can perform at the ages of thirteen to fifteen when confronted with the mathematical and scientific problems seem to elude the grasp of all but the most exceptional youngsters when they confront problems of equivalent difficulty in the realm of social and humanistic ideas, and even among that exceptional group the level is not achieved until the age of eighteen.

Some Conclusions for Teaching

To return to the question we began from: Can the teacher of adolescents learn something from these findings? Can they improve the way we teach social and humanistic subjects?

In the course of preparing this essay, I read a good deal of the technical literature on learning, on concept formation, on whatever seemed germane, giving especially close scrutiny to those writings—few in number, alas—that make some effort to apply what we have learned in the laboratory to the actualities of teaching the young. It is not an edifying experience. The will is there, the earnestness, even a certain bumptiousness. Yet almost invariably something seems to be lost in translation, and with the best will in the world, we seem generally unable to use empirical findings, even reliable ones, to provide useful counsel to the educator. I think it can be done, but it will not be done easily, and it will certainly not be done by those who, like myself, are not directly engaged in teaching primary and secondary school youngsters. For that reason, what follows is offered modestly, indeed timidly.

When I first began doing the studies reported in this paper, my next-door neighbor was a man who taught social studies at our local junior high school.

I soon found myself trying out my findings on him, and although I don't know whether my observations improved his teaching, his observations on my findings certainly sharpened my research. One day I consulted him about the following problem. The interview schedule contained several questions on taxes through which we had hoped to explore the child's understanding of the larger social functions of taxation, for example, to provide incentives or deterrents for certain economic or social activities, or to redistribute income. The power to tax is the power to destroy, as we all have been told; when does the youngster grasp this and equivalent ideas about the indirect functions of the taxing authority?

As soon as we began doing the interviews we became aware that we had overshot the mark, in that the child's understanding of taxes was far less developed than we had expected it to be. Some of the younger children among the ten and eleven-year-olds understood next to nothing, only that the tax was something collected at the store when you bought something or something that one's parents had to pay to someone. More commonly, children did understand that the function of taxes was to raise revenue for government, but few of them could tell us more than that, and only a handful understood much about the use of taxes as a means of channeling economic and other behavior. One day I mentioned to my neighbor the general nature of these findings and how surprised our research group had been to discover how little children understood about this topic. He thought for a moment, then said that he himself was not surprised. Taxation was a required subject matter in the ninth grade civics course he taught, and he had found that children had trouble with it, indeed so much so that he tended to give the topic short shrift, moving on to more engaging issues as soon as he had covered the fundamentals. But why do the children have trouble, I asked. He wasn't sure, but he suspected it was because they did not find taxes to be of any direct importance to them. It was seen as an "adult" concern, and as a consequence they were bored. Being bored, they would not learn the information. That was, I should say, a characteristic formulation by my neighbor; he tended strongly to a motivational theory of learning, holding that if the child's interest could be captured, learning would follow as the night the day. As for myself, I was then in the first flush of a newly acquired Piagetism and urged that perspective on him, suggesting that the youngsters were not cognitively ready for those materials and that their boredom and inability to learn reflected an underlying confusion due to conceptual immaturity.

I am now not at all sure that I was right and my neighbor wrong, or vice versa. I suspect that we were both partly right, in that we had touched upon the right dimension: interest or motivation, cognitive capacity, and information (or knowledge). In this essay I have stressed cognitive growth almost to the exclusion of other determinants of learning. I think that stress is legitimate given the general neglect of that outlook until recently. Yet it must be understood to represent only one element of a more complex process wherein capacity, knowledge, and motivation interact continuously. If the child is not ready cognitively to grasp a particular concept, he will be unsteady in his grasp of related information, and he will also fail to show much interest in the general topic; at the same time, a high level of interest may stimulate the acquisition of knowledge and enhance cognitive capacity. Within limits, the mind stretches to fulfill its intellectual needs. In that sense the approach represented here—cognitive developmental—does not represent anything new so far as education is concerned. To the contrary, if one reads Piaget's writings on education, for example, one is immediately struck by its closeness in spirit to the work of John Dewey.

What, then, can this approach do for us? With respect to practical teaching it can alert us to the sources of specific difficulties the child is likely to experience in learning new information and ideas. Conversely, it may alert us to otherwise unrecognized intellectual opportunities the child is ready for and may teach us how to teach the child to grasp those opportunities. Let me offer an example. We found that at the outset of adolescence the youngster cannot adopt an as-if or conditional attitude to social or psychological phenomena. What is, is, now and forever. Bad people are bad and good people are good. If a law is passed, the child assumes it will stay in place eternally, and he has a hard time understanding that it can be overturned; he has an even harder time grasping that it might be amended, that one part of a law might be retained and another part rejected: it is all or nothing. One of the unrecognized achievements of the adolescent period is the acquisition of the concept of amendment, which is itself part of a larger movement of the mind away from static, either/or conceptions of events, structures, and persons. The more inclusive concept of *mutability*—for example, of persons changing or institutions in flux, is not easily grasped until middle to late adolescence.

Now it seems to be vitally important that a teacher charged with the instruction of young adolescents would do well to keep that knowledge in mind, particularly since he is charged with teaching dynamic processes—that is, processes involving change—relating to persons and societies. If he is teaching about "laws" he ought, at the least, remain aware that although he may have in mind modifiable statutes passed by a legislative body, the eleven-year-olds he is talking to have in mind something like the Ten Commandments. One might, in general, want to avoid certain topics as being too difficult conceptually; or one might try to develop methods of finessing those limitations, doing an end run around them; or one might want to develop methods of overcoming them. That choice is up to the teacher, and to the deviser of curricula.

Probably the most common problem the child experiences in dealing with social and humanistic materials is achieving the proper degree of abstractness; and the most common error the teacher makes comes from a failure to recognize the child's problem or to take account of it. As I suggested earlier in this essay, the child has a remarkable mimetic capacity, an ability to use the language of abstractness without genuine understanding. He may use a word like "majority" confidently, yet once we begin to query him we find he has only the vaguest idea of its meaning. Another such word is "government." Another is "election." By the former term, the ten- or eleven- or twelve-year-old child may very well have in mind the governor or the mayor or some other figure cloaked in the robes of authority. The child at the same age may not really know what it means to be "elected." He does not necessarily connect it with an electoral process but confuses it with being appointed, or perhaps even being anointed, that is, with having somehow assumed the cloak of authority.

Looking back, it is painfully clear that many of our first interviewees did not understand the meaning of these and other terms; nevertheless, it took us a long time to realize it. A youngster would half recognize a term and answer with some appropriate cliche or stark response, one sufficiently plausible to allow the conversation to continue. After we had examined several of these half-on, half-off responses, it would dawn on us that something was not quite right, and we would then discern that there was a concept present somewhat beyond the ken of the youngsters in question.

Why did we not see this immediately? Because the language of social and humanistic disciplines so largely overlaps common parlance, and its principles so largely overlap both common sense and common experience. That is not likely to happen in more technical disciplines. If I quiz a youngster on the properties of the isosceles triangle, his ignorance and confusion will be evident immediately; but if I quiz him about law and government, he may well be able to improvise sufficiently to conceal these states of mind. It is not that the youngster aims to deceive his interlocutor; rather, he may only be aiming to please, to give the answers that are wanted. It is the examiner who does the rest, filling in the gaps and elisions, imputing to the child a level of understanding that is largely in the mind of the beholder.

I might say here, a bit parenthetically, that there seems to be a general tendency among adults to inflate the understanding of the child in these areas. I have no firm idea why this is so, but I've seen this tendency in myself— it took me a long time to accept what the transcripts were clearly saying about the cognitive capacities of the children. I have since seen other adults, with few exceptions, make the same error, generally saying something along these lines: the findings may be true for this particular sample of children but would not be true for the children they knew, referring tacitly to their own children. But if they were to give the interview to their own children, as I did to mine, they would discover, as I did, that the intellectual gestalt that the child offers, via an overall aura of brightness, simply conceals the actual (lower) level of cognitive capacity. I suspect that classroom teachers, who deal with a variety of youngsters through the day, are less likely to misappraise cognitive level quite so often or to the usual degree; yet, I also suspect that the direction of error is similar, that they perceive in the child a more advanced grasp than is truly the case.

That may not be a bad thing, so far as education is concerned, to teach up rather than down in terms of cognitive level. It seems to me it may be helpful to introduce concepts just beyond the easy reach of the youngster. The cautions here are obvious: the concepts should not be too advanced nor should there be so many of them to cope with that the child feels overwhelmed. But keeping these cautions in mind, the teacher ought not to refrain from the use of, let us say, abstract ideas, notions of historical influence, or any of the other concepts or perspectives we found to be difficult for children at the threshold of adolescence. In some cases, these are helpful in providing a framework—albeit a loose or hazy one—to help the child organize the more concrete ideas he is more comfortable with.

Take as an example the concept of democracy. If a youngster between the ages of ten and twelve is asked to give a definition of that word he will almost certainly be unable to do so satisfactorily. He may address the question in strictly emotive terms, pronouncing on its merits, or he may mix up specific aspects of democratic systems—elections of the legislature or the presidency—with the system itself. Yet, if you extend the conversation with the child, you may find that he has in his grasp most of the specific elements that make up democratic modes of government. It seems to me that the teacher would at this point do well to help the child connect what he can grasp—the more or less concrete aspect of government—to the more general concepts, such as democracy. Often the problem is less in the child than it is in the adult, because adults—almost reflexively—think abstractly when thinking about abstract matters, and when faced with incomprehension, tend to explain things by piling abstraction upon abstraction.

There is another reason that we may want to teach concepts the child is not quite prepared to grasp fully—when they embody values we deem vital. Many American youngsters at this age will, when prompted, use such phrases as "freedom of speech" or "freedom of religion" or—in a few cases—"Bill of Rights." Further discussion reveals that their understanding is incomplete or incorrect in important ways. They are certainly unable to grasp these ideas as abstractions. Yet these concepts are by no means empty of meaning to them. The child may well have an idea of First Amendment rights that is overblown or absurd; he may, for example, think that it means an utterly untrammeled tolerance for freedom of expression; but what is more important is that he has grasped, in however inchoate a fashion, the kernel of the idea of rights, and in time that idea will be placed in context, given resonance, qualified, and so on. What is more important is that some of the American reverence for "rights" has been communicated to the child.

Much the same can be said for the democratic rituals that the child is exposed to as part of his schooling. In trying to discuss the electoral process, some of our children adverted to the elections for student council or class president or most popular boy or girl that they had experienced. It was clear enough that the younger ones had only the dimmest notion of the connections, if any, between those processes and the electoral politics they learned about in the mass media. It is tempting to dismiss those exercises, precisely because they seem to be so hollow, so absent of genuine understanding. But talking to so many dozens of adolescent children myself and reading so many hundreds of their interviews has persuaded me that these presumably empty rituals do have an important socializing effect in habituating the child to the practices of democratic politics.

Part V
Psychology and Psychoanalysis

16

Psychology, Ideology, and the Search for Faith

Early in my career I lived in a small community, many of whose members were intellectuals or artists. I had just begun my own psychoanalysis, and because misery loves company I became an enthusiastic proselytizer, much given to attempts at persuading my colleagues to try it. It will do wonders for you, I said shamelessly. They were interested, even tantalized—psycho-analysis was then just on the verge of becoming fashionable—and yet they held back, for two reasons. First, it was thought that psychoanalysis might damage creativity. This was a time when the link between art and neurosis was the subject of much discussion in intellectual circles, witness Lionel Trilling's celebrated essay, or Edmund Wilson's *The Wound and the Bow*. To this I would reply that there was no evidence supporting the notion and that, to the contrary, psychotherapy more often unchained the talents con-stricted by neurosis. I would make precisely the same argument today, and with even greater confidence.

The second reason given ran along these lines: Although my friends admired Freud and thought him a genius, they were not at all sure about the ordinary working psychotherapist. They feared coming under the unwarranted influ-ence of an inferior mind, or provincial attitudes, or a world view lacking in power and sophistication. To this I would reply that they misunderstood psychotherapy, that the process was not preceptive but eductive, that is, its intention was not to indoctrinate but to explore. Indeed, I would go on, its essential merit was that it would not instruct nor mandate nor attitudinize; it provided instead a refuge, a quiet haven for the scrutiny of the self's vicis-situdes.

I would hesitate to offer that same argument today, in part because I can see that the issue is not so readily disposed of, that it is rather more complex than I once believed. But I would hesitate today for a more important reason; The psychotherapeutic scene itself has changed, and the ideal of value-neu-trality has been decisively eroded. In many ways, large and small, overt and covert, wittingly and unwittingly, gross and subtle, psychotherapy has become politicized. Indeed, much of the time it is a vehicle of unwarranted influence, involving silent but powerful indoctrination—just as my colleagues had once feared. And also as they had feared, as often as not the ideas transmitted are parochial or half-baked or merely modish.

A colleague of mine has recently observed that women are sometimes referred to her as patients because she has successfully combined career and family, and so would presumably provide a good role model. She is irritated by this, and rightly so, because such referrals are made on the grounds of gender and circumstance rather than competence. I might add that all my female colleagues, quite without exception, resent such referrals for precisely the same reason.

But there is an entirely different reason to be offended. I would like to ask why the referring analyst believes that it is his prerogative to determine what kind of model a patient needs. At the very least, such an assessment is premature, for it prejudges certain choices that should become evident only after psychotherapy, if then. What is even more troubling is the lighthearted arrogance expressed in the presumption that it is the psychologist's task to make such decisions. It is not. The psychologist is in no way licensed to offer moral pedagogy, even when it takes the form of tacit instruction about goals, roles, and life-styles. To get some perspective on the matter, consider what reaction would be forthcoming if the referring analyst had said something like this: "I am *not* going to send this woman to see you, because the last model in the world she needs is someone like you. She should see someone who would encourage her to be a good wife and mother and give up these foolish notions about a career." Yet the two instances are essentially the same, the only difference being that the idea of women having a career is now very much in fashion, just as it was very much out of fashion twenty years ago. In both instances, the real and the hypothetical, the psychologist has insouciantly taken on himself powers of decision that are not rightly his.

I would not wish to make too much of this example; the sin is venial. All therapists, in unguarded moments, have said similar things, or worse— thoughtlessly and generally harmlessly. I use it only to illustrate a more general problem: The ideal of disinterestedness—the separation of ideology from practice—is increasingly being abandoned, sometimes for the curious reason that because it cannot be perfectly achieved, one ought not to strive for it at all. The loss of this ideal is evident even in scholarship. One can no longer fully trust the probity of scientific research and commentary concerning a politically controversial topic. My own area of work has been the young in general and their politics in particular, one of the hot topics of the late 1960s, and my two decades of experience have induced an overwhelming skepticism about all writing on this topic, including at times my own. One learns to parse each sentence, to scrutinize each table, to recalculate each statistic. And as we all know, the same is true for other controversial issues in psychology, heredity and intelligence being the most obvious; more recently, the nature and innateness of sex differences. The great statement of the scholar's need for value-neutrality in his work is Max Weber's classic essay "Science as a Vocation." When I reread it recently, I was forced to conclude lamentably that things have not gotten better since Weber's time, and in some respects they have gotten worse.

But if the situation is troublesome in the social sciences, it is very nearly egregious in the practice of psychotherapy. One can easily see why. In science and scholarship, dialogues are public, and other voices can be heard; therapeutic interchanges are generally private. Science and scholarship involve conversations among peers; psychotherapy inherently involves inequality, even when we pretend otherwise. The tradition of objectivity is strong in the former case, relatively weak in the latter. All in all, in the practice and theory of psychotherapy we find fewer of the extrinsic constraints that might keep partisan impulses in check. Hence in a politicized and politicizing era, one in which messianic impulses run wild, the analytic attitude is lost. We are possessed by our presuppositions.

What is most disheartening is to see how the preceptive mode—the need to make judgments, to instruct, to legislate—preempts openness of heart and mind among so many students. I teach a graduate course in psychotherapy and find that a significant minority of my students, about a third, though only at the beginning of their learning seem already beyond its reach. They live within a cacophony of slogans, catchphrases, buzzwords, and other forms of cant; they are filled with an adversary passion. For example, to illustrate the workings of "transference" from patient to therapist in an uncomplicated case, I tell my students about a former patient, a young woman married to a successful and rising professional. Her marriage is a satisfying one; they have two preschool children, both of them happy and developing normally; they have just moved into a new home; their prospects could not be brighter. Nevertheless, just after their house had been built, she began to feel depressed. More serious still, she had developed an obsessive fear, which she herself understood to be irrational, that her husband would soon leave her for a younger and more attractive woman.

As I recount this rather ordinary story, I sense that a few of my students are unhappy, and after some conversation it becomes evident that they do not approve of her—she is too comfortably bourgeois, too comfortably domestic. They like patients they can feel sorry for, or sentimental about. Worse yet, as our colloquy develops it appears that they have arrived at certain conclusions about her problem, to wit, that she is leading a shallow suburban life, that she secretly hates being trapped in the role of housewife, that she resents her husband's dominance, that she should be encouraged to be assertive, and on and on, each and every one of the tired, thin, trite, superficial slogans of the phony social science of the television talk shows. One listens to this bemused at first, then impatient, and finally in despair, not merely because these formulas are, each and every one, utterly mistaken when applied to this patient but even more so because of the mixture of didacticism and moral superiority that informs the opinions. It is an attitude of mind that resists the particular; what is particular must be forced into the Procrustean bed of ideology. T. S. Eliot said of Henry James that he had a mind so fine that no idea could violate it, using the word *idea* in the sense of ideology; what we have now are minds not merely violated but entirely consumed.

The problem is compounded these days because the constituency for psychotherapy so often shares the ideologizing temper; hence the therapist and client enter into a sort of collusion, an agreement in restraint of therapeutic trade, so to speak, wherein certain questions will not be raised, certain assumptions never examined, certain conflicts never explored. Sometimes this is done quite directly, as when one is cross-examined about one's views on such matters as politics, religion, sexual preference; or penis envy; or when one is listed or blacklisted by various militant groups as either having or not having acceptable opinions on these or other matters.

But far more often the complicity is essentially unwitting, and even unwanted. Much of the time the patient does not have a clearly defined idea of what the problem is. The symptoms themselves may be diffuse or murky, or when they are sharply felt, the patient may be unable to place them in an acceptable framework of meaning. Thus the patient has been struggling to make sense of his personal situation even before entering the therapist's office, and the struggle persists in the introductory phases of the therapy—the patient searching for the language of motives that will be acceptable to the therapist so that their dialogue can begin. As any therapist can attest, these early hours are often critical because the patient, while trying to make himself understood both to himself and to the listener, is also listening, listening avidly to pick up a sense of the language that is to be common to them. Almost invariably, these early efforts at self-explanation further the resistance, at least partially; they are elaborations of the prevailing defensiveness, and the therapist must be ever alert to that possibility, particularly when the language chosen reflects the cliches of the patient's milieu, or of the therapist's.

Another example, again a fairly commonplace one: a woman in her early thirties, of aristocratic origins, married to a young academic. She is initially quite agitated. She recently and inexplicably has an anxiety attack, and although it was neither prolonged nor severe, she is terrified that she may be going crazy. She is a forceful woman, and she importunes me to tell her whether or not she is insane, and in either case to cure her rapidly. When I say "forceful," I mean that she shouts at me at the top of her lungs: the walls shake; I shake. I am later to learn that imperious anger is her customary way of controlling anxiety. But what she is so anxious about is not at all clear. In trying to understand seemingly sudden ruptures in the sense of well-being, a therapist usually begins by looking for losses or transitions, immediately past, or present, or pending. To be sure, her husband's prospects for achieving tenure are uncertain, and that worries her; she has just developed minor arthritic symptoms that may interfere with the sports that mean so much to her; but neither of these problems seem prima facie troubling enough to warrant the panic that now appears to possess her.

What really puzzles me in our early conversations is that I get no sense of how she locates herself in the life cycle, where she is, temporally speaking,and what she is moving toward. I raise the issue in the most general way, and she tells me, somewhat petulantly, that she has thought of having a baby. She is sure her husband wants one to carry on the family name, but she has decided she would not be a good mother, and it would interfere with her self-fulfillment. I am immediately alerted because the statement seems out of character, contrived; it is the first false note I have heard from her. One can almost hear the tumblers falling into place: baby, click; husband's pressure, click; self-fulfillment, click, click, click. An ideological trap is being baited, unconsciously; she thinks this is the language I want to hear, and if it serves her defenses, so much the better. And as matters turned out, to have taken the bait would have delayed at least and perhaps foreclosed the discoveries that were to come.

I will compress a long and fascinating period of therapy. The pressure to have a baby, we ultimately learned, did not come from her husband, who was in fact sympathetic to her wishes, but from within her and was imputed to him. More important, she did want the baby, desperately so, but was concealing a phobic anxiety about childbirth by pretending to herself that she was indifferent. And once we learned that, we learned the real secret: her mother had been hospitalized in a psychotic state immediately after she was born and had proved incompetent to care for her after being discharged, so that she was taken from her mother and put in the care of a nurse-governess. We were thus able to understand her fear of going crazy, and the conviction that she would prove an unfit mother. She felt she was destined to relive her mother's experience with her: to give birth, to go crazy, to be declared incompetent, and to have her own child taken away, as she herself had been. For those of you who like happy endings, she did have a baby, and proved to have prodigious maternal feelings. And for those of you who think I simply helped lock her into the nursery, the therapy also uncovered and resolved a long-standing intellectual inhibition; she is now enrolled in professional school. Those were her ambitions, not mine. Had she been content at the end of the therapy to return to the life of aristocratic ease in which she had been raised (she is the heiress to a substantial fortune) that would have been all right with me, too. Her goals are her business, not mine.

This struggle between the preceptive and eductive modes is by no means new to the history of psychotherapy; to the contrary, we find it appearing at the very onset of its history, in the responses of Jung and Adler to Freud's method. We have a brilliant exegesis of this conflict in Philip Rieff's *The Triumph of the Therapeutic*. He points out that "in their different ways both Adler and Jung sought in psychoanalysis a total theory, to which a patient could commit himself wholly. . . . More modestly, Freud sought to give men that power of insight which would increase their power to choose; but he had no intention of telling them what they ought to choose. . . . To make men do less harm than they might otherwise do was the limit of Freud's ambition. He had no interest in creating a doctrine of the good life, nor one of the good society." Rieff later notes that Adler's doctrine led into politics, and Jung's into religion; thus to an astonishing degree these psychologies prefigure the directions taken by current preceptive psychotherapies.

No one reads Adler today, and few read Jung, but you will find in Adler a complete anticipation of the politicized psychotherapies of our day; feminism, for example, is little more than warmed-over Adlerianism, with its emphasis upon power, super ordination, and even the "masculine protest." And you will find in Jung an equally complete anticipation of that incredible hodgepodge of semi- and pseudo- and quasi-religious therapies that will soon dominate the mass market for instant healing, though in all fairness I must emphasize the vast differences between the thin intellectual gruel of these latter-day derivatives and the erudition and variety found in Jung's writings.

It is this mass market for healing that increasingly dominates the practice of psychotherapy, and much of its theory. To a remarkable degree our clients are drawn from what we have come to call the New Class, that is, from that large and growing segments of the upper middle class devoted to the production and communication of knowledge and beliefs: college teachers (especially in the humanities and social sciences) and those working in the media, in entertainment, and in government and corporate bureaucracies devoted to knowledge or public relations. Though only a few create new knowledge, their social function is to be alert to what is novel and emergent, not merely ideas but also attitudes, moral postures, life-styles. This group is mobile, generally transient; with respect to origins, deracinated. It is both the carrier and the victim of modernity; having abandoned traditional values and restraints, members of the "new class" search restlessly for substitutes, generally making do with what is fashionable as causes or crusades, though unconsciously hungering for some kind of absolutism. It is no surprise that their children are so often drawn to political or religious tyrants.

The emergence and condition of this class was foreseen with uncanny prescience by our great predecessors in social theory: Durkheim, Weber, Schumpeter. What no one could foresee was the extent to which psychotherapy would be used as a replacement for lost faith. It was not until the appearance of Rieff's memorable writings that the interaction between psychotherapy and morality in the modern era came fully into view, and I would guess that even Rieff, writing a little over a decade ago, did not anticipate how rapidly and how pervasively the religious impulse—whether expressed in eccentric versions of traditional faith or in millennial political ideas—would transform psychotherapy. We can now see that practitioners and clients belonging to the same New Class, sharing the same sensibilities and suffering the same self-doubt, come together as priest and acolyte—not in search of self-knowledge but in search of a faith that will console them both.

17

The Self and Memory in *1984*

We do not think of George Orwell as a psychological novelist, and on the whole we are correct in that judgment. Orwell does not take us deeply into the inner life of his characters, nor does he deal with exotic psychological types, nor does he spend much time linking personal history to later behavior. At times he could be dismissive toward those who were in his view inappropriately "psychological." In his discussion of Arthur Koestler's *Arrival and Departure* he comes down hard on the novel's major idea, "that revolutionary activity is the result of personal maladjustment." That may be so, Orwell says, indeed it probably is so, but so what? "Actions have results irrespective of their motives." To be sure, he would sometimes use similar explanations when it suited his purposes, but most of the time he kept psychology firmly in its place. In his essay on P. G. Wodehouse, writing on what it is that led Wodehouse to broadcast for the Germans during the war, he seems to eschew any speculation on Wodehouse's personal motives, speaking instead of his "mentality," by which he means the author's limited and antiquated understanding of reality. It is a cognitive view of Wodehouse rather than a psychodynamic one. And in his many, many acerbic and disgusted observations of the perfidy of intellectuals, their appetite for the totalitarian state, I cannot recall a single comment having to do with their inner motivations, individually or collectively. Perhaps there are some we can find in that vast body of work, but it is fair to say that these are occasional. If Mr. Jones, who was once a Mosley Fascist, and later a member of the Communist party, and later still a convert to the Roman Catholic Church, now announces that he has given up politics and religion to become a vegetarian, Orwell may make note of that history, but only for what it reveals about the man's habits of mind— that is, his way of thinking—rather than for what it may say about his inner conflicts or his mental health. That reticence is refreshing, living as we do in a time and place simply besotted with psychology and psychologizing— much of it gratuitous, superficial, and vulgar.

So I did not think there would be much to say, even on a close rereading, about Orwell as a psychological writer. His work would prove to be interesting politically and morally but would provide little nourishment for those interested in the complications of mind. In *Sincerity and Authenticity*, Lionel

Trilling speaks of the common nineteenth-century judgment of the English, that their unique moral type was marked by "probity and candour." He quotes Emerson's *English Traits*, pointing to sincerity as the basis of their moral style: they "are blunt in expressing what they think and they expect others to be no less so." Probity, sincerity, candor—that summed up Orwell perfectly, as a man and as a writer: a quintessentially nineteenth-century English personality, honest, open, a bit innocent.

It is not a type much given to an agitated speculation on motives. But now imagine that personality cast adrift in another time and place, one marked in its politics by lies, dissimulation, contradiction, hypocrisy, duplicity. Imagine it to be this kind of place: Something that is said to have happened did not happen; something that did happen is said not to have happened. Someone who was there at the time, and saw that it took place, now says with complete conviction that it never did take place. He will swear to it. We must imagine what our nineteenth-century personality might ask himself: How is one persuaded to overcome memory? How is self-deception engineered, and once engineered, what are its consequences for the self? Conversely, what allows someone to resist falsehood? How is probity achieved, and what are its consequences?

Let me anticipate my argument: These questions haunt Orwell's writing from 1937, following his return from Spain, to the end of his life and the publication of *1984*, somewhat over ten years later. These questions begin from the shocked recognition of political lying, and what is worse, lying by the presumably progressive and humane elements in society. In pondering those question he was led—almost against his will, certainly against his native bent—to treat in his fiction many of the issues that torment modern psychology.

We are now so accustomed to political lying, it is so much a part of the climate of politics, that we find it hard to credit its traumatic effect upon Orwell. He went to Spain to fight a good clean fight against the Fascists, as so many other innocents did, and once there found that the Communist forces were far more eager to eliminate their rivals on the left than they were to win the war. The word "eliminate" is to be taken literally here, for the Communists meant to do more than win a political victory; they meant to get rid of their rivals by treachery and murder. That was bad enough. What made it worse for Orwell was his discovery upon returning from Spain that the story was not being told, that the slogans of revolution were being used to conceal a bloodbath directed against the revolution itself, that the liberal and left journals in England were quite deliberately telling their readers a pack of lies, which this audience was quite content to believe.

Confronting this state of affairs—the lies told abroad, the lies told at home—enraged Orwell, and ultimately made him a changed man. The first article he wrote on his return was entitled "Spilling the Spanish Beans," the first line reading: "The Spanish war has probably produced a richer crop of lies than any event since the Great War . . .," then going on to say that it was the "left wing papers . . . with their far subtler methods of distortion, that have prevented the British public from grasping the real nature of the struggle." Orwell then specifies the tactics through which allies are discredited, and are turned into political enemies, enemies so vicious indeed as to require elimination. "The logical end is a regime in which every opposition party and newspaper is suppressed and every dissenter of any importance is in jail." Quite clearly the ideas that were to find their way into *Animal Farm* and *1984* were already evident in 1937. Orwell found himself isolated in much the way he described, his journalism rejected for taking the wrong political line, as was his book on Spain, the great *Homage to Catalonia*, which was turned down by Orwell's publisher even before it was written, for the same reason. We begin to see Orwell's writing haunted by the theme of falsehood. In the year after he returned from Spain, almost every letter and review we have available adverts to it.

The war provided another experience that was to influence Orwell's thinking. It brought him into touch with the internecine rivalries of the international Left—much more savage than the British variety—and above all, it brought home to him the importance of the Moscow show trials, which exposed an entirely new dimension of political lying, the confession of error and treason by the losing side of the revolutionary party. Here were the revered figures of the Revolution, the Old Bolsheviks, the apostles, confessing abjectly to having betrayed that revolution, to having conspired with its enemies, and to having done so almost from the beginning. Here they were confessing to crimes that had not taken place, that were impossible psychologically, but beyond that, could not have been carried out because the historical record proved otherwise—Comrade X, confessing to a secret meeting with capitalist agents in, let us say Berlin, was in fact at that very moment at a party meeting in Leningrad, as official documents would show.

Show trials were later to become commonplace—routine rituals in totalitarian regimes—so we may find it difficult to appreciate the shock of their first appearance, that is, among those immersed in the politics of the Left. Of course, many believers kept on believing, blinded by faith or stupidity; and of course many believers did not believe, but pretended to because that was the progressive thing to do; but there were some deeply of the Left, like Orwell and Koestler, who understood quickly that the trials were a malevolent charade, the defendants having been coerced into false confessions. You then found yourself struggling with unexpected and perplexing psychological questions. How were the confessions induced? By physical means—torture and privation? By psychological means, and if so, which ones? New drugs, perhaps, or new methods of hypnosis, or more conventional means of persuasion? Those broken creatures on the stand, telling lies about themselves: Did they now believe what they were saying or did they keep one part of their minds clear and in touch with the truth, or were they now too confused or indifferent to know the difference between truth and untruth? What had happened to these men, as total human beings? These questions led in turn to others: Why did the regime feel it vital to have these men confess publicly? Why did it not merely murder them, secretly or openly, slowly or swiftly, as it was doing with hundreds of others? Did Stalin, in his paranoia, believe the lies he was forcing his opponents to confess to, thus making untruth into truth? Or was he inducing the confession of what he knew to be lies, as a display of consummate power?

So the Spanish war provided Orwell with a theme that was to inspirit his writing for the rest of his life: the political lie—its origins, its vicissitudes, its functions, its aims, its effects. Some of his most powerful essays examine its consequences for thinking and writing: the famous "Politics and the English Language" and "The Prevention of Literature." In "Writers and Leviathan," one of the last full-scale essays he wrote—on the relation of politics and writing—one finds, in a seven-page article, fourteen separate references to falsehood or self-deception. Even in his minor writing, the casual newspaper columns, we find him contemplating the lie, and its effects on the mind. In one of these brief pieces he offers some examples of what was later to be called "doublethink"—as he says, "the power of holding simultaneously two beliefs which cancel out. Closely allied to it is the power of ignoring facts which are obvious and unalterable, and which will have to be faced sooner or later." Orwell is obsessed by the lie, and I do not use the term pejoratively because the obsession is rational: Everywhere he looks, he finds that politics, and especially the high-minded politics of the intellectual, consists of people being lied to, and lying to others, and lying to themselves. As you read through the four magnificent volumes of his essays, journalism, and letters, you watch this calm, sardonic man overcome by exasperation— and perhaps some despair, and perhaps some smoldering rage—as he witnesses the triumph of falsehood in world politics. The obsession recedes only in the very last year of his life, when he was writing 1984, and which we will imagine was absorbing all he had left to say on those questions.

Through his preoccupation with the lie, Orwell was led in unwitting prescience to issues that were about to overtake psychology and psychiatry: the idea of the self, and its division into true and false sides. To deceive oneself, or to allow oneself to be deceived, without inner protest is to divide oneself. In dealing with a divided self, as he does in 1984, Orwell was looking ahead to psychologies not yet written. He was also—again I suspect unwittingly— looking back to the birth of modern psychology, in the latter part of the nineteenth century, when such writers as William James and Pierre Janet were trying to fashion a theory of the self, and a theory of inner division. That direction of thought, though never quite forgotten, had been put aside by the triumph and continuing hegemony of Freud's doctrine. Not that psychoanalysis was uninterested in the problem of how we deceive ourselves, to the contrary; but it was hostile to the concept of the self. It was, and in many ways it still is, for the self-concept is seen as a sly way of bringing back to life a moribund, discredited psychology of mere consciousness. Hence those psychologies that posited a self, or even implied it, came to be seen as anti-Freudian, in intention or effect—that is, as nondynamic, superficial, simpleminded, retrogressive. The history of Freudian polemics is for the most part a history of denunciations of those who tried to reintroduce the idea of the self, that is, the self not merely as a derivative of more fundamental processes but as an active, autonomous agent striving to fulfill aims of its own. So the self-theorists were slain, one after another, decade after decade—Adler, Horney, Fromm, Sullivan, all of the existentialists, most of the English school, such as Fairbairn and Winnicott, most recently Heinz Kohut—each slain, yet each arising again, in a new, generally improved version. In a way, it is a return of the repressed.

These theories rose again because they were willing to address a number of questions psychoanalysis would consider only late in its history, and even then uneasily. "What is the nature and source of the self, and of personal identity?" "How do we achieve and sustain the sense of self-worth?" "How do we understand and treat the divided self?" I have suggested that these questions have been with us from the beginning, that they were present at the creation of modern psychology, in the second half of the nineteenth century. William James's work is of particular interest to us here, in part because his writings on the self have remained amazingly contemporary, though nearly a century old, and in part because in his masterwork, *Varieties of Religious Experience*, he sets forth an analysis of the sick soul in search of its cure that provides, through ironic juxtaposition, some remarkable commentary on the failed voyage toward redemption recounted in *1984*.

At the very heart of James's book we come upon a cluster of chapters entitled "The Sick Soul"; "The Divided Self and the Process of Its Unification"; and "Conversion." In the first sentence of the first of the two chapters on conversion, James writes as follows: "To be converted, to be regenerated, to receive grace, to experience religion, to gain an assurance, are so many phrases which denote the process, gradually or sudden, by which a self hitherto divided, and consciously wrong, inferior, and unhappy, becomes unified and consciously right, superior, and happy, in consequence of its firmer hold upon religious realities." That sentence may serve us as a text for one understanding of *1984*.

When the novel opens, Winston Smith is a soul sick and divided, wrong, inferior, and unhappy, who seeks to be unified, to become right, superior, and happy. In James's language, he seeks "a process of remedying inner incompleteness and reducing inner discord." He is in a state of anhedonia, a term James brought to general awareness, and which he defined as "passive joylessness and dreariness, discouragement, dejection, lack of taste and zest and spring." He comes to life through his love for Julia, and then seeks to heal his sickness and inner division through a symbiosis with O'Brien. The faith he seeks eludes him; indeed his very seeking is turned against him, cruelly so, for in asking to be replenished, healed, and unified, he is at the end of his journey emptied and destroyed.

Orwell takes the traditional idea of conversion, as we find it in James, and turns it upside down. In its true religious meaning, conversion is a moment of epiphany, in which grace, insight, and conviction arise from within, unbidden, unforced, miraculous. In the brutal, climactic moments of *1984*, in the chilling dialogue with Winston, O'Brien uses the term twice, first to tell Winston that Julia has betrayed him, and that she did so quickly: "I have seldom seen anyone come over to us so promptly. . . . It was a perfect conversion, a textbook case." At another point in the interrogation, O'Brien tells Winston that he is not content "with the most abject submission. . . . We do not destroy the heretic because he resists us; so long as he resists us, we never destroy him. We convert him; we capture his inner mind; we reshape him. We burn all evil and all illusion out of him; we bring him over to our side, not in appearance, but genuinely, heart and soul." You may want to remember James's words on the outcome of conversion: "To be regenerated, to receive grace, to experience religion, to gain an assurance," and then listen to O'Brien's counterpoint, "Never again will you be capable of love, or friendship, or joy of living, or laughter, or curiosity, or integrity. You will be hollow. We shall squeeze you empty, and we shall fill you with ourselves." Throughout these terrible passages Orwell plays brilliantly upon traditional religious language. O'Brien tells Winston that "everyone is washed clean," and at another point, "always we shall have the heretic at our mercy, screaming with pain, broken up, contemptible—and in the end utterly penitent, saved from himself, crawling to our feet of his own accord."

The destruction of personality O'Brien proposes, undertakes, and achieves has already been prepared by the erosion of personal identity in Oceania, an erosion accomplished by the steady chipping away of memory by its institutions, by doublethink and the memory hole and the Ministry of Truth. The questions that had been nagging at Orwell since his return from Spain, as he witnessed the unchecked spread of deceit in politics, are at last answered in *1984*: to lie, to be lied to, to accept being lied to, or to rationalize and defend lying for the sake of a better world—all of that, taken to its extreme, will produce a sick and divided soul. The rewriting of history destroys any sense of past, and with it the sense of personal continuity. That is by no means a surreptitious theme in *1984*. At the thematic climax of the book, O'Brien asks Winston whether he believes that the past has real existence. He replies that it does, that it can be found in the records, in the mind, and in human memories. O'Brien counters that the Party controls all records and all memories, indeed controls the nature of reality, and to drive the point home undertakes the torture of Winston, forcing him to confess to a false reality, that two and two equal five.

Winston yields, but he has already been weakened, as we learn from his struggle throughout the book to remember his own past. From beginning to end, *1984* is taken up with Winston's efforts at recollection. At the beginning: "He tried to squeeze out some childhood memory that should tell him whether London had always been quite like this." We soon learn that he has bought a diary, so as to preserve a record of the past for the future, and he fills it with scattered recollections of his own past. Throughout the book he is tormented by a vain attempt to recover memories of his mother and sister, who had disappeared suddenly and without explanation, and at the end we have Winston recalling, unexpectedly, a happy childhood memory, one of reconciliation with his mother—a memory he dismisses as false, saying to himself, "Some things have happened, others have not happened." And if that sentence has a familiar ring to it, it is because it repeats Orwell's bitter complaints about the journalism of the Spanish war, that things happened that were not reported, and things did not happen that were.

Winston Smith's argument is Cartesian: "I remember, therefore I exist." To which O'Brien replies: "I control memory, and therefore your existence." As a number of commentators have pointed out, Winston can be understood as a last remnant of Western individualism, now about to be crushed by the megastate. He believes that he is unique and thus precious, in possessing a store of personal memory that defines him, and that cannot be taken away from him. It is a claim O'Brien dismisses contemptuously, telling him that men are malleable, and infinitely so. The debate between them is between two views of human nature—both of which can be said to underlie contemporary liberalism, and which account for much of the confusion and contradiction in current democratic thinking. Winston is a Pelagian, in that he believes in innate human goodness, and a Kantian, in that he believes man to have an intrinsic moral sense and thus an inherent moral dignity. O'Brien is the ultimate Lockean, believing that man is nothing beyond what the social order chooses to instill. As he tells Winston, "We shall squeeze you empty, and we shall fill you with ourselves."

18

Still Vital after All These Years

In an often-quoted letter to his publisher Henry Holt, written just as he was about to send off *The Principles of Psychology*, William James described the book as "a loathsome, distended, tumefied, bloated, dropsical mass." Don't believe it; falser words were never spoken. What that outburst tells us is that anyone, even a genius upon completion of a masterpiece, is capable of the most grotesque forms of authorial disgust and self-hatred—just like the rest of us.

That mass, that masterpiece, is now available in the definitive scholarly edition, published by the Harvard University Press ($75). There are three volumes, two of text totaling about 1,300 pages, and a remarkable third volume containing notes, emendations, references, James's corrections, and similar bibliographic aids. There are two splendid introductions, one by Gerald E. Myers, from the point of view of philosophy, and another by Rand B. Evans, from that of psychology; there is also a long, carefully detailed account of the writing and publication history of *Principles*. It has been put together by a distinguished team of scholars, led by the philosopher and James scholar Frederick Burkhardt, and by Fredson Bowers, one of the world's most famous bibliographic specialists. *The Principles of Psychology* is simply a stunning achievement, a triumph of U.S. scholarship.

Principles, first published in 1890, is the single greatest work in U.S. psychology. Among books written by psychologists, its only rival is Freud's *The Interpretation of Dreams*. It was James's first major work, and at the same time his last significant contribution to psychology; thus the same book stands as both his debut and swan song. The work took twelve years to complete, most of that time spent in psychological agony, in part because of the high standards James set for himself, in part because of the (possibly psychogenic) vision problems he suffered from at the time. Yet the book was successful from the start. James's peers in psychology—a handful in number but mighty in stature—sensed from the beginning that the work was something special, even when they did not like this or that about it, above all the breezy and offhand manner James would sometimes bring to bear on topics and personalities usually treated with great solemnity. The earlier reviewers of *Principles* make up a pantheon of those present at the creation of U.S. philosophy and psychology: among others, Charles Peirce, George Santayana, G. Stanley Hall, and John Dewey. Of these, only the irascible, eccentric Peirce was deeply negative; even Santayana, so alienated from James in temperament and outlook, treated the book respectfully. That critical success was soon matched by substantial sales and widespread acceptance as the standard text for the emerging discipline of psychology. Although it is difficult to trace the exact steps through which an early success survives the moment, becomes a standard, and then a classic, that brutally Darwinian process seems to have taken place with *Principles*. It *is* a classic; it is *our* classic.

Yet having said that, some questions remain. There are classics, and then there are classics. There are some we admire, even venerate, yet feel no impulse to read. We are content that they retain the nimbus of fame just so long as they stay safely on the shelf and out of our hands. There are other books we are drawn to; in the current jargon, they speak to us, that is, we find them to be germane to our own moment. A book may be great, yet its assumptions or concerns may be so removed from our own that we prefer to leave its reading and study to the scholarly specialists. In the Jamesian canon, there is at least one great work that has remained truly contemporary: *The Varieties of Religious Experience*. As the eminent philosopher William Barrett wrote recently, it "improves as a classic with each rereading"—never more so than at the present time, when the widespread revival of religious feeling, often taking bizarre forms, reminds us of the prescience and wisdom of James's attention to belief, faith, and religiosity.

Can we say the same of *The Principles of Psychology*? Is it contemporary in the sense that *Varieties* is, or Freud on dreams? Is it a book that we can profit from rereading now, and if so, in what ways, and if not, why not? Science ages very rapidly; has that happened to *Principles*, which was published nearly a century ago? Those were some of the questions put to me by our editors. I was to read through *Principles*, and offer the response of an ordinary psychologist, that is, not someone learned in philosophy, or in the history of psychology, or in those fairly narrow areas of experimental psychology that are discussed at length in the book. Indeed, I could if I chose write in a personal vein, an impressionistic account of my reactions. It was an offer too tempting to refuse, to write informally, essayistically about the most informal, most essayistic of all psychologists.

My first and most enduring response was to be reminded of James's literary genius. I believe that he was the most gifted writer of expository prose this country has ever had. I of course knew beforehand that James was a great writer, but somehow it had become lodged in the back of my head. I had somehow come to think of him as a crafter of memorable phrases ("blooming, buzzing confusion") or of set pieces, ranging from famous paragraphs to famous essays. For example, the extraordinary chapter "Habit" in this book, and in particular, the compelling paragraph beginning "Habit is thus the enormous flywheel of society. . . ." It is as though one were to admire Mozart only for his "highlights" rather than for his fecundity and variety. That may seem to be a strange conjunction—James and Mozart—but I think there is something to be said for it. In both cases we are struck by a seemingly infinite fertility of invention, along with the ability to work gracefully in all forms of the art.

James's versatility, as both writer and thinker, is evident at every point throughout this book. There is nothing out of his range. He will provide a lucid, masterful summary of the evidence bearing upon a given topic; will consider both the overt and tacit arguments involved in the research he is reviewing; will launch himself into what he calls "hortatory ethics," spelling out the moral or spiritual implications of a position he has taken; will dismiss a position he finds wrongheaded with a single sardonic brilliancy; and yet will devote dozens of pages to the exhaustive (and exhausting) examination of an argument that, he feels, deserves and requires careful scrutiny.

To use the distinction made famous by Isaiah Berlin—the hedgehog and the fox—James is the complete fox, someone who knew about and could write about everything in psychology. When one finishes this book, one feels that James knew everything there was to know at the time, and that it was perhaps the last time in the history of psychology when one man was able to know everything.

Though the sources of his literary genius are mysterious, as sources always are, it is not quite so difficult to account for his erudition. He was initially trained in science and medicine, then worked in the experimental psychology of the time (though listlessly), and ultimately found his metier in philosophy. We must not think of this in the twentieth-century way, as though James achieved his catholicity of knowledge by acquiring degrees of credentials. In fact his erudition was more directly the result of an astonishingly cosmopolitan earlier life. His father, the scion of an immensely wealthy family, and a prolific though unpublished writer in Swedenborgian philosophy, was intent on providing the perfect education for his children. In pursuit of this aim the family wandered over the civilized world, from the United States to Europe and back again, from country to country within Europe.

When William was thirteen, the family traveled from England to France to Switzerland to France to England and back to France (if I have counted my countries in the correct sequence), most of these stops being marked by enrollments in school, high initial expectations, parental disappointment, and abrupt departure. That restlessness was to mark James's intellectual apprenticeship in his later years, when he wandered from country to country and from one vocation to another. The peripatetic approach to education did not altogether please him because he felt it had deprived him of intellectual discipline; yet in all likelihood it was responsible for the dialectical tensions we find in so much of his writing, and above all in *Principles*. Moving from culture to culture, language to language, James was able to bring to his writing the fruits of international experience; French psychiatry (Charcot and Janet), British philosophy (Hume, Locke, the Mills, Spencer, Bain), German experimental psychology (Helmholtz, Windt, Fechner, Stempf); and both the old biology (Agassiz) and the new (Darwin and Huxley). *Principles* represents the cumulation and synthesis of these separate bodies of doctrine and learning; it is hard to imagine anyone else as perfectly positioned to write the definitive text on psychology as it moved from its philosophical to its scientific era.

In one sense, then, this book is a summa, the perfect conspectus of late nineteenth-century psychology. Yet its mere variety, range, and encyclopedic mastery give us little clue to its genius, which may be found in the conflicts and contradictions that, we sense, lie behind every chapter of this long book. All of the polarities of late Victorian thought are to be found therein, raging within James, and forming the essential dialectic of the work: faith versus skepticism, psychology versus philosophy, mind versus matter, materialism versus idealism, nativism versus empiricism.

Specialists in Jamesian thought have long been aware of these tensions, but I suspect that we ordinary readers have misled ourselves because we have been so captured by James's charm, both as a writer and as a personality. Once we allow ourselves to get into this book, reading it carefully and consecutively, we become fully aware of the intellectual heroism that went into its composition. James himself knew the magnitude of his ambition, and the barriers he had put before himself. In Ralph Barton Perry's magisterial biography, we learn of testimony to this effect from James's own correspondence during the years he was writing *Principles*. He complains that every problem "bristles with obstructions," that each sentence had to be forged "in the teeth of irreducible and stubborn facts," and that "it was no joke slaying the Helmholtzes as well as the Spencers."

That last phrase may evoke the usual Freudian wink among those given to vulgar forms of psychobiography. But an oedipal theory will not take us very far in understanding James's achievement. The dominant impression we carry away from a sustained reading is of a man determined to take nothing for granted, to think every important question through, as though for the first time. Reading *Principles* is exhilarating, yet it can also be exhausting—not because it is hard to read, far from it, but because of the sheer density of thought compressed into those elegantly balanced sentences. One has the sense of an intense, restless, questing mind at work. Not too surprisingly, James's students of this period remember him in much the same way. In dress and demeanor he was quite unlike the typical academic of the day—"more like a sportsman than a professor," one observer noted—unpretentious, democratic, full of wit and foolery. Yet what they remember even more vividly is the electricity of mind. Gay Wilson Allen's biography comments that "James was never satisfied with any theory, and was always exploring, examining, and experimenting." The words that recur are "intentness" and "vitality." A student remembers his classroom manner: "When he stood he was the nervous thoroughbred. If it had been possible to find and place beside him a man who was his perfect duplicate . . . the duplicate still would not have suggested James, because there would have been lacking the vital mind and tingling nerves." That vital mind, those tingling nerves, can be felt at every moment in reading this book.

So we have the first reason that we ought to read or reread *Principles*: it allows us to witness a magnificent mind, at the height of its powers, struggling with and ultimately conquering the most refractory materials. That brings us to the original question: Does the book speak to the contemporary reader? That does not allow a simple answer: largely yes, partly no.

To begin with, it is not essentially a prescient book, one of those that foretells, uncannily, the terms in which the future will understand itself. The nineteenth century produced a surprisingly large number of such writers and works: Tocqueville, Kierkegaard, Dostoevsky, and perhaps the James of *Varieties*. Nor is it the kind of book that launches a discipline, or a major new direction in thinking; the great nineteenth-century names here are of course Darwin, Marx, and Freud. Despite the high ambition James brought to the task, *Principles* was simply not destined to be either prophetic or path-breaking. James never quite abandoned the duty set for him by his publisher, to write a college textbook. We are reminded in the very first sentence of this work, in its preface, that it has "in the main grown up in connection with the author's classroom instruction in Psychology." That being the case, vast stretches of the book are given over to the exposition of evidence long since superseded and of controversies long since settled. James's literary genius is such as to compel our attention almost against our will; I still cannot quite believe that I read, semispellbound, nearly a hundred pages of text on the brain, all the time knowing that it was seriously out-of-date. Nevertheless, the contemporary reader, if he is determined to undertake this book from cover to cover, should be aware that a good portion of it—from a third to a half, I would guess—will be of interest largely to the historian of science.

Yet in a work of such size, that still leaves a great deal, indeed enough for two or three ordinary books. Fortunately, much of the material that "survives" is to be found in essentially self-contained chapters, some of them of monograph size. Hence it is a book that lends itself to browsing and selective reading. The following themes and topics continue to hold our interest, in some cases because they anticipate current or emergent developments in the field of psychology.

1. James's writing on the self, particularly the magnificent chapter 10, on the consciousness of self. Much of that chapter is given over to a complex, convoluted argument against philosophical positions that James found wanting, and the contemporary reader will probably not find it to be of much interest. Yet along the way we see numerous trails blazed, as James explores such questions as self-esteem, self-love, self-dissatisfaction, the extensions of selfhood to family and profession, the divided self, and the sense of personal identity. Much of what we now take for granted about the nature, origins, and pathology of the self was first discussed in *The Principles of Psychology*.

2. James's description of consciousness, of the stream of thought, has probably not been equaled since its writing. The psychologists of his time saw consciousness in static terms, as being made up of those separate elements—for example, sensations—discovered in introspective exercises. James saw it much as we do now, as a continuous flow, a more or less uninterrupted stream of experience: protean, ever-changing, selective in choosing what it will and will not attend to.

3. Throughout *Principles*, James wrote both as a philosopher and as a *philosophe* in the traditional sense, someone reflecting on human conduct in general. James never lost sight of the basic philosophical questions inherent in all psychological theory and research. Much of this book is an extended meditation upon some of the eternal issues of philosophical analysis, above all the mind-body interaction, and the question of how we learn to construe "reality." These contributions have stood the test of time, yet James's observations on human nature will probably prove even more enduring, and certainly more endearing. We find many of these in the set pieces I mentioned earlier, the chapters on habit and on instinct being the best known. These essays show James ranging at large, searching out the sources and effects of common modes of conduct: for example, the biological functions of habit and its social consequences; habit as a conserving agency, keeping society stable, yet at the same time limiting the individual's acquisition of new patterns of thought and work. The chapter on instinct, much influenced by Darwin, explores what is native to the species, and how that may be altered by education and experience. What captivates us is the freshness and percipience of so many, though by no means all, of James's observations.

That is the verdict of the present upon the past. It may be fitting to conclude by turning the tables: What would James's judgment be about us? What would our Founding Father think about his progeny? How would he view what has happened to the discipline he helped invent?

We know one part of the answer, from his very mixed feelings about psychoanalysis, occasioned by Freud's lectures at Clark University. At one point he seemed to feel that psychoanalysis would make up an important element of the future; yet a few days later wrote to a colleague that it was too narrowly focused, and too closely wed to psychopathology. We may suspect that James would continue to think so.

In all likelihood, James would be pleased by our understanding of brain physiology and biochemistry. He would admire Piaget, though here too he might be concerned about his conceptual narrowness—Piaget is the perfect hedgehog to the Jamesian fox. In general, however, I think he would be delighted by the emergence and growing strength of developmental psychology. And of course he would be gratified by the late blooming of cognitive approaches, all the while wondering why it had taken so long.

On the other hand he would be profoundly depressed by the long-sustained victory of positivism in U.S. psychology. Skinner and the Skinnerians would have given him fits—little doubt about that—but he would also have been impatient and sardonic about the continuing power of demi- and quasi-behavioristic approaches in the field. He would be miserable about the widespread ignorance of and indifference to philosophy, and mordant about the frantic empirical activity that so often takes the place of careful conceptual reasoning. Finally, he would be struck speechless by the abysmal standards of the U.S. university today. The contemporary reader will find it hard to believe that *Principles*—a great but difficult book—was addressed to undergraduates, went through eight printings, and reached a large general audience. Whatever we may have gained by the democratization of culture, that publication history reminds us of how much we may have lost.

19

The Dream as a Riddle

All dreams are riddles; they must be solved if they are to be understood. Indeed, all dreams in some sense intend to riddle; the defensive processes involved in the formation and reporting of the dream have as their aim to conceal some or all of its meaning. Why then should one propose, as this paper will, a special class of riddle-dreams? The answer is that in these cases the riddle element is more than the by-product of the defense; rather, it dominates the telling of the dream. One perceives on the dreamer's part an active, determined—though unconscious—effort to puzzle the therapist. The dream contains a secret, cast in the form of a conundrum, which the listener is tacitly challenged to uncover. Following is a report of two such riddle-dreams.

Case 1

The first dream arose out of these circumstances: I had shortly before told the patient, a housewife in her thirties, that I would be forced to interrupt her therapy for several months. I was then working in the East, and I was to go to the University of Michigan to undertake some research. Her reaction was ominously calm, ominous because she suffered an unusually intense fear of abandonment that she handled, in moments of crisis, by running away impulsively. This pattern had dominated the course of her life. As a very young child she had persistently run away from home, though never very far before being retrieved. But as she grew older her flights had become more elaborate and scandalous. In her early adolescence she had attempted to pawn some of her mother's jewelry in order to finance a trip to the West Coast. After her first semester in college she had eloped to marry her first husband, and several years later had run away from him to marry her second husband. She had then entered treatment because the impulse to flee had once again appeared. There were occasions when she got into her car not knowing whether she would be able to resist the urge to drive away and assume a new identity, never to return to her husband and children.

It was not difficult to discern that the impulse to run away was linked to the fear and expectation of being left behind, that it was, in fact, a counter-

285

phobic response to it. Her parents had been both neglectful and guiltily overindulgent. They lived for travel and had made it a practice to take an extended tour of Europe, without their children, at least once every two years, and more often when possible. Because they had found the children to be fretful before these departures, they had adopted the practice of concealing their intentions beforehand—leaving the children at the grandparents' home, presumably to spend the afternoon, and then letting the grandparents reveal that they would be gone for several months. When the parents returned home, they would shower gifts upon the children and promise to take them along the next time, which they never did. As the patient's history unfolded, we were able to see that her running away always followed or anticipated a parental trip. Her attempted flight to the West Coast, to cite one instance, had occurred shortly after her parents' visit there.

So we knew that departures were dangerous for her. If I were forced to miss an appointment with her, or even to change the time of a session, she reacted with rage, anxiety, and depression. In thinking forward as to how she might take my impending departure, I expected more of the same to appear, though more intensely. Not at all. Instead she settled into a bemused, restless affectlessness, the very mood I knew had preceded and portended her explosive departures in the past. Once this was clear, it seemed exigent that she come to grips with her disappointment and fury. But she could not, or would not. She spoke with her usual fluency, but only in the cold, remote, mildly sullen fashion that characterized her when at a willed distance from violent feeling.

It was at this juncture—with my time of departure approaching, with the therapy at an impasse, with my beginning to fear the worst—that she presented the following dream fragment:

> There was a piece of paper which had printed upon it the words, "CAROLINE, EDITOR." Although she could read the words without difficulty, she had the impression that the letters were printed erratically, some sideways and some upside down, as they might appear in a scrambled-words puzzle. It reminded her of a puzzle contest being conducted by a local newspaper.

Without hesitation she reported these associations: She had gone to a boarding school in North *Carolina*, and one of her friends there was a girl named *Caroline*. They had been co-*editors* of the school magazine. She then launched into reminiscences: about her work on the magazine, which she had enjoyed; about Caroline, whom she had liked but often clashed with; and about her life at prep school, which she had despised.

She spoke of these topics as she always did, graphically and amusingly, but as she went on it seemed plain that we were still not getting very far regarding the matter at hand, my imminent departure for Michigan and her feelings about it. Was there something else in the dream? Why did the letters seem to be scrambled? Was she hinting at something? I then recalled that in the puzzle contest she had alluded to, the names of cities were scrambled. It struck me that if one doubled the T, EDITOR was an anagram for DETROIT.

I mentioned this, rather diffidently. Did anything come to her mind about Detroit? She was startled, then burst into laughter. She had a confession to make. She had kept something from me. She had, in fact, been in touch with Caroline and had recently received a letter from her. Caroline now lived in Detroit, and had often asked her to visit her if she were in the region. Detroit, she knew, was only a short distance from Ann Arbor. The previous night she had had a fantasy that she would visit Detroit to see Caroline, and use her visit as a pretext to see me in Ann Arbor. But she had decided not to mention this because she was certain that I would forbid her to make the trip, just as her parents had refused to take her along on their voyages.

I told her it was certainly not my function to regulate her travels; for that matter, if she could arrange a trip to Michigan, I had no objection to having some therapy sessions there. She replied that, realistically speaking, she could not make the trip, but it was good to have me offer to see her. And then she was able to express, for the first time, her bitterness about the deceits her parents had practiced when they had gone on trips.

Case 2

The second dream was told by a professional man in this thirties. He had entered therapy because he was unable to marry. The one woman he had been in love with had married someone else. Many women had been and were now interested in him but he found them wanting in one way or another. His reasons were, as he himself recognized, often absurd: this one's ankles were too thick; that one wore dresses of the wrong color. Despite innumerable opportunities, he had never had sexual intercourse. There were, however, no psychoneurotic symptoms, nor were there signs of gross character pathology. He was at most moderately compulsive; he was too cautious, too prudent, too guarded, too blandly polite. These traits were by no means overdeveloped; they were, in fact, typical of many people in his professional milieu.

The therapy had begun well but after a few months had unexpectedly bogged down. We had been discussing some sexual activities about which the patient was ashamed. These involved an emphasis on seeing and being seen. An exaggerated—though not clearly perverse—interest in voyeuristic and exhibitionistic aims dominated his sexual fantasies and some of his behavior, coupled with an intense fear of being found out. We then came into a protracted period of resistance. He could do little more than report day-to-day trivia:

how things had gone at work, the concerts and films he had attended, news of the family, and so on. As this phase continued, he began to wonder whether he ought to continue therapy at all. Nothing seemed to be happening, and after all he did not really feel uncomfortable or unhappy.

This period of stasis was brought to an end when he reported a dream fragment consisting of the single word *steel*. I presumed the word to be *steel*, or perhaps *steal*. He said, however, "Isn't that the name of an English writer? An essayist, I believe."

At this moment I felt that I could grasp the meaning of the dream, and the probable source of the long period of resistance. I asked for further associations but there were none forthcoming. I then asked what he knew about Steele. He denied, with surprising vigor in view of his usual mildness, that he knew anything about Steele except his name. Now this was implausible; he had been educated in a tradition that stressed the study of English literature. I then decided to depart from customary practice and to lead the inquiry. What follows is a capsule summary of an interchange marked by grim pursuit and querulous retreat:

Q: With what writer was Steele always linked?

A: [after first silence and then a denial of knowing]: Addison.

Q: What was Addison's first name?

A: [after many protestations of ignorance]: Joseph?

Q: And what does that remind you of?

A: [resentfully]: Your name. I don't see what this has to do with anything.

Q: And what else?

A: *The Tatler*.

Q: So Steele conceals Addison which conceals Adelson, the spectator who might tattle? Are you worried about this?

This was followed by perplexity—chagrin—silence—a deep sigh. He then said that he would tell me something he had withheld, for he had been too embarrassed to talk about it. For some weeks he had worried about whether he could trust my discretion. He had seen me having lunch in a restaurant with someone he took to be a colleague. Though he could not hear what we were saying, he was convinced, from the animation of the conversation, that we were talking over our therapy cases, enjoying ourselves by telling prurient anecdotes about our patients. Since then he had found it very difficult to talk freely; on the other hand, he did not dare tell me so to my face. We went on to discuss the matter, and the treatment was resumed.

Do these dreams involve new or unusual processes of dream-formation? The construction of an anagram does show a high degree of verbal artifice, but no more so than other instances of clever wordplay in dreams. The "Steele" dream is based upon an extended but by no means extraordinary sequence of displacements. Both these dreams were distinguished not by their dreamwork but by their meaning in the therapeutic context, not by process but by purpose.

They appeared during periods of intense and prolonged resistance. The resistances were acute and stubborn for two reasons: first, the customary one, because a central and continuing conflict in the patient's life had been engaged; second, and perhaps more important, because the patient had lost faith in the therapist's integrity and goodwill. In each case the patient felt that the therapeutic contract was in doubt: in one instance because of an unexpected and arbitrary interruption of the treatment, in the other through a supposed failure of discretion. Thus the working alliance was disrupted; the therapist had lost his standing as a good object. In a therapeutic climate marked by a sense of betrayal, the patient may no longer wish to maintain his side of the compact, the agreement to speak openly. He will depend only on himself; he will secure his safety by secrecy. He composes a secret vow, a secret intention. In each case, the vow repeats an established habitual pattern of response of crisis; in the woman, a secret intention to take flight, to react to abandonment by counteraction; in the man, an intensification of caution and reserve, a secret determination to be silent and on guard.

If this were all, if there were no motive present other than the maintenance of secrecy, then the therapy would surely founder. But the will to secrecy meets the wish to confess, to restore the lost harmony between the therapeutic pair. Tension between concealment and confession produces its compromise in the dream as a riddle. Both sides of the tension are strongly expressed. On the side of the concealment, it should be noted that the dreamer does not participate in understanding the dream; on the contrary, he withholds his help. The therapist is then driven back to his own resources, forced to a tour de force. Yet the side of confession is also strong, and ultimately stronger. The solving of the riddle evokes a sudden decision to confess the secret. Why so easily? Because the dream itself is half a confession. The dreamer is like a criminal waiting and half-wishing to be captured. With the secret exposed, the impulse to confess is liberated, and the therapeutic alliance can be resumed.

These dreams concealed a vital secret; they also posed vital questions; "Will you let me go along with you?" and "Can I trust you to keep my secrets?" Unable to ask them directly, the patients turned to riddling. In doing so, they reverted to the archetypical function of the riddle. Nowadays one thinks of the riddle—if one thinks of it at all—as trivial and frivolous; it is, literally, child's play. But in the ancient societies, as Huizinga has shown, the deepest, most serious questions of the culture were approached through the riddle: questions of cosmogony, of life and death, of good and evil. "The riddle, we may conclude, was originally a sacred game, and as such it cut clean across any possible distinction between play and seriousness."[1] And: "The riddle-context is far from being mere recreation; it is an integral part of the ceremonial of sacrifice. . . . It forces the hand of the gods."[2] And: "The riddle is a sacred thing full of secret power; hence a dangerous thing. In its mythological and ritual context . . . you either solve [it] or forfeit your head. The player's life is at stake."[3]

These patients, in a playful but desperately serious way, were forcing the hand of the therapist. What was at stake was not life itself but the patient's continuing life in therapy. The riddle had to be solved if doubt were to be resolved and if mutual trust were to be restored.

Notes

1. Johan Huizinga, *Homo Ludens: A Study of the Play Element in Culture* (Boston: Beacon Press, 1955), p. 110.
2. Ibid., pp. 107–8.
3. Ibid., p. 108.

20

Letty in Pogrebinland

Growing Up Free: Raising Your Child in the 80's
by Letty Cottin Pogrebin

This is a book about an imaginary society—an anti-utopia—which goes unnamed in the text but which I will name, in honor of its inventor, Pogrebinland. It is the author's conceit to suggest to us that she is writing about our own country; yet it is clear immediately that this is merely a literary device, and that no such country has ever existed. Another such device is to pretend that the book is a guide for parents; but here again it is evident that the parents and children depicted are products of the author's fertile imagination. The actual intention of the book is to recount the trials and tribulations of its heroine, Letty, as she struggles against the blight that has enveloped Pogrebinland.

That blight is sexism, here represented as eternal, ubiquitous, and infinitely malevolent. It is the primary source of all human error and discord. Sexism wrecks marriages. It causes crime. It causes war. It stifles creativity. It pollutes language. It causes children to hate their fathers and despise their mothers. It makes boys stupid; it also makes girls stupid. It even causes bedwetting in both sexes, the boys and the girls because they resent not being boys.

Strangely enough, the blight seems not to have limited Pogrebinland's material culture. Despite the universal devastation of intelligence and creativity, the country seems to be prosperous and technologically advanced. Nevertheless, each and every artifact, event, and institution of the society is deployed relentlessly to reinforce sexcoding. All methods of communication—newspapers, magazines, books, movies, and television (termed ''sexistvision'')—all modes of education, all toys and leisure activities are given over to a single purpose—to sustain or induce sexual stereotypes. Through the keen eyes of her heroine, Letty, the author takes us through a tour of an ordinary household in that troubled land, showing us the many insidious ways in which sexist messages are introduced. There is, for example, a three-page analysis and denunciation of the following colors—pink, orchid, fuchsia, purple, magenta, mauve, blue, tan, brown, and gray—centering on their sexist connotations. Letty herself has managed to overcome the problem, and has decorated her home to be "free of gender color-coding." Her daughter's room, like her son's is "bright and functional, forest green, orange, and yellow."

It is here, in the depiction of family life, that the reader is most often struck by the imaginary nature of Pogrebinland, and its departure from the ordinary experience of most of us. Most actual parents will worry if their children eat too much junk food, or are too fat or too thin, or are rude at the dinner table; in Pogrebinland these problems do not seem to exist, and parents are largely concerned with forcing their male children to eat steak and potatoes, so as to make them beefy and aggressive, while encouraging girls to eat lettuce sandwiches, to help them retain their daintiness. Most real-life parents are content if their children bathe fairly regularly, and do so without splashing water on the bathroom floor; in Pogrebinland parents urge boys not to bathe too often, or at all, but pour oils, lotions, and other perfumed essences upon their female children. In our society the common toy store contains thousands of items, the vast majority of which have no evident association with gender; in Pogrebinland these stores seem to be divided by sex, the girls' side containing dolls, toy carriages, layettes, and copies of household appliances, the boys' side displaying only pistols, rifles, shotguns, bayonets, tanks, missiles, instruments of torture, and precise copies of nuclear weapons. In our society parents are overcome with joy (and undue pride) if their offspring show any sign of competence in any domain of learning; in Pogrebinland parents become profoundly anxious when a daughter gives any evidence of talent in mathematics or the sciences.

Unfortunately I have been able to provide only the briefest sampling of the many curious customs the author describes—although the book is long, invention never flags. She relies not only upon her own vivid imagination, but also upon the many (presumably) fictive authorities she cites—e.g., the report of two experts on sexuality that parents are not troubled by masturbation in boys under twelve, only in girls; or the report from another expert that 44 percent of children prefer television to their fathers. We must turn now to another facet of the author's literary strategy, the pretense that this is a guidebook for parents. Her talent for satire is evident at once: she calls the book *Growing Up Free*, yet the volume is made up largely of rules, prohibitions, warnings, commands, and threats. Examples: "Ten Commandments for Nonhomophobic Parenthood." "Nine Rules of Sex Stereotyping." "Twelve Dos and Don'ts for Promoting Free-Flowing Gender-Blind Alliances."

Yet it is not hard to understand why the author's approach is proscriptive. For the truly devoted parent, life in Pogrebinland can be demanding. Most of one's waking hours are given over to self-examination (for hidden or disvowed signs of sexism) and to the scrutiny of one's spouse, friends, children and children's friends. Self-testing begins even before one has become a parent.

We are provided a checklist of ten questions to assess "bias before birth," that is, to determine whether one harbors a secret wish to have a boy rather than a girl ("Have you practiced or would you practice sex-selection methods if perfected?" "During pregnancy did/do you and your mate refer to the fetus as 'he'? Sometimes? Usually? Always?"). Such self-scrutiny continues through the life cycle. The author advises parents to test themselves by testing their children. A number of objects—e.g., egg beater, pliers—are placed before the children in random order, and they are asked whether the object in question is anybody's, or Mommy's, or Daddy's. If a child should reply that the pliers, let us say, belong to Daddy, then some heavy thinking is called for. It is not altogether clear what rites of confession and contrition are available—the author finds no current church fully acceptable to her—but there is little doubt that the more concerned residents of the country spend much of their time in shame and guilt.

Aside from testing and being tested, the major parental devotion involves keeping an eye on the children for signs of backsliding. A little boy may, for example, refuse to play with the doll carriage his mother has thoughtfully provided, saying that only sissies play with dolls. The parent must swing into action immediately, correcting both the sexism and the odious language. The author reminds us that the term "sissy" is not merely sexist, it is also homophobic, and goes on to point out that given the connections between sexism and racism, it is the exact equivalent of a racial slur. The responsible parent also keeps her ears open for sex stereotyping, since it may appear at any time in the spontaneous play of children—in the rhymes, chants, and songs, most of these offensively sexist—which is part of the tragic heritage of Pogrebinland.

Yet the parents' work need not be exclusively negative; there are positive tasks as well. This book's heroine, Letty, keeps stationery handy at the side of the sexistvision set, and the children are encouraged to write letters of complaint to the networks and their advertisers. We are told a heartwarming story about Letty's daughter Abigail, who saw a sexist Wheaties commercial in July 1973, wrote a letter of protest to the company and, dissatisfied with the response, boycotted Wheaties (along with lettuce, grapes, and Gallo wine) for two years, until the commercial was replaced.

These are some of the benign short-term effects of intervention against sexism. The long-run effects, in the minds and hearts of the young, are seen impressively in a vignette about Letty's son David. He has just heard a presentation from the director of a summer camp the family is considering for the children, and the following colloquy takes place:

"It's nice," he [David] said. "But it's sexist."

"Funny, we didn't notice anything," Bert [Letty's spouse] replied. "Boys and girls seem able to do the same things."

"Yes," agreed David. "But the director said they had a 'manmade lake.' "

(We assured him that was an expression, not an admission of sex bias, but David still turned the camp down.)

What makes this anecdote especially poignant is the reader's knowledge that Letty's son David has been the only troublesome member of an otherwise ideal family. We know almost nothing about Bert, her spouse, since he seems to do little but agree with her; but there is no sign at all that he has been less than admiring. Letty's two daughters, Robin and Abigail, are very close to perfect—indeed, they are Letty-clones, writing letters to the networks, and taking part in boycotts and demonstrations. When they reach pubescence they will, we are certain, be instructed carefully in the arts and sciences of contraception and the features and function of the sexual anatomy—for a parent to do otherwise, the author tells us, is to submit to the sexist conspiracy which pervades Pogrebinland.

Yet David has been a problem, in that we perceive in his very being the possibility of original sin, that is, of a reversion to the atavistic state of male chauvinism. David has had the best of everything—a vigilant mother reminding him constantly of the evils of sexism, two sainted sisters engaging him in catechism on the absence of sex differences, a complaisant and liberated father—hence, a continuing exposure to a Babel of virtuous voices, and beyond that, a home in which every possible reminder of gender bias has been removed.

Yet despite these advantages, the old Adam will out. Toward the end of the book we learn the mournful truth about David. Unlike his sisters, who have never shown any such interest, he has had a "definite fascination with guns." He has pleaded for "a fancy toy tank or shiny revolver," and his play "sometimes has included pretend finger games, war whoops, and 'bang, bang you're dead.' " And as an older child he produced "meticulously detailed drawings of artillery, bombers, and gunboats."

What are we to make of such aberrant behavior? The author cannot quite make up her mind. She seems unable to decide, here as elsewhere, whether males are naturally brutal, or whether they have fallen victim to the sexist conditioning they receive in Pogrebinland. Did David love guns "because he is a boy, or because he's seen guns everywhere defined as accoutrements of male power and glory?" The question preoccupies the author quite as much as guns preoccupy David. Indeed the book begins with an extended discussion of whether or not men are innately aggressive, and the issue continues to torment the author throughout her many discussions of rape, wife beating, child abuse, incest, violent crime, sadistic pornography, torture, warfare, and other characteristic expressions of the ordinary male nature. Women are customarily free of aggression, one is led to understand, though it is acceptable in the service of anti-sexist justice. We are told it is permissible to "humiliate" or "bully" some proponents of sexism.

One cannot but admire Letty's candor in discussing her embarrassing family problem—David's atavisms—and we sense that the author shares our admiration. Although she makes every effort to remain objective in her account of Letty, she cannot quite conceal from us the awe she feels for this heroic woman. We have already taken note of her accomplishments in such fields as child-rearing, interior decoration, psychological testing, and political activism. What this brief review can only hint at is the extraordinary range of her achievements in such fields as psychoanalysis, anthropology, developmental psychology, folklore, linguistics, theology, art history, literary criticism, legal studies, film theory, hormone biology, pedagogy, moral philosophy, and many many more. In each of these areas we can count on Letty to come up with forceful opinions and startling new perspectives.

In theology, we learn of her disavowal of the faith she was raised in (Judaism) because of its excessive emphasis on such male personalities as Abraham, Isaac, and Jacob. She displays a mastery of psychoanalytic theory which permits her to sum up its basic ideas in a few pungent sentences. Her explorations in the history of art bring to our attention such pivotal figures as Sofonisba Anguissola, Elisabetta Sirani, and Lady Jane Butler. In the field of comparative iconology, she raises some profound questions as to the bias which encourages textbook writers to mention Mozart and Bach, while ignoring such luminaries as Phyllis Wheatley and Molly Pitcher.

The book concludes with a rather clever jape, one so subtle it may escape the attention of many readers. This may be the most heavily footnoted trade book ever published. There are 79 pages of notes, containing over 1,700 items, mentioning several thousand references. The first reaction of the ordinary reader will be that he has come across some solid scholarship, and since the notes are printed in very small type, he will most likely pass up the chance to examine them carefully. That will be a mistake, for he will thereby forgo many hours of entertainment. If he reads the references carefully, he will see that the author has achieved a *tour de force* of parody, for the citations have only the most remote connection to the text, or to common canons of scholarship. Each reader will have his own favorites. My own are these: a reference to a presumably scientific survey, which reads (in full) "J. B. Ra, quoted in *National Enquirer*, Oct. 12, 1976," and the reference to Fisher and Greenberg's 502-page volume, discussing hundreds of studies in support of psychoanalysis, here cited to confirm the view that there is "not an iota of evidence" for the theory.

One might say that it was quite clever of the author to conclude her book with this attenuated joke; one might also say that her book is a joke from beginning to end.